Lecture Notes
in Business Information Processing

375

Series Editors

Wil van der Aalst ⓘ
RWTH Aachen University, Aachen, Germany
John Mylopoulos ⓘ
University of Trento, Trento, Italy
Michael Rosemann ⓘ
Queensland University of Technology, Brisbane, QLD, Australia
Michael J. Shaw
University of Illinois, Urbana-Champaign, IL, USA
Clemens Szyperski
Microsoft Research, Redmond, WA, USA

More information about this series at http://www.springer.com/series/7911

Petr Doucek · Josef Basl ·
A Min Tjoa · Maria Raffai ·
Antonin Pavlicek · Katrin Detter (Eds.)

Research and Practical Issues of Enterprise Information Systems

13th IFIP WG 8.9 International Conference, CONFENIS 2019
Prague, Czech Republic, December 16–17, 2019
Proceedings

Springer

Editors
Petr Doucek (iD)
University of Economics
Prague, Czech Republic

Josef Basl
University of Economics
Prague, Czech Republic

A Min Tjoa (iD)
TU Wien
Vienna, Austria

Maria Raffai (iD)
Szechenyi University
Gyor, Hungary

Antonin Pavlicek (iD)
University of Economics
Prague, Czech Republic

Katrin Detter
TU Wien
Vienna, Austria

ISSN 1865-1348 ISSN 1865-1356 (electronic)
Lecture Notes in Business Information Processing
ISBN 978-3-030-37631-4 ISBN 978-3-030-37632-1 (eBook)
https://doi.org/10.1007/978-3-030-37632-1

This Springer imprint is published by the registered company Springer Nature Switzerland AG
The registered company address is: Gewerbestrasse 11, 6330 Cham, Switzerland

International Conference on Research and Practical Issues of Enterprise Information Systems

13th IFIP WG 8.9 Working Conference, CONFENIS 2019

December 16–17, 2019,
University of Economics, Prague, Czech Republic

Preface

The 13th edition of the IFIP WG 8.9 Working Conference (CONFENIS 2019), was held during December 16–17, 2019, at the University of Economics in Prague, Czech Republic.

This year's CONFENIS brought together academic researchers, practitioners, as well as eminent representatives from industry, academia, and public administration to present and discuss the most recent ideas and findings facilitating the exchange of ideas and developments in the various aspects of Enterprise Information Systems (EIS).

CONFENIS 2019 was mainly focused on aspects of EIS and Industry 4.0, Technical Architecture and Applications for EIS, Theory and Methods, Collaborative Networks, Project Management and Security and Privacy issues. After a rigorous peer-review process, a total of 13 papers were accepted. We believe that the findings presented in the selected papers of this proceedings will trigger further EIS research and applications.

We would like to thank all authors for their valuable contributions as well as the Program Committee members for their reviewing work. At the same time, we would like to acknowledge the great support by the CONFENIS 2019 organization team; in particular Antonin Pavlicek and Katrin Detter for the timely support, organization, and the many contributions that made this edition of the conference proceedings possible.

Finally, we hope that CONFENIS 2019 served as a platform for both academia and industry to discuss the various, current issues concerning EIS, and that this event will further trigger innovative approaches in the many different EIS areas.

December 2019

Maria Raffai
A Min Tjoa
Petr Doucek
Josef Basl
Antonin Pavlicek
Katrin Detter

International Conference on Research and Practical Issues of Enterprise Information Systems

13th IFIP WG 8.9 Working Conference, CONFENIS 2019

Preface

Organization

International Conference on Research and Practical Issues of Enterprise Information Systems – CONFENIS 2019

General Chair

Petr Doucek   University of Economics in Prague, Czech Republic

Program Chairs

A Min Tjoa   Vienna University of Technology, Austria
Maria Raffai   Szechenyi University, Hungary
Josef Basl   University of Economics in Prague, Czech Republic

Publication Chair

Katrin Detter   Vienna University of Technology, Austria

Organization Chair

Antonin Pavlicek   University of Economics in Prague, Czech Republic

Program Committee

Ba Lam Do   Vienna University of Technology, Austria
Raffai Mária   Szechenyi Istvan University, Hungary
Larissa Bulysheva   Old Dominion University, USA
Christine Strauss   University of Vicnna, Austria
Antonin Pavlicek   University of Economics in Prague, Czech Republic
Sohail Chaudhry   Villanova University, USA
Amin Anjomshoaa   Massachusetts Institute of Technology, Austria
Fajar J. Ekaputra   Vienna University of Technology, Austria
Subodh Kesharwani   Indira Gandhi National Open University, India
Petr Doucek   University of Economics in Prague, Czech Republic
Young Moon   Syracuse University, USA
Frederik Gailly   Ghent University, Belgium
Lisa Seymour   University of Cape Town, South Africa
Wu He   Old Dominion University, USA
Zhuming Bi   Indiana University Purdue University Fort Wayne, USA
Wenjun Zhang   University of Saskatchewan, Canada

Contents

Security and Privacy Issues

EIS and Industry 4.0

Analysis of Selected ERP 4.0 Features and Proposal of an ERP 4.0 Maturity Model

Josef Basl[✉] and Marketa Novakova

Prague University of Economics, W. Churchill Sq. 4, Prague, Czech Republic
{basl,novm29}@vse.cz

Abstract. The paper deals with new trends in ERP enterprise information systems that are related to the general trends of Industry 4.0. These trends are covered under the topic of ERP 4.0 in this paper. They are analysed based on a literature review. Selected ERP 4.0 trends are analysed from the point of view of their penetration into the offers of ERP suppliers and the expectations of users in companies. Finally, the main trends identified in ERP 4.0 are reflected in own ERP 4.0 maturity model.

Keywords: Enterprise resource planning · ERP 4.0 · Industry 4.0 · Maturity model · AI · Internet of things · IoT · IS/ICT innovation · Digital innovation

1 Introduction

Industry 4.0, with all its attributes, has become a constant concern of suppliers and users of related components and solutions in recent years. However, Industry 4.0 also remains the subject of many research articles. Their focus is gradually changing as knowledge and experience in this area is developed and refined and there is an associated need for further research. In connection with Industry 4.0, not only the focus of research topics is changing, but also the focus of interest of individual authors is changing.

One of the co-authors of this paper is an example of such internal evolution. His publishing activity has gradually reflected interest from general perspectives on Industry 4.0 awareness to business readiness and business ICT vendor readiness in recent years. This article logically results in a focus on ERP 4.0 and its maturity model.

Specifically, these articles were:

(a) Analysis of the preparedness of enterprises in industry 4.0, both in the Czech Republic and in comparison with Poland - in 2015/2016 [1, 2]
(b) Analysis of the preparedness of companies and their business IS for trends 4.0 in 2015/2016 [3].
(c) Analysis of ERP application vendor Industry 4.0 readiness in 2015/2017 [4].
     In addition to the state of preparedness of enterprises and their business IS for Industry 4.0, the author of the article subsequently discussed the models of maturity 4.0

P. Doucek et al. (Eds.): CONFENIS 2019, LNBIP 375, pp. 3–11, 2019.
https://doi.org/10.1007/978-3-030-37632-1_1

(d) Analysis of maturity models 4.0, in particular from the perspective of available models with subsequent formulation of principles applicable to own maturity models, in 2017/2018 [5].

(e) Formulation of a metamodel that identified areas, i.e. certain "gaps" where maturity models 4.0 are still missing (one of which was focused on ERP 4.0), also in 2017/2018 [6].

This article focuses specifically on an ERP 4.0 maturity model and is linked to the work above in previous years, especially those dealing with maturity models and identification of potential gaps. Its formulation is based on a pilot analysis of the main 4.0 trends, which can be applied in ERP 4.0.

The following research questions were chosen for this article:

1. What are the main industry 4.0 trends reflected in ERP 4.0?
2. What results will the verification of the state of the current supply and demand of trends of ERP 4.0 in the pilot survey on the Czech market?
3. Can these trends be used to specify the ERP 4.0 maturity model?

These three questions are covered in the following sections of this paper. The first question is formulated on the basis of a review by the second co-author of this article.

The second one was also conducted via survey by the second co-author of this article. The third question - the formulation and design was based on a previously conceptually designed maturity model for ERP, based on a general model formulated on the basis of earlier work by the first co-author [6].

2   ERP 4.0 – 4.0 Trends in ERP Applications

2.1   ERP 4.0 Methodology

This article focuses primarily on the area identified as ERP 4.0, which is not generally defined, and sometimes other terms are used. Examples of definitions include postmodern ERP [7] or intelligent ERP by SAP. In general, the ERP 4.0 system can be considered as an ERP system that provides the necessary functionality for Industry 4.0. ERP 4.0 is directly based on ERP system functionality, but it takes it to a higher level. ERP 4.0 is strongly supported by Industry 4.0. It must take advantage of all the important 4.0 trends while supporting most of the industry's requirements for industry [8].

Research of available sources was used for analysis of 4.0 trends in applications from articles as well as suppliers and users and more than 30 literary sources were analysed. Criteria (categories) were used by various authors who generally describe the area and typical features for 4.0 trends and Industry 4.0 [7].

These are:

(a) trends dominated by the onset of 4.0 - such as cloud computing, IoT integration, blockchain usage, digital twins, edge computing,

(b) trends that are dynamically developing in connection with 4.0 - artificial intelligence, business analytics, application mobility, big data, social networks, virtual and augmented reality.

2.2 Results – Main ERP 4.0 Features

To evaluate the results of the ERP 4.0 trend analysis, an analysis of the frequency of occurrence of individual trends was used. According to the resulting frequency, the following trends can be classified as the most recent trends in ERP systems [7]:

- Cloud computing used in ERP systems is the most frequently reported trend [8–12]. Cloud ERP is mentioned as a gateway to modernization, mainly because of lack of innovations available in older traditional solutions.
- Internet of Things (IoT) is a term meaning the connection individual physical devices via the Internet without the active involvement of a person. IoT technology can improve accuracy and expand data availability, resulting in intelligent and more flexible ERP systems [13]. By combining ERP with attached devices (IoT), businesses can use real-time data from any device in the world to gain a competitive advantage [14–16].
- Artificial intelligence and machine learning are among the most frequently mentioned trends. They have already rocked many areas of business, but when it comes to key business functions, the use of artificial intelligence is still in the early stages. Artificial intelligence ERP solutions can take on routine tasks performed so far by humans, design more efficient work processes, or communicate with customers. This could reduce operating costs and increase efficiency.

With lesser frequency, the following digital twin trends emerged in the survey, promising to provide better responses to change, help extend asset life and optimize performance. And also the trend of implementing blockchain technology into ERP systems. It turns out that the most common application of blockchain is to use it as an online book of account records that stores transactions made by users. Combined with cryptography, it can ensure anonymity of operations and prevent unauthorized transactions. The use of Blockchain in ERP promises to change industry by enabling confidence, providing transparency and reducing friction between business ecosystems, potentially reducing costs, reducing transaction clearing time and improving cash flow [8].

Other identified trends include Big Data and their interconnection with ERP and the combination of ERP solutions with Business Intelligence tools. The use of In-Memory Computing (IMC) in ERP is gradually expanding. IMC enables the user to process massive amounts of data at a rate faster and with significantly shorter latency in access to information. Last but not least, mobile ERP applications were often mentioned in the survey. Mobile ERP applications can help companies to improve service quality, improve business relationships, increase employee productivity, and make communication with customers easier and faster [17]. In recent years, social ERP, a system that includes traditional ERP functionality but has integrated social media tools, has been a trendsetter. These tools are built into the system in such a way that both internal employees and external suppliers, customers or other partners can work together.

It is expected that in the future it will be possible to communicate with the ERP system using voice commands. This will again speed up, because a person can say up to 150 words in a minute, but can write only 40. In addition, voice interaction is more natural, efficient and convenient for a person. So there is no reason not to communicate with the ERP system in this way with the help of simple queries, for example, to find the number of sales in the database for the last quarter.

3 Analysis of Supply/Demand View on the Most Important Attributes of ERP 4

3.1 Methodology of Data Collection

The analysis was carried out on the basis of findings from the search part in the form of a questionnaire [7]. The questions were focused mainly on the main trends mentioned by other authors:

cloud [18]
internet of Things (IoT) [19], and
artificial intelligence [20].

In total, the questionnaire contained 17 questions and the Google Forms cloud service was used to create it. The questions concerned the offer of each trend by its supplier in full or partial range at present, or its planned delivery in the 2 or 5 years horizon. These questions were supplemented by questions determining their overall familiarity with the topic on the one hand and the question of whether customers are interested in the questioned 4.0 trends in connection with ERP.

Respondents were selected from the professional portal SystemOnLine.cz from the overview of ERP systems. The collection of replies was closed on 31 March 2019. The response to the survey was 30.2%. A total of 86 ERP system suppliers were addressed, of which 26 companies replied to the questionnaire.

3.2 Results from Analysis

ERP and Cloud
The first set of questions related to the cloud ERP trend. All ERP vendors surveyed said they were familiar with the trend (23% said they had a general idea and 79% of respondents were well versed in this issue).

Answers from 26 companies suggest that 65.4% of ERPs are cloud-based (30.8% of enterprises offer cloud ERP in SaaS, and 34.6% offer cloud ERP solutions in another model). While 75% of companies offer a full ERP functionality in a cloud solution, 6.3% offer hybrid ERP systems where only certain functions are transferred to the cloud, and 18.8% offer both solution options.

The remaining 34.6% do not currently offer any cloud ERP solutions. Of these, 22.2% plan to offer a cloud ERP system within 2 years and 33.3% are considering deploying within 5 years. Roughly half (44.4%) of those who do not offer ERP in the cloud today do not plan to do so in the future.

Investigating this trend showed that companies evaluate customer interest in it on a scale of 1 to 5 (from min to max) fairly evenly and indefinitely at a certain value, with an average value of interest of 2.5.

ERP and IoT (Internet of Things)

The second group of questions concerned the use of the Internet of Things in ERP systems. The term Internet of Things itself has never been encountered by 3.8% of companies, 3.8% are aware of this issue, but do not know exactly what it means, 46.2% have a general idea and the same 46.2% well orientated. It can be seen that this trend is somewhat less known to businesses than the previous cloud ERP trend.

A 26.9% of companies are actively extending their ERP system using IoT technologies, 23.1% of companies plan to expand the ERP system using the Internet of Things within 2 years and 15.4% plan to do so within 5 years. The remaining one third (34.6%) of companies do not use IoT in their ERP solutions, nor do they plan to use it in the future.

If the company stated that it is actively extending its ERP system through the Internet of Things, a supplementary question followed on the functional areas in which the Internet of Things is applied. There were multiple answers to this question and there was also the possibility to add your own answer. Most respondents said they used the Internet of Things to track inventory levels, half of IoT companies used predictive maintenance, a third of respondents reported location and shipment tracking, and one company used IoT to plan production.

At the same time, the company assesses the interest of companies in this trend as low (average value of 1.8) and roughly one half rated them as 1, i.e. as little to no interest.

ERP and Artificial Intelligence

The third group of questions was focused on the use of artificial intelligence in ERP systems. Most companies are familiar with this term (53.8% of companies say they are well versed in this issue and 42.3% of enterprises have a general idea of artificial intelligence). Only 3.8% of companies have never encountered this term. In terms of using AI in ERP, none of the companies indicated that artificial intelligence was at the core of their ERP solution. However, about a quarter (23.1%) said they are actively expanding their ERP system with artificial intelligence. The same percentage (23.1%) of companies plan to extend the ERP system using AI within 2 years and 19.2% within 5 years. Around a third of businesses reported that their ERP system does not use artificial intelligence, nor do they plan to do so.

For companies that said they were actively expanding their ERP system through artificial intelligence, most respondents said they used artificial intelligence in predictive inventory management, two-thirds used it in data analysis and processing, and decision support. One third of AI businesses use conversational systems and digital assistants. Only one company has introduced artificial intelligence in predictive maintenance. Customer interest in ERP solutions using AI is similar to the IoT trend. The average result is just above 2 and so far, customers have not been interested in this trend. To summarize the main findings of the analysis, it should also be remembered that ERP systems were not evaluated qualitatively, as it was important from the point of view of research methodology whether the trend was even offered. The survey results therefore do not reflect the quality of the provider's offer, but only its relation to selected ERP trends.

According to the results of the questionnaire, we can generally say that awareness of given trends among providers is quite good, only some companies have not heard about the Internet of Things and Artificial Intelligence.

It was again confirmed that the world of ERP is quite conservative and quite resistant to change. The cause is not primarily on the suppliers' side, but primarily on the ERP users' side. Customers are often not interested in new trends and technologies, which is mainly due to the low willingness to change their habits and knowledge. In the case of Czech providers, it is also necessary to realize that they are targeted primarily at small and medium-sized enterprises. They do not have as high functional requirements for ERP systems as multinational companies. In addition, they may be discouraged by large initial costs, for example in the case of the introduction of the Internet of Things and artificial intelligence.

4   ERP 4.0 Maturity Model

4.1   Methodology of Maturity Model

The research findings and analyses described above were reflected in the refinement of the ERP 4.0 maturity model. In fact, the key trends of 4.0 can be described from the ERP perspective as 4.0 key enablers. It will enable ERP applications to provide improved and expanded capabilities in traditional functionality of ERP (in the original meaning of ERP – Enterprise Resources Planning):

(a) Improved enterprise resource planning - which will be able to leverage data from IoT sensors, apply the potential of machine learning and artificial intelligence to handle job fulfilment needs more quickly and with more available data, including integration and planning requirements from predictive maintenance. Also interesting is the idea of abandoning the central, centrally conceived role of a plan in ERP, which opens the way to decentralization and autonomy of enterprise planning.

(b) Better decision support - which also builds on decision-making based on more data (thanks to IoT), digital twin data and much data from outside enterprise sources and non-business databases, has already been outlined by the Competitive Intelligence (CI) trend in the previous decade; the integration of social networks and the increasing digital footprint.

(c) Better information sharing - thanks to the "tracing" of orders, generally goods, throughout the logistics chain, but also to the "tracing" of the customer and their requirements and needs with a high share of mobile applications

(d) Higher automation and robotization of all processes, i.e. by supporting administrative processes and not only production and transport robots and automation.

These functional trends of ERP will be reflected in the key model dimensions, i.e. the columns of the proposed maturity model (see Table 1). Its overall concept is based on the previous work and studies of the first co-author [6]. They are based on an analysis of 27 different maturity models, formulating the concept of the model and approach to determine dimensions (columns) and degrees of maturity (rows).

Maturity is evaluated on a 6-degree scale from 0 to 5, where 5 is the highest value and represents the highest possible degree at a given time under given technological, economic, environmental, social, political, legal, health and other important conditions. Lower steps then mean partial fulfilment of the highest possible degree and then the way to it.

4.2   Proposal of ERP 4.0 Maturity Model

In accordance with the ERP 4.0 maturity model described above and exploration of the analysis of ERP 4.0 trends, the following dimensions have been proposed for the ERP 4.0 maturity model:

- The overall model of providing ERP services aiming at cloud
- Integrated technology trends 4.0 aiming at IoT, digital twin, blockchain, etc.
- Improved core functionality of ERP like planning and decision support
- Increasing levels of automation and robotization of business processes supported by ERP.

Table 1. Picture 4: ERP 4.0 maturity model

	Business Model – on promise/cloud	Technology – 4.0 trends	Data – planning and decision support	Processes – digitization and automation
0	Own solution	Based on relational database	Data integration within ERP	Basic ERP processes automated
1	Partly own, partly on promise	Internet connection, mobility of solutions	Data integration with other application	Some new processes digitized and automated
2	Complex on promise	In memory computing	Data analysis	Some new 4.0 processes digitized and automated
3	On promise, partly cloud	Social integration, mobile solutions	Business Intelligence (BI)	Selected new 4.0 processes digitized and automated
4	Complex as a service	IoT, digital twin	Competitive Intelligence	All key 4.0 processes full automated
5	Complex cloud solution	Blockchain, edge computing, quantum computing	Artificial Intelligence (AI) RPA	All business processes full automated

The model design includes the key factors monitored by the analysis - i.e. cloud ERP, IoT and artificial intelligence. In terms of their importance today, they are placed in the highest stages of maturity in the model. The technology dimension is complemented at the highest level by trends like blockchain and edge computing.

The use of the proposed maturity model ERP 4.0 is not only in the as-is state mapping, but also in the to-be state formulation and the overall trajectory of digital transformation and innovation in the enterprise.

5   Conclusion

The analysis helped to formulate the maturity model content for ERP 4.0 applications. This article is based on the assumption that an ERP 4.0 system can be considered as an ERP system that provides the necessary functionality for Industry 4.0. ERP 4.0 is also based on the ERP system's functionalities, but it has moved up to a higher level thanks to the applications of 4.0 trends. The main identified 4.0 trends from the literature review were also verified in the survey among ERP suppliers in the Czech Republic.

References

1. Basl, J.: Pilot study of readiness of czech companies to implement the principles of industry 4.0. Manag. Prod. Eng. Rev. **8**(2), 3–8 (2017). https://doi.org/10.1515/mper-2017-0012. ISSN 2080-8208
2. Basl, J., Sasiadek, M.: Comparison of industry 4.0 application rate in selected polish and czech companies. In: IDIMT-2017 Digitalization in Management, Society and Economy. Poděbrady, 06–08 Spetember 2017, pp. 401–410. Trauner Verlag Universität, Linz (2017). ISBN 978-3-99062-119-6.Available: http://idimt.org/wp-content/uploads/proceedings/IDIMT_proceedings_2017.pdf
3. Basl, J., Kopp, J.: Study of the readiness of czech companies to the industry 4.0. J. Syst. Integr. **8**(3), 40–45 (2017). https://doi.org/10.20470/jsi.v8i3.313
4. Basl, J.: Penetration of industry 4.0 principles into ERP vendors' products and services – a central european study. In: Tjoa, A.M., Zheng, L.-R., Zou, Z., Raffai, M., Xu, L.D., Novak, N.M. (eds.) CONFENIS 2017. LNBIP, vol. 310, pp. 81–90. Springer, Cham (2018). https://doi.org/10.1007/978-3-319-94845-4_8
5. Basl, J.: Analysis of industry 4.0 readiness indexes and maturity models and proposal of the dimension for enterprise information systems. In: Tjoa, A.M., Raffai, M., Doucek, P., Novak, N.M. (eds.) CONFENIS 2018. LNBIP, vol. 327, pp. 57–68. Springer, Cham (2018). https://doi.org/10.1007/978-3-319-99040-8_5
6. Basl, J., Doucek, P.: Metamodel of indexes and maturity models for industry 4.0 readiness in enterprises. In: IDIMT-2018 Strategic Modeling in Management, Economy and Society. Kutna Hora, 05–07 September 2018, pp. 33–40. Trauner Verlag Universität, Linz (2018). ISBN 978-3-99062-339-8. https://idimt.org/wp-content/uploads/proceedings/IDIMT_proceedings_2018.pdf
7. Novakova, M.: Trends of enterprise information systems in 4.0 conditions. Diploma Thesis, University of Economics, Prague (2019)
8. Gartner, Inc.: Gartner Identifies the Top 10 Strategic Technology Trends for 2019 (2018). https://www.gartner.com/en/newsroom/press-releases/2018-10-15-gartner-identifies-the-top-10-strategic-technology-trends-for-2019. Accessed 24 Feb 2019
9. Srubar, J.: QAD system and its support by industry 4.0. Diploma Thesis, University of Economics, Prague (2019)
10. Accenture: 2019 ERP Trends (2018). https://www.accenture.com/t00010101T000000Z__w__/gb-en/_acnmedia/PDF-90/Accenture-Unleashing-Exponential-Evolution-PDF.pdf. Accessed 25 Feb 2019
11. Philips, Ch.: Here Are the Biggest Cloud ERP Trends of 2018. Charles Phillips (2018). https://charlesphillips.me/here-are-the-biggest-cloud-erp-trends-of-2018. Accessed 25 Feb 2019

12. Rust, O., Martinez: 5 Enterprise Resource Planning (ERP) Trends to Watch in 2019 (2018). https://www.pcmag.com/article/351807/5-enterprise-resource-planning-erp-trends-to-watch-in-201. Accessed 25 Feb 2019
13. Stark, Ch.: The history of cloud computing. Cetrom Information Technology, Inc. (2012). https://www.cetrom.net/uncategorized/the-history-of-cloud-computing.   Accessed   10mar 2019
14. Quirk, E.: The latest trends in enterprise resource planning (2018). https://solutionsreview. com/enterprise-resource-planning/erp-trends-2018/. Accessed 25 Feb 2019
15. Macola Software: 8 ERP Trends for 2018 (2018). [https://macola.com/images/pdf/8-erp-trends-macola.pdf?utm_source=macola_com&utm_medium=pdf&utm_campaign=8_erp_trends&utm_term=click. Accessed 26 Feb 2019
16. I-SCOOP: Artificial intelligence in business: challenges and recommendations. i-SCOOP (2018).   https://www.i-scoop.eu/artificial-intelligence-cognitive-computing/artificial-intelligence-business-ai-4-business-summit-belgium. Accessed 28 Mar 2019
17. Lee, I., Lee, K.: The internet of things (IoT): applications, investments, and challenges for enterprises. Bus. Horizons 58(4), 431–440 (2015). https://doi.org/10.1016/j.bushor.2015.03. 008. ISSN 0007-6813
18. Xu, X.: From cloud computing to cloud manufacturing. Robot. Comput.-Integr. Manuf. 28 (1), 75–86 (2012)
19. Wang, S., Wan, J., Li, D., Zhang, C.: Implementing smart factory of industrie 40: an outlook. Int. J. Distrib. Sens. Netw. 10 p (2016). Article ID 3159805. http://dx.doi.org/10. 1155/2016/3159805
20. Zach, A.: How AI Is shaping the future of ERP software. Software Advice (2018). https:// www.softwareadvice.com/resources/ai-erp. Accessed 28 Mar 2019

Systematic Literature Review:
Effects of Digital Technology
on Business Models and Sustainability

Doroteja Vidmar(✉) and Andreja Pucihar

Faculty of Organizational Sciences, University of Maribor,
Kidriceva cesta 55a, 4000 Kranj, Slovenia
doroteja.vidmar@um.si

Abstract. In recent years we are observing two simultaneously ongoing transformations in enterprises. Through systematic literature review we explored existing literature that combines digital technology, business models and sustainability. Using protocol that we placed beforehand we assessed collected papers, classified them and analyzed them focusing on the methodology used, common themes, open research questions and theoretical background.

Keywords: Digital technology · Business model · Sustainability

1 Introduction

In recent years we are observing two simultaneously transformations in the enterprises. Transformation towards sustainable and transformation towards digital - two continuous, ongoing processes that are developing under internal and external pressures and result in changes of the elements of business model (BM). BM can be used as an analytical unit to help us explore the logic and economics of production and consumption in fulfillment of specific needs through specific artifacts [1]. We will be examining the processes of transformation towards sustainable and towards digital in the observed enterprises through the lens of BM.

Globally, humans are not making enough progress in addressing sustainability issues [2], and with time, these challenges are only getting more severe, while our time and options for action are only getting slimmer [3]. Viewing sustainability as the ability to fulfil the present needs without restricting the ability to fulfil those needs in the future [4], combined with the triple bottom-line perspective, according to which sustainable value is a balance between economic, environmental and social value [5] – implies that responsibility and profit should be shared equally between everyone involved in production, consumption and the aftermath of the product/service.

In today's economy the financial capital is overvalued, human capital undervalued and natural capital is not valued at all [6]. Our society lets enterprises privatize profits and socialize costs of their irresponsible use of resources [6, 7]. This economical model needs to be replaced with more sustainable alternative. Wealth inequality needs to be reduced and prices, taxes and incentive systems adapted in such way, that they take into account the real costs that consumption imposes on our environment [2].

© IFIP International Federation for Information Processing 2019
Published by Springer Nature Switzerland AG 2019.
P. Doucek et al. (Eds.): CONFENIS 2019, LNBIP 375, pp. 12–23, 2019.
https://doi.org/10.1007/978-3-030-37632-1_2

In the time when impact of information technologies (IT) on business is already enormous and still growing, reaching digital maturity through digitalization is imperative for enterprises to ensure their competitiveness on the market [8, 9]. Resource-efficiency can be achieved through the use of IT [10], but information systems (IS) sustainability research needs to go beyond Green IT and energy-informatics, that deal primarily with increasing energy-efficiency of technologies [11]. The effects of IT on sustainability are still underestimated and understudied [12]. However, with the growing use of IT, it's influence on innovation for sustainability and thus sustainability is rising as well [13]. This is the time for IS scholars to view sustainability as the imperative in their research agenda and act with the urgency [14].

Our interest in reaching sustainability in enterprises stems from the limited ability of the consumers to reach sustainability in their lives. Sustainability of an enterprise can be reached only if the whole supply chain, or at least parts below it, act sustainably [11]. This implies that a consumer, the link in the traditional supply chain that most chains lead to, can be only as sustainable as the enterprises from which they are consuming products/services. This un-sustainable predisposition of our whole economy is in dire need of change. We argue that IS' strategic roles (automation, information and transformation) can lead our society towards sustainability [11, 13].

The need for inter-disciplinary research on sustainability and IS was previously observed by other researchers [11, 14, 15] and it is becoming more visible in business, where emerging sustainability-oriented BMs (e.g. PSS (product-service systems), CE (circular economy)) are driven by widespread use of IT [13, 16] and enterprise information systems (EIS).

We chose BM perspective to evaluate change that IT is causing in sustainability of enterprises. In this paper we aim to asses existing inter-disciplinary research on the effects of IT on sustainability performance, through use of business model innovation (BMI). We aim to identify current research gaps, search for possible contributing variables and explore interconnections between them. Findings from this paper will be used as a base for further research.

The paper is organized as follows: in the Sect. 2 findings from existing literature are presented, in Sect. 3, we present methodology, including selection protocol and quality assessment criteria. In the Sect. 4 we present the results of systematic literature review and in Sect. 5, we discuss the findings and present limitations, possible further research directions and conclusions.

2 Previous Literature Reviews

While searching for literature, we found a handful of literature reviews exploring the connections between IT, sustainability and BM. Literature reviews were published between the years of 2007 and 2018, they tackled the topics from various angles, emphasizing very different areas and were of various rigor and relevance. In Table 1 we present in chronological order those that were of relevance to us.

Table 1. Previous literature reviews.

Reference	Journal	Content
[17]	MIS Quarterly	Demonstrating and advocating a research agenda to establish subfield of IS tackling the issue of high energy use; focus on research opportunities for IS scholars; proposed framework for »energy informatics«
[12]	MIS Quarterly	Focus on environmental sustainability; developing research agenda for IS innovation for sustainability; author demonstrated IS can play a key role in shaping attitude, enabling and transforming economic and environmental sustainability in organizations; belief–action–outcome (BAO) framework
[18]	ERSCP-EMSU Conference	Technology is discussed as a driver of BMI; focus on BMI as strategic factor that supports the adoption of more sustainable products, processes, supply chains; moving closer to conceptualization of sustainable BMs
[11]	Journal of Strategic Information Systems	Authors developed sustainability framework based on resource-based-view (RBV); examined strategic roles of IS (automate, informate, transform and infrastructure); call for IT to move beyond reducing energy consumption
[1]	Journal of Cleaner Production	Advancing research on sustainability by adopting BM perspective; authors examined literature on BMs, proposed requirements a BM should meet in order to support innovations for fostering sustainability and proposed a set of questions that should guide future research agenda
[19]	Business Horizons	Exploring whether »sharing economy« is only a trend or a real shift in consumption of goods; authors discuss the role of technology, shift in values of consumers, potential of sharing BMs
[20]	Sustainability	Investigating the opportunities and challenges digitalization brought to public transport and possible contributions towards sustainability; authors discuss economic, environmental and social perspectives through studied literature
[21]	PICMET Conference	Exploring the impact of Internet of Things (IoT) has on innovation for sustainability; authors aimed to examine enablers and barriers in innovation for sustainability; discuss the potential of internet of things (IoT)
[22]	Technological Forecasting & Social Change	Through study of literature authors identified a research gap on integration between circular economy (CE) and large data; proposed a framework; set foundations for future research

Through literature reviews we can observe how research on reaching sustainability through the use of IT in organizations developed – first steps in 2010 were solely about IS scholars helping decrease energy use in and lessen environmental degradation. Technology is already seen as one of the drivers for sustainable advancement and sustainable BMs are already mentioned.

In 2011 we notice the need to broaden the contribution of IS to sustainability, which meant including economic, environmental and social sustainability. In 2013 scholars argued for advancements in research through BM perspective.

After 2016 we observe shift in consumer values, causing rise of novel BMs and foci of research being how specific types of BMs, fields and technologies tackle sustainability.

2.1   Key Findings from Literature

What we can learn from the literature is that sustainability advancements of society are not likely without improving sustainability in organizations [23]. Significant sustainability impact can be reached through the use of technologies or through BMI [21], meaning that not only what organizations do for business, but complete shift in the way the business is conducted is required [24]. BMs are seen as key initiators [23] or at least support for systematic and continuous changes in corporate sustainability [18, 24].

Relating to technology, BMs are seen as mediators between how technology is made, technology itself and how it is eventually used [1]. Its »role as a market device« can manifest in different ways: creation of new business models through which tech nologies are used, adoption of new technologies in existing BMs, existing BM triggering technological innovation or technologies triggering creation of new BMs [1].

Not much of the research focused on the role of technology to address issues of sustainability [11, 21], but in existing research, technologies are seen as key, often undervalued and underused, factors enabling the implementation of sustainable BMs [12, 21]. »Increased digitalization is seen to provide multiple value creation mechanisms and possibilities by enhancing the more effective use of resources« [21]. It is well established that IT resources enable various business capabilities, from what we can argue that IT resources may be critical to develop capabilities to tackle sustainability issues [11] – and these connections should be explored in order to develop body of knowledge and improve sustainability [12].

Even though the environmental perspective of sustainability tends to be most commonly addressed, social implications of business need to be considered as well. Through transformation of supply chain businesses can stimulate social changes (e.g. decreased poverty, improved health, gender equity, life quality) [21].

All three dimensions of sustainability need to be balanced, which poses a major challenge [21]. It has been shown that environmental and economic performance reinforce each other [11] and enterprises focus firstly and mostly on economic sustainability and then on environmental sustainability – while social implications tend to stay unaddressed [11]. To tackle this issue of not-addressing social sustainability, every enterprise should tackle sustainability from two organizational departments: human resources and operations [11]. While both departments should be concerned with economic sustainability, operations should additionally consider environmental sustainability and human resources social sustainability.

Our global economic system is set for enterprises, who are not held responsible for full cost of their unsustainable activities – if they were, they would have the incentive to act sustainable [17]. Market regulation, along with BMI and technological progress are seen as three essential drivers of innovation for sustainability [18] – implying that markets need to be regulated for sustainability.

Research agenda for IS and sustainability should focus on »informing beliefs, enabling actions, and transforming outcomes« [12]. And while humanity faces rising threats that are caused by unsustainable actions of individuals and enterprises, enterprises are experiencing threats of changed business environment. Changes are now caused in large part by rising digital maturity of competitors [8] whose use of IT is enabling innovative BMs. Fast growth of these potentially more sustainable BMs [25] is fueled by shift in values of individuals, who turn more and more toward »liquid and adaptable lifestyle«. Possession is no longer seen so much as commodity but as constraint to mobility - causing the dramatic drop in the value of ownership [19].

It should also be noted that changes in consumption of individuals might influence sustainability positively or negatively [25]. In order to tackle this issue, access to accurate and timely information is necessary [20]. In transport system one of the key examples when talking about sustainable BMs, IT is used to continuously monitor the data and use it to support decisions of system operators and users [26]. Collection and analysis of information is the activity that IS/EIS can bring to other fields and help drastically improve sustainability efforts simply by informing [12, 17, 22].

3   Methodology for Systematic Review of Literature

Based on various guidelines for conducting systematic literature reviews [27–29], we outlined the protocol for conducting systematic literature review. The protocol must be in place beforehand in order to protect us from literature bias [28]. Unfortunately, this does not protect against publication bias, which needs to be accounted for [28].

3.1   Review Protocol

Based on the recommendations [28, 29] we decided to include the following steps:

Research Question. Goal of this literature review is to assess scope, nature and quality of academic literature on inter-disciplinary research combining the fields of sustainability, effects of IT and BMI. Our focus is on the role of IT in BMI towards sustainability. We aim to identify gaps in research, explore interconnections between contributing factors and prepare a base to be used for further inter-disciplinary research.

Search Strategy. Everything needs to be documented! (To ensure that the search for obtained literature is at least partially repeatable.)

Search was conducted exclusively through electronic sources. We searched in the top IS digital libraries (Web of Science, Scopus, Science Direct, IEEExplore) and AIS Senior Scholars' Basket of Journals (European Journal of Information Systems,

Information Systems Journal, Information Systems Research, Journal of AIS, Journal of Information Technology, Journal of MIS, Journal of Strategic Information Systems, MIS Quarterly).

All papers from digital libraries were retrieved through queries covering all three areas of interest: IT (digital transformation, digital maturity, digitalization, digitization), sustainability (sustainability, sustainable innovation, innovation for sustainability), BMI.

We developed keywords and constructed search strings including all three areas of interest. Search strings were adapted based on the demands of search mechanisms of different databases to ensure optimal collection of results. Papers retrieved directly from journals were obtained by custom search strings combined with manual search. Search strings were adapted based on the search mechanisms of each webpage.

Additionally, we performed backward literature search procedure, based on papers that were obtained through search in digital libraries that passed the practical screen and quality assessment. Lists of references were searched for additional papers.

Practical Screen. Field of IS unique for combining qualitative and quantitative research, guiding towards adapted systematic literature review (SLR) procedure [29]. Once the search results are obtained, they need to go through screening process to establish their relevance [28]. In this step we provide a set of inclusion/exclusion criteria we used to determine whether the obtained papers should be included in the literature review.

All papers included in literature review needed to be: accessible (we need to be able to gain full access), written in English, include topics of information technology, sustainability and business models (based on title, keywords and abstract).

Quality Assessment. Papers obtained through described search strategies and not excluded through practical screening process were subjected to additional quality assessment. Criteria that we selected for quality assessment of papers are: were all three topics of interest addressed? Was paper published in scientific journal or conference proceedings? Papers that didn't meet the selected criteria were excluded, since objective of quality assessment is to exclude papers that passed practical screen, but their focus is not in the areas that are of interest to us, or the quality of paper is questionable.

For us, quality assessment was especially important, since term sustainability is often used in two different meanings. We are focused on sustainability related to the Brundtland commission definition [4] and focusing on at least one of the scopes of the triple bottom line – environmental, social and economic profit [5] Often, sustainability is mentioned only as long term survival of organization – this is not sustainability that we are focused on, and papers focusing on this aspect of sustainability were excluded.

Quality Classes. All papers will be classified [27] into two categories: Class A papers - papers published in impact factor journal and Class B papers – professional reports, papers published in less-reputable journals and in conference proceedings.

Data Extraction and Analysis. Aim of this review is to assess scope, quality and maturity of papers written on topics of digital transformation, need for sustainability and their impact on BM.

Papers were classified into 2 quality classes described above, and for each paper we checked the following: where was the paper published; year of publication; methodology; is problem clearly defined; is problem statement answered; are crucial terms clearly defined; what methods and approach were used; are there any theories mentioned; what were the main factors mentioned; did authors identify any research gaps?

4   Results

After completing the search for papers through electronic databases and AIS Senior Scholars' Basket of Journals, practical screen and quality assessment of obtained papers was conducted. Backward search for additional papers through the references of all included papers was conducted. Additionally, practical screen and quality assessment of papers identified through backward search was conducted. In the end, we were left with 23 papers that were relevant to us.

Papers that we decided to include in our review were published from 2007 to 2018.

All included papers were divided into 2 quality classes, A and B, adapted from [27], we have 12 class A papers (published in high impact factor journal) and 11 class B papers (professional reports, papers published in less-reputable journals and conferences – as can be seen from Table 2.

Table 2. Papers included in systematic literature review.

#	Title and reference	Year	Class
1	A new electronic service for UK theses: access transformed by EThOS [30]	2007	A
2	The fourth wave of digitalization and public transport: opportunities and challenges [20]	2016	A
3	How GoGet CarShare's product-service system is facilitating collaborative consumption [16]	2017	A
4	Driving business transformation toward sustainability: exploring the impact of supporting IS on the performance contribution of eco-innovations [13]	2017	A
5	What makes a sustainable business model successful? An empirical comparison of two peer-to-peer goods-sharing platforms [31]	2018	A
6	Unlocking the circular economy through new business models based on large-scale data: an integrative framework and research agenda [22]	2017	A
7	Getting smart about urban mobility – aligning the paradigms of smart and sustainable [26]	2016	A
8	Information systems and environmentally sustainable development: energy informatics and new directions for the IS community [17]	2010	A
9	Information systems innovation for environmental sustainability [12]	2010	A
10	From green to sustainability: information technology and an integrated sustainability framework [11]	2011	A

(continued)

Table 2. (*continued*)

#	Title and reference	Year	Class
11	Business models for sustainable innovation: state-of-the-art and steps towards a research agenda [1]	2013	A
12	Sharing yet caring [25]	2018	A
13	Innovative business models for smart cities: overview of recent trends [32]	2012	B
14	Crowdsensing-based transportation services - an analysis from business model and sustainability viewpoints [33]	2016	B
15	Developing disruptive innovations for sustainability: a review on impact of internet of things (IOT) [21]	2017	B
16	Exploration of simulation-driven support tools for sustainable product development [34]	2017	B
17	Metals industry: road to digitalization [35]	2017	B
18	Second-movers' advantage of utilizing big data to enhance sustainability performance: the case of elevator industry [36]	2016	B
19	An industry 4.0 research agenda for sustainable business models [37]	2017	B
20	Re-distributed manufacturing to achieve a circular economy: a case study utilizing IDEF0 modeling [38]	2017	B
21	Towards a conceptual framework of business models for sustainability [18]	2010	B
22	Organizational self-renewal: the role of green is in developing eco-effectiveness [39]	2012	B
23	Developing smart services by internet of things in manufacturing business [40]	2018	B

5 Qualitative Assessment

Methodological approaches that were most commonly used were literature review and case-study. Rigor of literature reviews in class A and class B varied.

The most prominent difference between classes A and B was in case-study approach, where authors of class A papers used mixed approach, combining case-studies with other methods or at least provided reader with multiple case-studies, in-depth explanation and cross-case analysis.

In one instance case-study was conducted in the same enterprise multiple times over the course of 2 years and combined with 15 in-depth interviews [16].

One article cross-analyzed case-studies from 8 different enterprises and described methodology and results in great depth [13].

Theories were not commonly mentioned in selected papers. Those that were mentioned, are: Theory of two-sided (and multi-sided) markets [31, 33], resource-based view (RBV) [11, 13], product life-cycle [34, 37], sociotechnical theory [26], technology acceptance model (TAM) [12], and agency theory [25].

Worth mentioning is that theory of two-sided markets is often used with platform economy, while resource-based view is sometimes mentioned if the study focuses on ecological sustainability and limited resources.

Recurring themes are platform economy (also collaborative economy, sharing economy, collective economy), public/communal transport, (PSS), (CE).

Sustainability is in most cases understood as triple bottom line perspective [5] – environmental, social and economic gains – 6 instances, or as ecological/environmental perspective - in 5 cases. Interestingly, even though not very popular, economic and environmental perspective are sometimes considered combined and economic perspective is sometimes considered as sole sustainability perspective. Social perspective on sustainability is mentioned only as a part of triple bottom line trio.

Regarding definitions of **BM**, there were three general options: either no definition of BM is offered, a type of BM is mentioned, or other authors' definitions are given as an example. The only exception to this was viewing BM as an analytical perspective that helps us understand economic logic of need-fulfilment through artefacts [1], [18].

We already spoke about duality of term sustainability. Additionally, we soon noticed that not many papers mention term **digital transformation**. Instead the use of IT and the effects of IT on business practices is often mentioned, as well as digitalization or even digitization and their effects. Often state of the art technologies are mentioned - IOT, big data, smart.

We see no need to use the term digital transformation, or even digital maturity, as the term in itself only describes the effects that IT has on business environment. We therefore included all results that dealt with interconnections between sustainability, BMs and IS or IT.

In the next step, we identified **moderating and mediating variables** from the research. We only found one possible **mediating variable (MeV) – BMI**. BMI connects IT and demand for sustainability, creating hybrid solutions, which can be deployed on a larger scale than without the use of IT [13], potentially reaching higher impact on overall sustainability performance.

We identified several **moderating variables (MoV)**, which we sorted into two groups:

MoVs Affecting Relationsip Between Green IT and BMI: proactiveness of IT stance [13]; use of supporting IS [13]; organizational aspiration level of eco-innovation use [13].

MoVs Affecting Relationsip Between BMI and Sustainability: putting pro-social objectives first, in order to attract users [16]; adequate/critical mass of users [16, 31, 33]; crowdsourcing [33]; hybrid business/social models [13, 16]; offering complementary activities instead of radical adoption of new technologies to reach sustainability objectives [16]; design and execution of BMs [31]; strategic agility [31]; constant BMI [31].

6 Discussion of Key Findings

Focus of this research is to determine whether IT can act as an enabler and driver of increased sustainability through BMI. The reasoning behind the idea is that enterprises are rarely leading the sustainability movement – and through the presence of mostly unsustainable products and services on the market they affect customer choice. Therefore, they are not only responsible for their own non-sustainability, but are co-responsible for non-sustainability of customers, that they affected through lack of sustainable options and adequate disposal methods.

Inter-disciplinary research on the topic of sustainability, BMs and IT is still in its birthing stage, which is evident from low number of relevant results, lack of diversity and choice in methodology, gap in methodology pointing toward the need to conduct more qualitative research and eventually quantitative research.

However, literature obtained from high impact journals shows that the interest of academia for inter-disciplinary take on proposed subjects deserves attention.

Researchers from IS community often act ignorant about the fact, that they too can tackle the problems of sustainability [17]. Some researchers focus on research opportunities, so that other information systems scholars can focus on delivering solutions [17]. Research on contribution of IT and EIS for sustainability is limited and rarely stretches beyond reducing the consumption of energy [11] and additional insight on how to use IS to transition to sustainability is needed [15]. In first attempts, information systems scholars focused on energy and resource reduction (Green IT or Green in IT), or the practices where IT is a contributor towards sustainability [13]. Almost a decade later, IT is seen as a possible solution that will enable us to reach sustainability (therefore we will become Green by IT). Some authors [23] propose research on how BMs for sustainability evolve in the process leading to industry transformations. They believe that insight is needed on how impacts of such BMs can be managed or measured.

"The economics of sustainability need not be permanently set for organizations. As regulations change, the economics change and markets can become mechanisms for sustainability" [17]. We are observing these changes in economy through occurrence of new and changed BMs. A pattern emerges from the literature, proposing IT is often seen as a driver and enabler of BMI, which is used to reach sustainability of enterprises.

Acknowledgements. This research was supported by the Slovenian Research Agency; Program No. P5-0018—Decision Support Systems in Digital Business.

References

1. Boons, F., Lüdeke-Freund, F.: Business models for sustainable innovation: state-of-the-art and steps towards a research agenda. J. Clean. Prod. **45**, 9–19 (2013)
2. Ripple, W.J., et al.: World scientists' warning to humanity: a second notice. Bioscience **67** (12), 1026–1028 (2017)
3. Broman, G.I., Robert, K.-H.: A framework for strategic sustainable development. J. Clean. Prod. **140**(1), 17–31 (2017)

4. World Commission on Environment and Development: Report of the World Commission on Environment and Development: Our Common Future (1987)
5. Elkington, J.: Cannibals with Forks: The Triple Bottom Line of 21st Century Business. Wiley, Hoboken (1997)
6. Potočnik, J.: Keynote speech: transition to a sustainable economy – the critical role of digital transformation. In: 31ST Bled eConference Digital Transformation: Meeting the Challenges (2018)
7. University of California and Vox, Climate Lab S1 E2: Going green shouldn't be this hard (2017)
8. Kane, G.C., Palmer, D., Phillips, A.N., Kiron, D., Buckley, N.: Achieving digital maturity (2017)
9. Kane, G.C., Palmer, D., Phillips, A.N., Kiron, D., Buckley, N.: Coming of age digitally: learning, leadership, and legacy (2018)
10. Gholami, R., Sulaiman, A.B., Ramayah, T., Molla, A.: Senior managers' perception on green information systems (IS) adoption and environmental performance: results from a field survey. Inf. Manag. **50**, 431–438 (2013)
11. Dao, V., Langella, I., Carbo, J.: From green to sustainability: information technology and an integrated sustainability framework. J. Strateg. Inf. Syst. **20**, 63–79 (2011)
12. Melville, N.P.: Information systems innovation for environmental sustainability. MIS Q. **34** (1), 1–21 (2010)
13. Hanelt, A., Busse, S., Kolbe, L.M.: Driving business transformation toward sustainability: exploring the impact of supporting IS on the performance contribution of eco-innovations. Inf. Syst. J. **27**(4), 463–502 (2017)
14. Seidel, S., et al.: The sustainability imperative in information systems research. Commun. Assoc. Inf. Syst. **40**, 3 (2017)
15. Malhotra, A., Melville, N.P., Ross, S.M., Watson, R.T.: Spurring impactful research on information systems for environmental sustainability. MIS Q. **37**(4), 1265–1274 (2013)
16. Tan, F.T.C., Cahalane, M., Tan, B., Englert, J.: How GoGet CarShare's product-service system is facilitating collaborative consumption. MIS Q. Exec. **16**(4), 265–277 (2017)
17. Watson, R.T., Boudreau, M.-C., Chen, A.J.: Information systems and environmentally sustainable development: energy informatics and new directions for the IS community. Source MIS Q. **34**(1), 23–38 (2010)
18. Lüdeke-Freund, F.: Towards a conceptual framework of business models for sustainability. In: Knowledge Collaboration and Learning for Sustainable Innovation – Conference Proceedings, 14th European Roundtable on Sustainable Consumption and Production (ERSCP) and 6th Environmental Management for Sustainable Universities (EMSU), 25–29 October 2010
19. Kathan, W., Matzler, K., Veider, V.: The sharing economy: your business model's friend or foe? Bus. Horiz. **59**(6), 663–672 (2016)
20. Davidsson, P., Hajinasab, B., Holmgren, J., Jevinger, Å., Persson, J.: The fourth wave of digitalization and public transport: opportunities and challenges. Sustainability **8**(12), 1248 (2016)
21. Nasiri, M., Tura, N., Ojanen, V.: Developing disruptive innovations for sustainability: a review on impact of internet of things (IOT). In: 2017 Proceedings of PICMET 2017: Technology Management for Interconnected World (2017)
22. Jose, C., Jabbour, C., De Sousa Jabbour, A.B.L., Sarkis, J., Filho, G.: Unlocking the circular economy through new business models based on large-scale data: an integrative framework and research agenda. Technol. Forecast. Soc. Chang. **144**, 546–552 (2019)
23. Schaltegger, S., Hansen, E.G., Lüdeke-Freund, F.: business models for sustainability: origins, present research, and future avenues. Organ. Environ. **29**(1), 3–10 (2016)

24. Bocken, N., Short, S.W., Rana, P., Evans, S.: A literature and practice review to develop sustainable business model archetypes. J. Clean. Prod. **65**, 42–56 (2014)
25. Hildebrandt, B., Hanelt, A., Firk, S.: Sharing yet caring: mitigating moral hazard in access-based consumption through IS-enabled value co-capturing with consumers. Bus. Inf. Syst. Eng. **60**(3), 227–241 (2018)
26. Lyons, G.: Getting smart about urban mobility - aligning the paradigms of smart and sustainable. Transp. Res. Part A Policy Pract. **115**, 4–14 (2018)
27. Ali, S., Li, H., Khan, S.U., Zhongguo, Y.: Practices in software outsourcing partnership: systematic literature review protocol with analysis. J. Comput. **13**(7), 839–861 (2018)
28. Kitchenham, B., Charters, S.: Guidelines for performing systematic literature reviews in software engineering (2007)
29. Okoli, C., Schabram, K.: A guide to conducting a systematic literature review of information systems research. Sprouts Work. Pap. Inf. Syst. **10**(26) (2010)
30. Troman, A., Jacobs, N., Copeland, S.: A new electronic service for UK theses: access transformed by EThOS. Interlend. Doc. Supply **35**(3), 157–163 (2007)
31. Piscicelli, L., Ludden, G.D.S., Cooper, T.: What makes a sustainable business model successful? An empirical comparison of two peer-to-peer goods-sharing platforms. J. Clean. Prod. **172**, 4580–4591 (2018)
32. Molinari, F.: Innovative business models for smart cities: overview of recent trends. In: Proceedings of the 12th European Conference on eGovernment (2012)
33. Heiskala, M., Jokinen, J.-P., Tinnilä, M.: Crowdsensing-based transportation services—an analysis from business model and sustainability viewpoints. Res. Transp. Bus. Manag. **18**, 38–48 (2016)
34. Jaghbeer, Y., Hallstedt, S.I., Larsson, T., Wall, J.: Exploration of simulation-driven support tools for sustainable product development. Proc. CIRP **64**, 271–276 (2017)
35. Merluzzi, A., Brunetti, G.: Metals industry: road to digitalization. In: 2017 40th International Convention on Information and Communication Technology, Electronics and Microelectronics, MIPRO 2017 - Proceedings (2017)
36. Ng, A.W., Wong, A.K.L., Wut, T.M.: Second-movers' advantage of utilizing Big Data to enhance sustainability performance: the case of elevator industry. In: Proceedings of the International Conference on Industrial Engineering and Operations Management (2016)
37. Cornelis De Man, J., Strandhagen, J.O.: An industry 4.0 research agenda for sustainable business models. Proc. CIRP **63**, 721–726 (2017)
38. Moreno, M., et al.: Re-distributed manufacturing to achieve a circular economy: a case study utilizing idef0 modeling. Proc. CIRP **63**, 686–691 (2017)
39. Hedman, J., Henningsson, S., Selander, L.: Organizational self-renewal: the role of green is in developing eco-effectiveness. In: ICIS 2012 Proceedings (2012)
40. Cedeño, J.M.V., Papinniemi, J., Hannola, L., Donoghue, I.: Developing smart services by internet of things in manufacturing business. LogForum **14**(1), 59–71 (2018)

IS Research Theoretical Foundation: Theories Used and the Future Path

Nastaran Hajiheydari[1(✉)], Mohammad Soltani Delgosha[2], and Mojtaba Talafidaryani[3]

[1] Management School, University of Sheffield, Sheffield, UK
n.hajiheydari@sheffield.ac.uk
[2] Business School, UWE Bristol University, Bristol, UK
mohammad.soltanidelgosha@uwe.ac.uk
[3] Faculty of Management, University of Tehran, Tehran, Iran
mojtabatalafi@ut.ac.ir

Abstract. The way a scientific field applies theories shapes its intellectual structure and determines its development and survival as a discipline. Information Systems (IS) with its multidimensional nature and innovatory essence has a different contingence with its original theories, which are basically rooted in a diverse spectrum of fields. This research is designed to investigate which theories have been deployed in different IS research streams in the last decade, and by analyzing the perceived gap, how it might be changed in the future. To this aim, a data-driven method for analyzing the published papers' cited references in the top two IS journals is designed and implemented. This study is directed based on the co-citation network analysis, text analysis, and investigation of the highly cited references in MISQ and ISR from 2009 to 2018. The analysis of the top-cited references co-citation network revealed six distinct clusters representing the research areas in our field including IS Value, IS Research, E-commerce, IS in Organization, Social Network Analysis, and IS Usage. Further, text analysis and interpretations disclosed the main and the dominant theoretical foundation in each cluster and their linkages. By examining the relationships between the clusters and their theories, the eminent theoretical gap in E-commerce cluster is distinguished. Subsequently, some fact-based hypotheses about what would be changed in this cluster in the future are represented. Considering a wider timespan, including data from basket of 8 journals and deeply analyzing all clusters, this study could be continued.

Keywords: IS theory · Theoretical foundation · IS research clusters · Co-citation analysis · Text analysis

1 Introduction

Information Systems (IS) field of research has been the subject to identity crisis during the time [1–3]. The multidisciplinary nature of this field raises lots of debates about the main origin, focus, and scientific contribution of IS and how it could survive and grow as a discipline [4]. Although the importance of IS in value creation and how it affects business success and competitiveness are proven [5, 6], the way its intellectual

© IFIP International Federation for Information Processing 2019
Published by Springer Nature Switzerland AG 2019
P. Doucek et al. (Eds.): CONFENIS 2019, LNBIP 375, pp. 24–39, 2019.
https://doi.org/10.1007/978-3-030-37632-1_3

structure founded and its scientific originality are continuously controversial. Based on its nature, IS field of research is rooted in different basic fields such as psychology, sociology, system science, management, economics, and strategy and these fields have contributed toward IS emergence and growth [7]. As a very rapidly changing knowledge domain, scientific focus in this field has been shifted from time to time and the researchers' concentration changed frequently [8]. IS research also covers wide range of topics including IS usage/adoption, IS design and development, e-commerce/e-business, IS research, knowledge management, IS evaluation, software and programming languages, IS functional applications, telecommunication and networking, and internal/external environment of IT [8], which are diverse and different in concept and impact. The diverse nature of IS and how its semantic structure is shaped from one side, and the emerging concepts and technologies on the other side make this field both complicated to comprehend and essential to be examined.

The multidimensional essence of IS besides the variant typology for discussing the nature of theory in this field [9] cause the increasing level of ambiguity in the discourse of IS theory. Although some debates about the role and the importance of theory in IS are stated [10], there is no doubt that theoretical foundation of each scientific discipline is very crucial for shaping the semantic structure of discipline, for moving further than the patterns and simply for explanation, and prediction of the associated phenomena [11]. Additionally, IS scholars' ability to understand and contribute to theory is considered an essential qualification in research practice [11]. Generally, it is perceived that the theory foundation in any scientific field is the main platform for the growth and the survival of the discipline; and IS field is not an exemption. A theory is mainly perceived as a systematic explanatory scheme for describing the patterns and regularities in a discipline [12].

There are several of grounds for believing that examining the theories used in IS research is both essential and timely. Firstly, IS, as an ever-changing field of research, periodically needs to take the stock and represent how the core theoretical ideas are developing. It seems that the previous theories becoming out of date or ill-suited mainly due to major and radical change in type of data [13]. Secondly, calls continue for "next-generation information systems theories" principally based on the fundamental change in the core phenomenon, which is becoming increasingly intelligent, interconnected, and infused through all the contexts [14]. Finally, looking at the previous trends might help in depicting a better picture of what would happen in the future in a research discipline [15]. Therefore, investigation of theories applied in the IS field, understanding their connections and the foundational gaps make essential contributions in clarification of IS context and its backbone, hence are important for the scholars.

1.1 Literature Review and Related Works

The theoretical foundation of IS has been an issue in the field occasionally [16–20]. Researchers followed different approaches to study cornerstone theories in IS research ranging from pure quantitative technical methods including n-gram analysis [19], complex network analysis [17], statistical methods [18], to mixed approaches [16], and even absolutely subjective and judgmental investigation [20]. Soper, Turel and Geri [19] reported on the list of IS field's most commonly used theories, their co-occurrence and their priority in the top three IS journals from 1990 through 2011. They applied the measurement model considering the "relative frequency" of a theory in the literature, which might be biased in reflecting the real importance and effect of a theory. Similarly, Lim, Saldanha, Malladi and Melville [17] tried to investigate the type of theories are borrowed in IS by analyzing the published papers during 1998–2006 in MISQ and ISR and their analysis is limited to the top five theories in each IS stream. Moody, Iacob, Amrit and Müller [18] conducted comparable analysis using the reference lists of all papers published in the five leading IS journals over 5 years (2003–2007) and they revealed the top 10 influential sources including six important theories and four significant research method sources. Although, de Vaujany, Lesca, Fomin and Loebbecke [16] used a different approach by concentrating on the General Editorials Statements (GES) of the top 30 IS journals for the years 1997 and 2007. They reported on the words with similar repetition and related concepts in these two different time horizons and their study showed that not the expectations by journals from researchers have changed and nor the lexical diversity increased over time. Considering the limitation of GES in representing IS foundations, the ultimate change during the time could not be discovered by their study. Weber [20] was seeking to propose a framework with which evaluation of the quality of an existing theory could be facilitated. The result of this qualitative research does not assist in choosing the focal phenomena and the ways these phenomena might be conceived.

Considering the recent major evolution in our field due to the massive technological enhancement during the last decade, and regarding the intrinsic limitation of the previous studies, this research is designed to investigate the highlighted theoretical base of the recent IS studies and to indicate what might be changed in the future.

1.2   Motivations and Contributions

This study is defined to represent the recent and probable future status of the IS theoretical background deploying a systematic and data-driven approach in analyzing the highly cited references in the two top IS journals in the last ten years. Considering the contribution of clarifying the theoretical context of any discipline in defining its boundaries and recalling the more interconnected economy and society and the recent data revolution, we are motivated to define this research to answer the following major questions:

1. Which prominent theories formulate the intellectual core of the IS research streams in the last decade?
2. What would be the probable future contribution of distinctive theories in the different IS research areas?

These important issues not only contribute massively toward our discipline intellectual structure definition, also are the basic concern of scholars in IS, which necessitate this study focusing on the recent publications and applying innovative mixed method.

2 Research Method

This research is conducted in five steps shown in Fig. 1. In the first step, the bibliographic data of scholarly articles published in *MIS Quarterly* (MISQ) and *Information Systems Research* (ISR) journals during the last decade (from 2009 to 2018) are retrieved through the Web of Science database. Since the selected journals are two pioneering research journals in IS discipline [9], the analyses are anchored on data extracted from these journals' publications. The chosen timespan implies that the research questions needed pretty recent scientific evidence to be addressed. Concerning the research aim, from all the bibliographic attributes in the result dataset, we used the cited references attribute, which represents the references cited in the articles published in the mentioned journals and timespan (target articles).

Fig. 1. An overview on the research design

In the second and the third steps, the references cited together are analyzed applying co-citation analysis, and the hidden clusters based on the co-citation relationships are revealed. To this end, 154 cited references with the highest number of citations in the target articles are selected and their co-citation network is prepared. The appropriate number of the nodes is determined based on the software's default suggestion alongside the authors' judgment about other numbers. In the co-citation network, each node represents a cited reference that its size is defined based on the number of reference's citations, and the edges between references indicate their co-citations. Since the visualization of the network is distance-based, the more proximity of references cues to their more co-citations and consequently, their more content relatedness. Therefore, it is expected that a group of adjacent nodes forms a cluster of related cited references. The cluster analysis determines these groups and differentiates them with different colors. The apt number of clusters is defined based on the interpretability of different networks with varying numbers of clusters. These two steps are performed using VOSviewer software [21].

It is worth to mention the VOSviewer unified approach based on the compendious discussion provided by Van Eck and Waltman [22]. VOSviewer accomplishes three major tasks, including normalization, mapping, and clustering to generate any variant of clustered bibliometric network, such as a clustered co-citation network. Firstly, VOSviewer takes the association strength normalization, which is extensively explained by Van Eck and Waltman [23], to normalize the high variances between nodes in the number of links they have. Secondly, it maps the normalized network based on a distance-based approach in a two-dimensional space. For this aim, VOSviewer employs the VOS mapping technique discussed by Van Eck, Waltman, Dekker and van den Berg [24] in detail. This technique tries to solve a minimizing problem using a kind of Scaling by MAjorizing a COmplicated Function (SMACOF) algorithm similar to Borg and Groenen [25]. The problem is to minimize a sum of the squared Euclidean distances between all pairs of nodes, in which the squared distance between a pair of nodes is weighted by the similarity between them, subject to the constraint that the average distance between two nodes must be equal to one. Finally, VOSviewer clusters the nodes in the mapped network in such a way that a cluster comprises a group of closely related nodes without any overlap with any other cluster. The VOS clustering technique is completely described by Waltman, Van Eck and Noyons [26]. In this technique, VOSviewer solves a maximizing problem using the Smart Local Moving (SLM) algorithm introduced by Waltman and Van Eck [27]. The problem is to maximize a weighted and parameterized type of the modularity function introduced by Newman and Girvan [28]. In other words, the VOS clustering is a kind of modularity-based clustering. Therefore, VOSviewer solves an optimization problem in both mapping and clustering tasks. There is a notable mathematical relationship between the problems, which is the basis of a unified approach used by VOSviewer to map and cluster the nodes in a bibliometric network.

In the fourth step, the abstracts of cited references appeared in the network are collected. For references without an abstract, the titles have been substituted. Then, the authors attempted to process resulting corpus using text-processing techniques to analyze the references' content. To this aim, firstly, pre-processing tasks have been conducted by python coding to cleanse the corpus. These tasks include conversion of upper cases to lower cases, removing punctuations and digits, stripping from double-spaces, elimination of stopwords, and stemming. Then, WordItOut[1], which is an online application for a word-cloud generation, is used to produce clusters' word-cloud of the clean corpus. Each word-cloud depicts about 100 words with the highest number of frequencies in the corresponding text, in which the size and color of words are defined based on their repetition. RapidMiner software is utilized to analyze words' occurrences in the clusters' clean corpus. Thus, the top 20 meaningful words with the highest number of occurrences in the corresponding text for each cluster are detected.

In the last step, the results are evaluated and interpreted. To increase the validity of the results, the authors conducted this step separately and then, they crosschecked the findings and discussed to reach consensus. The dominant research subjects in IS discipline are identified using the text analysis results and scrutinizing the titles and the abstracts of the references appeared in the network. It is expected that combining both quantitative and qualitative findings bring forward some senses which neither of the two methods can achieve solely [29]. Hence, applying both quantitative text-mining techniques and authors' qualitative judgments in this research led to improved findings. Furthermore, the originating or seminal articles of well-known theories used in the IS research are identified by thorough analyzing the network's references. In this case, the pertinent literature in IS theories are considered for the inquiry [17, 30–32]. By doing so, at the end of this step, in addition to the dominant research subjects, prominent theories applied in IS studies are identified for each cluster to address the research questions.

---

[1] worditout.com.

3 Analysis and Results

Overall, the 929 retrieved articles analyzed contain 41916 bibliographical cited references. This represents an approximate average of 45 references per work. Concerning the numbers, it is impossible to conduct a co-citation analysis of the whole cited references. McCain [33] suggested that a cut-off point could be established to select the most influential studies. Therefore, the current study selected 154 references, which had been cited at least 20 times by the target articles. This threshold is considered based on the software's default suggestion. The 154 most cited references by MISQ and ISR during the last decade are analyzed in this study.

The co-citation network of the highly cited references identifies and illustrates an overall view of the recent IS discipline structure and knowledge groups containing both dominant research subjects and prominent cited theories (see Fig. 2). The size of bubbles represents the normalized number of citations received by the target articles and the thickness of links shows the strength of co-citation ties. The color of a bubble indicates the cluster with which the bubble's reference is associated. Each bubble is labeled by the author(s) and the publication year of the respective document. As shown in Fig. 2, the co-citation network formed six clusters and analysis of the clusters discloses the groups of references with similarities.

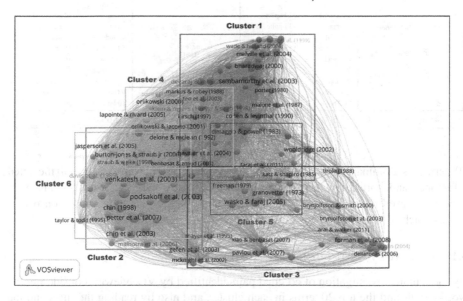

Fig. 2. Top cited references co-citation network with clusters

In Table 1 the word clouds show specific common terms that are frequently mentioned in the abstracts (or titles) of the clustered cited references. Each word cloud comprises around 100 items with the highest number of repetitions, in which the color and size of each word is based on its frequency. Additionally, Table 1 includes the top

Table 1. Word clouds and top 20 terms stemmed from the abstracts of the clustered cited references

Word cloud	Top 20 terms		Word cloud	Top 20 terms	
	1. Firm	11. Manag		1. Model	11. Develop
	2. Inform	12. System		2. Data	12. Form
	3. Technolog	13. Capabl		3. Statist	13. Inform
	4. Develop	14. Invest		4. Use	14. Relationship
	5. IT	15. Empir		5. Analysi	15. Structur
	6. Use	16. Model		6. Measur	16. Theori
	7. Perform	17. Valu		7. Construct	17. Method
	8. Resourc	18. Process		8. System	18. Estim
	9. Analysi	19. Competit		9. Valid	19. Techniqu
	10. Data	20. Knowledg		10. Effect	20. Adopt
Cluster 1			Cluster 2		
	1. Product	11. Market		1. Use	11. IT
	2. Onlin	12. Implic		2. Inform	12. Develop
	3. Use	13. Purchas		3. Organ	13. Interact
	4. Consum	14. Theori		4. Theori	14. Natur
	5. Inform	15. Review		5. Technolog	15. Process
	6. Model	16. Firm		6. Analysi	16. Social
	7. Behavior	17. Internet		7. System	17. Empir
	8. Trust	18. WOM		8. IS	18. Work
	9. Data	19. Commerc		9. Chang	19. Form
	10. Effect	20. Sale		10. Structur	20. Design
Cluster 3			Cluster 4		
	1. Inform	11. Use		1. System	11. Support
	2. Network	12. Impact		2. Use	12. Belief
	3. Organ	13. Implic		3. User	13. Develop
	4. Social	14. Influenc		4. Model	14. Intent
	5. Develop	15. Knowledg		5. Behavior	15. Organ
	6. Model	16. Resourc		6. Inform	16. Theori
	7. Effect	17. Structur		7. Technolog	17. Perciev
	8. Support	18. Motiv		8. Accept	18. Individu
	9. System	19. Commun		9. Usag	19. Implic
	10. Theori	20. Benefit		10. Influenc	20. Practic
Cluster 5			Cluster 6		

20 terms as dominant concepts stemmed from the abstracts (or titles) of the cited references and sorted by their occurrences. In other words, the word clouds were generated based on frequencies, but the top 20 terms were identified based on occurrences, each of which has own meaning and provide specific contribution.

3.1 Perceived Recent Intellectual Structure of IS

By meticulous investigation of co-cited pairs identified by VOSviewer, considering the word clouds and the top 20 terms in each cluster, and also by reading the titles and the abstracts of the documents, the dominant research subjects in IS discipline were revealed. Additionally, reflecting the majority of references and carefully reading the whole content of the top 5 cited references in each cluster, we labeled the six clusters shown in Table 2, ranked based on the number of documents they contain and the total number of citations. The first two clusters are the most prominent, jointly representing

42.7% of the documents in the co-citation network and obtaining 44.8% of the citations. Meanwhile, the distribution of documents and citations are almost uniform in other clusters.

Table 2. Documents, citations, and dominant research subjects of clusters

Cluster	No. of documents	% of documents	No. of citations	% of citations	Dominant research subject
1	38	24.7	1038	22.8	IS value (in red)
2	28	18	994	22	IS research (in green)
3	23	15	598	13	E-commerce (in blue)
4	22	14.3	621	13.7	IS in organization (in yellow)
5	22	14.3	569	12.5	Social network analysis (in purple)
6	21	13.7	723	16	IS usage (in cyan)
Total	154	100	4543	100	

The visualization of the density view based on the items proximity analysis carried out by VOSviewer provides a new view of the influential references in IS studies. This particular view allows us to acquire an overview of the general structure of a map and identify specific items, which are at the center of very dense co-citation networks. According to Van Eck and Waltman [21], the density of a point in a map depends on the number of its neighbors and also on the weights of these neighbors. The larger the number of the neighbors and the smaller the distances between them, the more the point density. Point densities are then translated into colors, red corresponds with the highest density and blue relates with the lowest one. The colors indicate the amount of attention researchers pay to the items located in the various areas of the map. In this sense, Fig. 3 shows that there are strong relations between clusters 1 (IS Value), 2 (IS Research), 4 (IS in Organization), and 6 (IS Usage) implying that studies in these clusters use common theories and share a set of cited references heavily. Alongside there are some bridges between clusters 1, 4, and cluster 5 (Social Network Analysis). It represents that these clusters are interrelated and the researchers reciprocally use theories from each other. By contrast, cluster 3 (E-commerce) appears more disconnected from clusters 1 and 4 and it just has some fragile neighborhood and weak links with clusters 2, 5, and 6, which indicates fragmented use of theories in the cluster. The next section will focus on this gap and deeply investigate the relationship between studies in this cluster with theories in other clusters to see if any perceived theoretical gaps could be found.

3.2   Theoretical Foundation of IS Research

Cluster 1 brings up many interesting insights on the underlying strategic dimensions related to the IS practices, such as the contribution of IS in achieving competitive advantages and the IS value in organizations. Studies in this cluster have been mainly built on strategic effects and values theories. Dynamic capabilities [34–36], resource-based view [34], theory of competitive strategy [37], theory of administrative behavior [38], absorptive capacity theory [39], and diffusion of innovations theory [40] are the most important theories which have been applied in the cluster 1 studies.

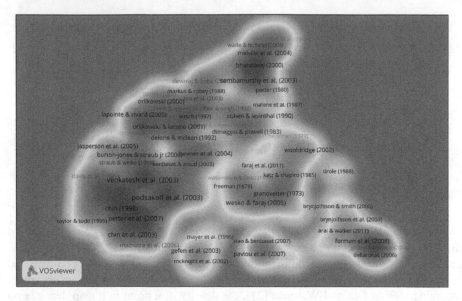

Fig. 3. Top cited references co-citation network with density-based visualization

Cluster 2 is named IS research which focused more on the major research issues, methods, and techniques in IS. With the proliferation of Structural Equation Modeling (SEM) methods [41], many IS scholars deployed them as the key multivariate analysis methods to conduct their studies. Therefore, in the second cluster, studies largely cited to the publications about SEM methodologies, issues, or errors. Since some studies in this cluster used psychological metrics, methods, or measurements, theories that were exploited by IS researchers for this purpose are psychometric theory [42, 43] and general deterrence theory [44].

During the last two decades, research about e-commerce aligned with its dramatic growth has been significantly increased. In the target articles, it is perceived that researchers mainly studied e-commerce adoption covering online trust and e-marketing issues including the impact of e-WoM and recommender systems in online customer purchase decisions. Most influential references in the field of e-commerce have been enlisted in cluster 3, and the theory of industrial organization [45] and prospect theory [46] are the two most important theories cited by the target articles.

The main subject of cluster 4 is IS in organization. The research theme of this cluster is primarily about implementing IS in organizations and its effects on organizational performance, structure, business processes, and employees. Design theory [47] and adaptive structuration theory [48] were extensively utilized and also many scholars applied grounded theory [49] to conduct their studies.

According to the popularity of social media as an important part of the people's daily life, academics, and practitioners increasingly observe social networks, and it becomes the focus of attention in recent studies. Cluster 5 represents a number of studies directed to investigate the relationships, interactions, knowledge sharing, and social structures in different virtual platforms. Social network theories [50–54], organizational ambidexterity [55], and diffusion of innovations theory [56] are the influential theories in this cluster.

Due to the huge amount of investment in IS, identifying influential factors on IS usage and technology acceptance across different settings have been an important and focal interest in IS scholarship (cluster 6). With these purpose, IS academics mainly refer to Unified Theory of Acceptance and Use of Technology (UTAUT) [57], Technology Acceptance Model (TAM) [58, 59], DeLone and McLean IS success model [60, 61], theory of planned behavior [62], task-technology fit [63], and computer self-efficacy [64].

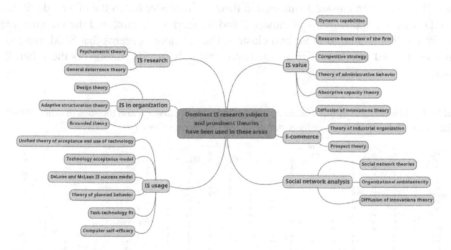

Fig. 4. Mind-map of dominant IS research subjects with respective prominent theories

In summary, Fig. 4 shows the mind-map of dominant IS research subjects and prominent theories have been exploited in these areas, which is produced using MindMup[2] software.

3.3   The Eminent Theoretical Gap and the Future Direction

Meticulously consideration of the publications in each cluster reveals that studies in cluster 3, e-commerce, used fewer theories and it seems that a strong theoretical base has not yet evolved in this cluster. Therefore, a theoretical gap could be perceived in applying the fundamental related theories by the research in this cluster. To objectively

---

[2] mindmup.com.

examine this cluster in-depth, we built a table to check the strength of the co-citation links by mapping cited references in cluster 3 with the extracted theories in the other clusters (Table 3)[3]. Accordingly, the codes are assigned to the cited references in cluster 3 and the applied theories in other clusters (Appendix 1).

In accordance with the density view (Fig. 3), which mentioned before, the results of Table 3 show that e-commerce studies are almost disintegrated from theories in clusters 1 and 4. However, dynamic capabilities (18 points) and design research (14 points) have been used in some e-commerce studies. For the other clusters, it is noticeable that social network theories (66 points) have been used comparatively more in e-commerce research. Acceptance models such as UTAUT (53 points), TAM (48 points), and IS success models (40 points) are the other highlighted theories that were applied in this field. Also, some e-commerce studies were found in examining trust, which especially exploited psychological metrics (37 points) for measuring knowledge, abilities, attitudes, and personality traits.

Generally, our analysis divulged that besides social network theories, there are some links between cluster 3 studies and theories in cluster 6. On the other side, it can be seen that the applications of cluster 1 and 4 theories are thin, and the e-commerce research is less related to those two clusters. Furthermore, it seems that SEM methods have been used much less in e-commerce research in comparison to the other IS studies.

Table 3. The strength of links between cited references in cluster 3 and theories in other clusters (The color scale of matrix's cells is defined based on their values.)

	T1	T2	T3	T4	T5	T6	T7	T8	T9	T10	T11	T12	T13	T14	T15	T16	T17	T18	T19	Sum
R1	1	0	0	0	0	0	0	0	2	0	0	2	0	0	0	0	0	0	0	5
R2	0	0	1	0	1	1	0	0	0	1	0	12	1	2	1	0	0	0	0	20
R3	1	0	0	0	0	0	1	0	0	0	0	2	0	0	0	0	0	1	0	5
R4	3	1	1	0	0	0	2	0	0	0	0	0	0	0	1	2	0	0	0	10
R5	0	0	0	0	0	1	0	0	1	1	0	0	0	1	1	2	0	0	0	7
R6	0	0	0	0	0	1	0	0	1	1	0	8	0	0	0	0	0	0	0	11
R7	0	0	1	0	0	0	0	0	1	0	0	6	2	1	0	0	0	1	0	13
R8	0	0	0	0	0	0	0	0	1	0	0	1	0	0	0	0	0	0	0	2
R9	0	0	0	0	0	0	0	0	0	0	0	0	0	1	1	0	0	0	0	2
R10	0	0	0	0	0	1	1	0	1	1	0	12	0	2	1	1	1	1	1	25
R11	2	0	0	0	2	2	7	2	1	1	0	1	1	11	11	4	6	2	6	59
R12	0	0	0	0	0	0	0	0	0	0	0	2	0	0	0	0	0	0	0	2
R13	0	0	0	0	0	0	2	0	0	0	0	0	0	6	5	2	1	1	1	18
R14	0	0	0	0	0	0	0	0	1	0	0	1	0	1	1	0	0	0	0	4
R15	0	0	0	0	0	0	0	0	0	1	0	2	0	0	0	0	0	0	0	3
R16	1	0	1	0	1	1	5	0	0	1	0	4	0	3	4	4	2	0	3	30
R17	0	0	1	0	0	1	8	0	1	0	0	3	0	6	5	6	3	2	3	39
R18	1	0	0	0	0	1	4	0	1	0	0	0	0	8	8	5	5	3	2	38
R19	3	0	1	0	1	0	4	1	0	0	0	1	0	1	4	2	2	2	1	23
R20	2	0	1	0	1	0	1	2	0	0	0	1	0	5	3	4	2	3	1	26
R21	4	2	2	1	3	0	0	0	0	0	0	0	2	0	0	0	0	0	0	14
R22	0	0	1	0	0	0	2	1	2	1	0	6	1	5	2	6	0	3	0	30
R23	0	0	0	0	0	0	0	0	1	0	0	2	0	0	0	0	0	0	0	3
Sum	18	3	10	1	9	9	37	6	14	9	0	66	7	53	48	40	22	19	18	

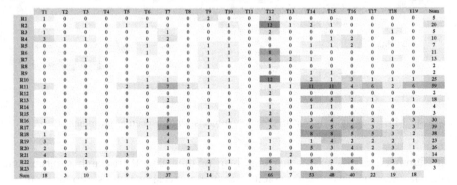

4   Conclusion

In this research, we tried to shed light on the IS theoretical foundation in the last decade, especially with respect to how different groups of studies interrelate with one another in the context of the theory exploitation. One of the innovations of this research

---

[3] In the case of co-citation links between cited references, the strength of a link indicates the number of publications in which two references are cited together.

is applying a mixed method, which provides us an objective tool besides qualitative interpretation to identify the main research streams and the potential new directions within the field under investigation. Six different clusters in the co-citation network were identified as the pillars of the semantic structure shaping the IS discipline: IS Value (Cluster 1, in red), IS Research (Cluster 2, in green), E-commerce (Cluster 3, in blue), IS in Organization (Cluster 4, in yellow), Social Network Analysis (Cluster 5, in purple), and IS Usage (Cluster 6, in cyan). Among these groups, cluster 1 and cluster 2 have the most citations and documents. It shows strategic theories such as dynamic capabilities and theory of competitive advantage and IS research methods and theories are prominent cited theories in the recently published articles in MISQ and ISR. Investigating theories used in each cluster shows that some of the IS research streams have stronger theoretical foundations than the others. Alternatively, studies in these weaker clusters might be getting published in other journals. By analyzing inter-cluster linkages, the other contribution of this research is clearly emerging the fact that some clusters have more theoretical relations with each other. It means that studies in these clusters have extensively applied theoretical foundations of each other. In contrast, few relations of cluster 3 (E-commerce) with other clusters were discovered that demonstrates interrelated theoretical gap in this type of studies. Examining the relationships of cited references of e-commerce studies with explored theories in the other clusters let us suppose that future research in this area could mainly focus on theoretical foundations which were used less in the recent years. So as the final contribution, we propose some hypotheses about the application of the prominent theories related to clusters 1, 2, and 4 in e-commerce future studies. Firstly, the relationships between e-commerce and strategic values and competitive advantages (cluster 1) could be better analyzed by future studies through focusing on aspects that are either internal or external to the firms. Also, using of SEM methods or other IS research methods (cluster 2) in this group of studies might be more considered. Finally, capturing complexity of e-commerce in organizations and societies (cluster 4) is another probable research theme that could be followed.

4.1 Limitations and Future Research

This study only set out the starting point for further analyses that aim at a better understanding of the current IS theoretical foundation and its future destiny. Therefore, some limitations in the current study have to be mentioned. The source data in the last decade from MISQ and ISR does not consist of all the research articles in our discipline. Future research could include the AIS "basket of eight" IS journals[4] and expand the timespan to 20 years. We tried to minimize subjectivity by adopting a consistent procedure but a little bit of human opinion and interpretations were needed to make the results meaningful. In future research, other complementary quantitative methods along the co-citation networks could be exploited to assess intra- and inter-cluster analysis.

---

[4] http://aisnet.org/?SeniorScholarBasket, accessed 26-04-2019.

Appendix 1. Cited Theories in Clusters 1, 2, 4, 5, and 6

Theory	ID	Theory	ID
Dynamic capabilities	T1	Grounded theory	T11
Resource-based view of the firm	T2	Social network theories	T12
Competitive strategy	T3	Organizational ambidexterity	T13
Theory of administrative behaviour	T4	Unified theory of acceptance and use of technology	T14
Absorptive capacity theory	T5	Technology acceptance model	T15
Diffusion of innovations theory	T6	DeLone and McLean IS success model	T16
Psychometric theory	T7	Theory of planned behaviour	T17
General deterrence theory	T8	Task-technology fit	T18
Design theory	T9	Computer self-efficacy	T19
Adaptive structuration theory	T10		

References

1. Agarwal, R., Lucas Jr., H.C.: The information systems identity crisis: focusing on high-visibility and high-impact research. MIS Q. **29**, 381–398 (2005)
2. Benbasat, I., Zmud, R.W.: The identity crisis within the IS discipline: defining and communicating the discipline's core properties. MIS Q. **27**, 183–194 (2003)
3. Galliers, R.D.: Change as crisis or growth? Toward a trans-disciplinary view of information systems as a field of study: a response to Benbasat and Zmud's Call for returning to the IT artifact. J. Assoc. Inf. Syst. **4**, 337–351 (2003)
4. Teo, T.S., Srivastava, S.C.: Information systems (IS) discipline identity: a review and framework. Commun. Assoc. Inf. Syst. **20**, 518–544 (2007)
5. Kohli, R., Grover, V.: Business value of IT: an essay on expanding research directions to keep up with the times. J. Assoc. Inf. Syst. **9**, 23–39 (2008)
6. Melville, N., Kraemer, K., Gurbaxani, V.: Information technology and organizational performance: an integrative model of IT business value. MIS Q. **28**, 283–322 (2004)
7. Raghupathi, V., Weiser Friedman, L.: A framework for information systems metaresearch: the quest for identity. Commun. Assoc. Inf. Syst. **24**, 333–350 (2009)
8. Palvia, P., Kakhki, M.D., Ghoshal, T., Uppala, V., Wang, W.: Methodological and topic trends in information systems research: a meta-analysis of IS journals. Commun. Assoc. Inf. Syst. **37**, 630–650 (2015)
9. Gregor, S.: The nature of theory in information systems. MIS Q. **30**, 611–642 (2006)
10. Avison, D., Malaurent, J.: Is theory king?: questioning the theory fetish in information systems. J. Inf. Technol. **29**, 1–10 (2014)
11. Mueller, B., Urbach, N.: Understanding the why, what, and how of theories in IS research. Commun. Assoc. Inf. Syst. **41**, 349–388 (2017)
12. Beller, S., Bender, A.: Theory, the final frontier? A corpus-based analysis of the role of theory in psychological articles. Front. Psychol. **8**, 1–16 (2017)

13. Rai, A.: Editor's comments: beyond outdated labels: the blending of IS research traditions. MIS Q. **42**, 3–6 (2018)
14. Burton-Jones, A., Butler, B., Scott, S., Xu, S.X.: Next-generation information systems theories. MIS Quarterly Call for Papers (2018). http://www.misq.org/skin/frontend/default/misq/pdf/CurrentCalls/NextGenerationIS_Full.pdf
15. Asatani, K., Mori, J., Ochi, M., Sakata, I.: Detecting trends in academic research from a citation network using network representation learning. PLoS ONE **13**, 1–13 (2018)
16. de Vaujany, F.X., Lesca, N., Fomin, V.V., Loebbecke, C.: The espoused theories of IS: a study of general editorial statements. In: Proceedings of the 29th International Conference on Information Systems, pp. 1–18. AIS, Paris (2008)
17. Lim, S., Saldanha, T.J., Malladi, S., Melville, N.: Theories used in information systems research: insights from complex network analysis. JITTA J. Inf. Technol. Theory Appl. **14**, 5–44 (2013)
18. Moody, D.L., Iacob, M.E., Amrit, C., Müller, R.: In search of paradigms: identifying the theoretical foundations of the is field. In: Alexander, P.M., Turpin, M., van Deventer, J. P. (eds.) Proceedings of the 18th European Conference on Information Systems, pp. 1–13. AIS, Pretoria (2010)
19. Soper, D.S., Turel, O., Geri, N.: The intellectual core of the IS field: a systematic exploration of theories in our top journals. In: Sprague Jr, R.H. (ed.) Proceedings of the 47th Hawaii International Conference on System Sciences, pp. 4629–4638. IEEE, Waikoloa (2014)
20. Weber, R.: Evaluating and developing theories in the information systems discipline. J. Assoc. Inf. Syst. **13**, 1–30 (2012)
21. Van Eck, N.J., Waltman, L.: Software survey: VOSviewer, a computer program for bibliometric mapping. Scientometrics **84**, 523–538 (2010)
22. Van Eck, N.J., Waltman, L.: Visualizing bibliometric networks. In: Ding, Y., Rousseau, R., Wolfram, D. (eds.) Measuring Scholarly Impact: Methods and Practice, pp. 285–320. Springer, New York (2014). https://doi.org/10.1007/978-3-319-10377-8_13
23. Van Eck, N.J., Waltman, L.: How to normalize cooccurrence data? An analysis of some well-known similarity measures. J. Am. Soc. Inf. Sci. Technol. **60**, 1635–1651 (2009)
24. Van Eck, N.J., Waltman, L., Dekker, R., van den Berg, J.: A comparison of two techniques for bibliometric mapping: multidimensional scaling and VOS. J. Am. Soc. Inf. Sci. Technol. **61**, 2405–2416 (2010)
25. Borg, I., Groenen, P.: Modern Multidimensional Scaling. Springer, New York (2005). https://doi.org/10.1007/0-387-28981-X
26. Waltman, L., Van Eck, N.J., Noyons, E.C.: A unified approach to mapping and clustering of bibliometric networks. J. Informetr. **4**, 629–635 (2010)
27. Waltman, L., Van Eck, N.J.: A smart local moving algorithm for large-scale modularity-based community detection. Eur. Phys. J. B **86**, 1–33 (2013)
28. Newman, M.E., Girvan, M.: Finding and evaluating community structure in networks. Phys. Rev. E **69**, 1–16 (2004)
29. Ivankova, N.V., Creswell, J.W.: Mixed methods. In: Heigham, J., Croker, R.A. (eds.) Qualitative Research in Applied Linguistics: A Practical Introduction, pp. 135–161. Palgrave Macmillan, New York (2009)
30. Dwivedi, Y.K., Wade, M.R., Schneberger, S.L.: Information Systems Theory: Explaining and Predicting Our Digital Society. Springer, Dordrecht (2011). https://doi.org/10.1007/978-1-4419-6108-2
31. Larsen, K.R., Eargle, D.: Theories Used in IS Research Wiki (2015). http://IS.TheorizeIt.org

32. Lim, S., Saldanha, T.J., Malladi, S., Melville, N.: Theories used in information systems research: identifying theory networks in leading IS journals. In: Nunamaker Jr, J.F., Currie, W.L. (eds.) Proceedings of the 30th International Conference on Information Systems, pp. 1–10. AIS, Phoenix (2009)
33. McCain, K.W.: Mapping authors in intellectual space: a technical overview. J. Am. Soc. Inf. Sci. **41**, 433–443 (1990)
34. Barney, J.: Firm resources and sustained competitive advantage. J. Manag. **17**, 99–120 (1991)
35. Eisenhardt, K.M., Martin, J.A.: Dynamic capabilities: what are they? Strateg. Manag. J. **21**, 1105–1121 (2000)
36. Teece, D.J., Pisano, G., Shuen, A.: Dynamic capabilities and strategic management. Strateg. Manag. J. **18**, 509–533 (1997)
37. Porter, M.E.: Competitive Strategy. Free Press, New York (1980)
38. March, J.G., Simon, H.A.: Organizations. Wiley, New York (1958)
39. Cohen, W.M., Levinthal, D.A.: Absorptive capacity: a new perspective on learning and innovation. Adm. Sci. Q. **35**, 128–152 (1990)
40. Rogers, E.M.: Diffusion of Innovations. Free Press, New York (1995)
41. Gefen, D., Rigdon, E.E., Straub, D.W.: Editor's comments: an update and extension to SEM guidelines for administrative and social science research. MIS Q. **35**, 3–14 (2011)
42. Nunnally, J.C.: Psychometric Theory. McGraw-Hill, New York (1978)
43. Nunnally, J.C., Bernstein, I.H.: Psychometric Theory. McGraw-Hill, New York (1994)
44. Straub, D.W., Welke, R.J.: Coping with systems risk: security planning models for management decision making. MIS Q. **22**, 441–469 (1998)
45. Tirole, J.: The Theory of Industrial Organisation. MIT Press, Cambridge (1988)
46. Kahneman, D., Tversky, A.: Prospect theory: an analysis of decision under risk. Econometrica **47**, 262–291 (1979)
47. Hevner, A.R., March, S.T., Park, J., Ram, S.: Design science in information systems research. MIS Q. **28**, 75–105 (2004)
48. DeSanctis, G., Poole, M.S.: Capturing the complexity in advanced technology use: adaptive structuration theory. Organ. Sci. **5**, 121–147 (1994)
49. Glaser, B.G., Strauss, A.L.: The Discovery of Grounded Theory: Strategies for Qualitative Research. Aldine, Chicago (1967)
50. Burt, R.S.: Structural holes: the social structure of competition. Harvard University Press, Cambridge (1992)
51. Constant, D., Sproull, L., Kiesler, S.: The kindness of strangers: the usefulness of electronic weak ties for technical advice. Organ. Sci. **7**, 119–135 (1996)
52. Freeman, L.C.: Centrality in social networks conceptual clarification. Soc. Netw. **1**, 215–239 (1979)
53. Granovetter, M.S.: The strength of weak ties. Soc. Netw. **78**, 1360–1380 (1973)
54. Wasserman, S., Faust, K.: Social Network Analysis: Methods and Applications. Cambridge University Press, New York (1994)
55. March, J.G.: Exploration and exploitation in organizational learning. Organ. Sci. **2**, 71–87 (1991)
56. Rogers, E.M.: Diffusion of Innovations. Free Press, New York (2003)
57. Venkatesh, V., Morris, M.G., Davis, G.B., Davis, F.D.: User acceptance of information technology: toward a unified view. MIS Q. **27**, 425–478 (2003)
58. Davis, F.D.: Perceived usefulness, perceived ease of use, and user acceptance of information technology. MIS Q. **13**, 319–340 (1989)
59. Davis, F.D., Bagozzi, R.P., Warshaw, P.R.: User acceptance of computer technology: a comparison of two theoretical models. Manag. Sci. **35**, 982–1003 (1989)

60. DeLone, W.H., McLean, E.R.: Information systems success: the quest for the dependent variable. Inf. Syst. Res. **3**, 60–95 (1992)
61. Delone, W.H., McLean, E.R.: The DeLone and McLean model of information systems success: a ten-year update. J. Manag. Inf. Syst. **19**, 9–30 (2003)
62. Ajzen, I.: The theory of planned behavior. Organ. Behav. Hum. Decis. Process. **50**, 179–211 (1991)
63. Goodhue, D.L., Thompson, R.L.: Task-technology fit and individual performance. MIS Q. **19**, 213–236 (1995)
64. Compeau, D.R., Higgins, C.A.: Computer self-efficacy: development of a measure and initial test. MIS Q. **19**, 189–211 (1995)

Technical Architecture and Applications for EIS

The State of Agile Software Development in the Czech Republic: Preliminary Findings Indicate the Dominance of "Abridged" Scrum

Michal Dolezel$^{(\boxtimes)}$ ⓘ, Alena Buchalcevova ⓘ, and Michal Mencik

Faculty of Informatics and Statistics, University of Economics,
Prague, W. Churchill Sq. 4, 130 67 Prague, Czech Republic
{michal.dolezel,alena.buchalcevova,menm00}@vse.cz

Abstract. This paper presents preliminary results from a survey focused on the state of agile method adoption in the Czech Republic. To this end, an initial survey sample (N = 120) was analyzed. Scrum is the most frequently used agile software development method, reported by 46.7% of respondents as the agile method of choice. However, the results indicate that Scrum seems to be introduced through cherry-picking of those practices that are quite easy to implement. Specifically, the only widely-spread Scrum practice is the maintenance of Product backlog. To the contrary, the teams are rarely cross-functional and the Scrum master role frequently absents. This suggests that in many organizations, Scrum might be invoked due to being a valuable "brand name", rather than due to professionals' subscribing to core Scrum values and assumptions. Our results contribute to the body of empirical knowledge on the state of agile software development initiatives. Our findings confirm the theoretical proposition that in the real world, the implementation of software development methods is often patchy and rarely done "by the book".

Keywords: Software project management · Agile methods · Agile practices · Scrum practices · Scrum variations · Agile method tailoring · Hybrid methods

1 Introduction

Software development and deployment activities are at the heart of many information systems initiatives. The academic disciplines in the field of computing have long been interested in the conceptual means that practitioners employ to manage those activities in everyday reality [1, 2]. Of particular interest are presently agile software development methods (ASDMs), which are rapidly spreading across the world, irrespective of what the company's core business is [3]. Thanks to this advance, the interest in agile methods is growing also in a number of interrelated research areas, including Enterprise Resource Planning and business administration [4, 5].

Striving to characterize the state of ASDM adoption, both scientists [3, 6–11] and practitioners [12] put effort into exploring the agile territories. However, only very limited data are available to speak about the up-to-date state of ASDM adoption in the Czech Republic. To close that gap, we designed and conducted a survey among Czech agile practitioners. On this basis, the present paper provides an overview of ASDMs

© IFIP International Federation for Information Processing 2019
Published by Springer Nature Switzerland AG 2019.
P. Doucek et al. (Eds.): CONFENIS 2019, LNBIP 375, pp. 43–54, 2019.
https://doi.org/10.1007/978-3-030-37632-1_4

used by them. To deliver preliminary findings, we analyze our initial survey sample (N = 120) gathered over the period of 5 weeks. (At the time of writing, the survey was still on-going.)

At this stage of research, we have been particularly interested in the connection between ASDMs and software project management [13]. To this end, in this paper we present two categories of findings: (i) an overall summary of the coverage of different ASDMs in the Czech Republic; (ii) the data that characterize the local nature of Scrum, a generic software project management framework [14]. We then discuss the ways in which Scrum seems to be currently implemented in the surveyed population. As a matter of fact, we found a highly reductionist version of Scrum seeming to dominate in practice. We contribute to the body of knowledge by (i) describing the present state of ASDMs in the Czech Republic; (ii) a brief analysis of the Scrum adoption pattern observed. Our findings are useful for understanding the nature of differences between *ideal* ASDMs, viewed as generic templates, and the *real instances* of ASDMs as implemented by practitioners.

The paper is organized as follows. Following the Introduction, Sect. 2 reviews related work. Next, Sect. 3 describes our research approach. Section 4 then presents the survey results. Finally, Sect. 5 provides discussion and concluding remarks.

2 Related Work

To understand the current usage of ASDMs, a number of research strategies have been adopted. Typically, either qualitative [15, 16] or quantitative methods are employed. Less commonly, researchers also use action research frameworks [7]. To limit our focus only on the quantitative side, researchers make use of national-level surveys [11], global reach surveys [17] and surveys probing into a selected set of agile practices of certain kind [8]. A significant influence within the domain of industry practice is attributed to practice-based surveys which are administrated by large vendor and consulting companies [12]. Given the space constraints of this paper, we review below only the most relevant contributions from both categories, forming a conceptual basis for our research. We firstly take a look on relevant surveys from abroad (Sect. 2.1), followed by the surveys previously carried out in the Czech Republic (Sect. 2.2).

2.1 State of ASDM Adoption Worldwide

Generally speaking, a significant amount of survey results that describe the current state of ASDM adoption are available, but the coverage of various geographic territories highly differs. In 2012, among the first (see also [17]), Finish researchers conducted a large scale survey to portray the initial picture of ASDMs in an European context [11]. Similar surveys have been conducted also in entirely different geographical areas such as Brazil [18, 19]. In addition, researchers have tried to reach English-speaking populations across the globe by offering them survey instruments in English [10, 17]. Starting quite recently, valuable work has been carried out within the Hybrid dEveLopmENt Approaches (HELENA) research community. The goal of the initial phases of the initiative was to collect data on the nature of hybrid methods adoption, including both the sequential and agile ones. The survey was available in several languages and thus more accessible to non-English speaking practitioners [3]. Unfortunately, the survey did not attract attention of respondents from the Czech Republic.

In the world of business practice, the "State of Agile" survey with a global reach has been conducted by VersionOne (later CollabNet VersionOne) annually since 2006. Today, the survey is well-known to many agile practitioners. The recent (13th) edition [12] was carried out between August and December 2018. However, when considering the results reported by similar surveys, one should be cautious. In essence, many times those surveys may be designed in a way to support the core business of the vendor [11]. Also, the research method adopted may lack the necessary level of rigor.

2.2 State of ASDM Adoption in the Czech Republic

The results that would describe the state of ASDM adoption in the Czech Republic are quite rare. Yet, initial attempts to map the area were carried out in 2006 and 2009 [20, 21]. In 2013, two surveys were executed. The Czech company Etnetera replicated the VersioneOne survey in the Czech Republic [22]. Then, Tománek [23] collected data for his survey within a global logistics company. Although his findings have limited generalizability, he proposed that Czech practitioners seem to be among the laggards in ASDM adoption.

3 Research Method

In this section, we provide details on the construction and execution of our survey. In Sect. 3.1, we describe survey design. Then, in Sect. 3.2, we discuss the method of data collection.

3.1 Survey Design

The survey instrument contained 18 questions, including a large section devoted to concrete practices, and 4 optional (mostly free-text) answers. We divided the instrument into three logical parts:

- The first part consisted of (i) General demographic characteristics of respondents; (ii) Primary ASDM that the team uses; (iii) Estimated level of method tailoring; (vi) Perceived benefits of method use;
- The second part consisted of (i) Used agile practices (34 practices were offered – see below); (ii) Frequency of their usage within the team (a three-point Likert scale: "Used", "Used to a certain extent", "Not used", complemented by a "Don't know/Cannot be evaluated" option); (iii) Respondent's subjective scoring of the importance of the practices;
- Concluding demographics questions.

The analysis presented in this paper is centered around the list of 34 practices, derived by a synthesis of previous research [3, 19] and practitioner literature [12]. We put a particular attention to the practices introduced by the Scrum and XP originators

[14, 24]. Giving some extra attention to DevOps, we added certain practices to the list. For example, we expected to capture significant differences in popularity among various "Continuous *" methods [25], and we therefore conceptually differed among them.

The survey form contained an instruction to relate the answers concerning the practices to a current or quite recent project (run either by their team, or a team that the respondents "work with"). Inversely, the respondents were asked to think about a potential importance of the practice from their personal perspective, i.e. irrespective of the fact whether the practice was currently used or not used by the team (this aspect is not analyzed here). The survey was available in the Czech language. However, for the sake of clarity and respondents' convenience, it contained also English equivalents of the names that commonly characterize the surveyed agile practices (e.g. "Tabule Kanban" was supplemented with "Kanban board" in smaller letters). The reason behind was that as part of their jargon, many Czech practitioners commonly use the original English terms instead of their formal Czech equivalents.

3.2 Data Collection and Analysis

Given certain pragmatic constraints (e.g. additional costs, current European privacy laws etc.), we opted for convenience sampling [26] in which social networks played a dominant role. While such a strategy suffers from clear drawbacks, it is relatively common in our domain of research.

In two waves, we shared the link to the survey in 17 professional and alumni LinkedIn and Facebook groups containing ca. 20,000 members (who were mostly Czechs or Slovaks) in total. This was followed by sharing the link with our industry contacts (ca. 50), either via LinkedIn messaging or by email. Here, we analyze the answers collected during the first 5 weeks (ending on 17 August 2019). We applied descriptive statistics.

4   Results

This section presents some initial results derived from the data sample described above. First, we give a summary of participant demographics (Sect. 4.1). In Sect. 4.2, we demonstrate what ASDMs are adopted, and to what extent. In Sect. 4.3, we take the dominant method (i.e. Scrum) and discuss the way in which the method seems to be implemented.

4.1 Participant Demographics

Table 1 provides an overview of the survey respondents (only respondents who completed the survey, i.e. answered all mandatory questions, were included in our analysis). To give some additional details, our respondents were mostly from the domain of Information Technology/Software Development (40.0%) and Finance (10.8%). Other domains were less frequent (6% or less each).

Table 1. Respondents' job position and years of experience

Job Position / Experience with ASDMs	No hands-on experience	< 1 y.	1 to 2 y.	3 to 4 y.	5 or more y.	Total
Product owner		1	6	5	6	18
Agile coach / Scrum master			6	10	6	22
Member of the dev. team	1	7	17	16	7	48
Other managerial IT role		3	3	4	8	18
Other managerial role	1	1	1	3	1	7
Other business role				1	2	3
Other		2			2	4

4.2 Agile Methods Usage

Figure 1 shows usage of various agile methods, as reported by our respondents. The most widely used agile method is Scrum, reported as the method of choice by 46.7%. Scrum altogether with its agile extensions (i.e. Scrum/XP hybrid and Scrumban) counts for 65.0%. Interestingly, the representation of Scrum combined with Waterfall (commonly called also Water-Scrum-Fall [27]) accounts only for 8.3%. Large scale agile methods [7] were reported to be used by 16.7% of respondents.

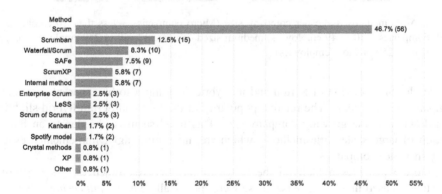

Fig. 1. Agile methods usage

The dominance of Scrum is in line with the CollabNet VersionOne survey [12], where Scrum (54%) and agile Scrum hybrids (together with Scrum account for 72%) were reported as the most widely-practiced agile method(s). The leading position of Scrum (87%) was confirmed also by the Etnetera local survey [22] in 2013. Nevertheless, it is not possible to directly compare the relative representation of various agile methods with the latter survey. The reason is that Etnetera adopted a multi-choice questioning strategy regarding this aspect, while we opted for single-choice, being in-line with CollabNet VersionOne.

Figure 2 portrays what agile methods are used in companies of various sizes. At this point, we aggregated data for two common hybridized agile methods (i.e. Scrumban, ScrumXP), being represented by the *Hybrid agile methods* category. As obvious, *Waterfall/Scrum* forms a separate category. (We consider those implementations "not fully agile".) The category titled *Large-scale agile* includes Enterprise Scrum, LeSS, SAFe, Scrum of Scrums, and Spotify model.

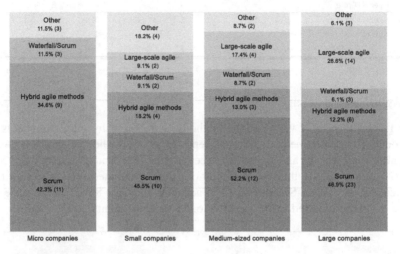

Fig. 2. Agile methods usage per company size (Micro companies – less than 10 employees; small companies – 10 to 49 employees; medium-sized companies – 50 to 249 employees; large enterprises – 250 or more employees)

The leading position of Scrum and its hybrids continues to be apparent across all company size segments. The relative popularity of the Waterfall/Scrum hybrid slightly falls down with the growing company size. This trend seems to be due to an introduction of large scale agile methods, which are, not surprisingly, implemented especially in larger companies.

Figure 3 provides a look on the usage of 34 surveyed practices. As the term "practice" is used in a broad sense, these were specifically either *engineering practices* (e.g. Pair programming), *organizational practices* (e.g. Iteration planning) and *organizational patterns* (e.g. Open office), or *team-work tools* (e.g. Kanban board). Product backlog is by far the most used agile practice utilized by almost all teams (98.3% use it fully or partially). By contrast, Behavior Driven Development (BDD) and Test-Driven Development (TDD) are the least used agile practices (only 22.5% use fully or partially BDD, and 28.3% TDD).

Next, we analysed the practices reported by CollabNet VersionOne [12] as the *most widely used* within two specific categories. First category covers three *organizational practices* (termed by their survey as "agile techniques") and second category contains three *engineering practices*. In Table 2, we compare those data with the relevant data from the former Czech industry survey conducted by Etnetera [22], the HELENA study

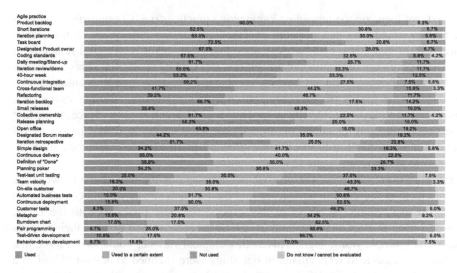

Fig. 3. Agile practices usage

[6], and our survey. Except for the comparison with HELENA (see below), there are no striking differences in the category of *organizational practices* among the surveys. An interesting finding is that in the Czech Republic the usage of the three top agile techniques slightly increased between 2013 and 2019 (as reported by Etnetera and our survey respectively). This may speak for agile implementations becoming more mature.

Table 2. Usage of top-3 organizational and engineering practices (a comparison with VersionOne as a baseline)

	VersionOne (World)	Etnetera (CZ)	HELENA (World)	Our study (CZ)
Organizational practices				
Daily standup	86%	79%	79.7%	**88.4%**
Sprint/iteration planning	80%	86%	82.4%	**93.3%**
Retrospectives	80%	69%	77.9%	**76.7%**
Engineering practices				
Unit testing	69%	67%	86.7%	***55.0%***
Coding standards	58%	41%	93.4%	**90.0%**
Continuous integration	53%	55%	84.5%	**86.7%**

As of the usage of *engineering practices*, the differences among the surveys are significant. Notably, the differences between the Etnetera survey and our survey are of interest. First and foremost, it is surprising to see the low adoption rate of unit testing, as reported by our respondents. Given that unit testing has long been considered a vital practice in software development, one may certainly wonder why so many surveyed teams (37.5%) do not employ such practice at all (Fig. 3).

Next, we focus on the remaining engineering practices (i.e. Continuous integration and Coding standards) and possible explanations for the differences in the results between 2013 and 2019. First, we speculate that there might be a causal relationship between the high use of Continuous Integration and Coding standards. This could be an effect of the following pattern: Checking compliance to coding standards automatically (i.e. through the means of the continuous integration process – during every code commit) is nowadays considered, in general, a good practice [28]. Hence, regarding those two engineering practices, we broadly assume that the increased proportion of their use may go hand-in-hand with the growing popularity of continuous software engineering in the recent years [25].

Looking from a different perspective, we propose that the differences between the research methods adopted in our survey and the Etnetera survey might account for an alternative explanation. In our case, the respondents were provided with the Likert scale described in Sect. 3.1. By contrast, Etnetera seems to had queried their respondents using a simple yes/no logic. This methodological variance could have caused that a number of undecided respondents in our study were inclined to answer "Used to a certain extent" instead of "No". In our understanding, such respondents or their teams might be currently just experimenting with the practices.

The reason for employing the 3-point scale was to give respondents a possibility to indicate that the practice was not (yet) fully instituted. A similar approach was chosen in the HELENA study, in which even a more complex scale ("rarely used", "sometimes used", "often/always used") was implemented [6]. In essence, we wanted to understand whether there is a possibility to discriminate between "easy" and "complicated" practices. In that regard, we want to briefly highlight the following fact. The practices with the lowest "Used to a certain extent"/"Used" ratio (exact calculations are not included here) are Product backlog and Open office. These appear to be easily implementable practices. The practices scoring with high ratios (e.g. Small releases or Refactoring) are arguably technically demanding and teams might struggle with their implementation.

Regarding an additional comparison with HELENA, it is important to highlight that the interest of the HELENA study has not been limited to agile projects. That means, the HELENA data contain also such responses collected concerning hybrid projects (i.e. projects with a presumable planning-oriented component). Interestingly, except for unit testing, the differences between the presented HELENA results and our results are not very significant. This finding, however, applies only to six practices from the presented baseline. Looking beyond that would allow for rendering additional significant differences (e.g. regarding the usage of Burndown chart).

4.3   Nature of Scrum

Table 3 allows for deriving certain conclusions about the form of Scrum the teams use in practice.

To derive stronger conclusions, we wanted to differ deep-rooted practices from those used by the teams only rarely or those which might be considered as dysfunctional. Hence, differently from the above analysis of agile practices, at this point we focus on the answers that indicate confidence in the usage of a practice (i.e. when the

Table 3. Usage of agile practices in teams with "pure" Scrum (N = 56). Q1: dominant practices (used by 75–100%); Q2: mainstream practices (used by 50–75%); Q3: marginalized practices (used by 25–50%); Q4: absenting practices (used by 0–25%).

	Scrum practice	Used	Used to a certain extent	Total
Q1	Product backlog	85.7% (48)	10.7% (6)	96.4% (54)
	Iteration planning	67.9% (38)	28.6% (16)	96.4% (54)
	Iteration backlog	67.9% (38)	16.1% (9)	83.9% (47)
	Daily meeting/Stand-up	67.9% (38)	17.9% (10)	85.7% (48)
Q2	Short iterations	64.3% (36)	32.1% (18)	96.4% (54)
	Designated Product owner	62.5% (35)	26.8% (15)	89.3% (50)
	Iteration retrospective	57.1% (32)	23.2% (13)	80.4% (45)
	Iteration review/demo	51.8% (29)	32.1% (18)	83.9% (47)
	Definition of "Done"	44.6% (25)	35.7% (20)	80.4% (45)
Q3	Designated Scrum master	37.5% (21)	42.9% (24)	80.4% (45)
	Cross-functional team	33.9% (19)	50.0% (28)	83.9% (47)
Q4	Burndown chart	16.1% (9)	21.4% (12)	37.5% (21)

practice was reported as "Used"). We took all common Scrum practices [14, 29] from our list of 34 practices and grouped them into four quartiles, according to their representation (see the table caption for details).

Based on this framing, the only practice considered as dominant is keeping of *Product backlog*. By contrast, the practice which absents from use is *Burndown chart*, i.e. the visual tracking of remaining development work. For many, this finding may be surprising. Given that the Scrum originators argue that projective practices "have proven useful" [29], we consider the latter practice an important part of Scrum.

As marginalized we label the practices as follows: *Cross-functional team, Scrum master, Definition of "Done"*. The low usage of the former practices is particularly interesting, because it indicates the way in which Scrum is implemented from an organizational standpoint. The originators of Scrum claim [29]: "Scrum Teams are self-organizing and cross-functional"; "The Scrum Master is responsible for promoting and supporting Scrum as defined in the Scrum Guide". In our survey, we did not explicitly ask for a pattern of self-organization. However, we did guide respondents in terms of stating that cross-functional teams are "usually self-organized". Indeed, the above data seem to portray a picture of ritual-centred implementations of Scrum [30], cherry-picking only those practices that are easy to implement. The truth is that a shift from directive management styles to self-organization have proven difficult for some enterprises [15]. Moreover, the frequent absence of Scrum master–a servant, non-directive leadership role–reported by our research seems to confirm the proposition. In that regard, an interesting question to ask is: Who is the keeper of the agile spirit in such teams? If this is the project manager, the question is whether we can still talk about Scrum in the sense of what Scrum originators have been using the term for [29].

In general, previous research shows that core responsibilities and the form of authority of the Scrum master role highly vary across different companies [16].

Surprisingly, the present study reports that combinations of Scrum and Waterfall (i.e. less-purist versions of Scrum) are employed infrequently. Together, this seems to show that many practitioners might be entirely unknowledgeable about the original intentions of Scrum originators, and the underlying values and assumptions they have promoted. In that sense, instead of "being agile", the practitioners might be just "doing agile" [31].

5 Discussion and Conclusion

Today, research into software development and project management methods represents an important theme in a number of academic disciplines. This paper presents preliminary results that characterize the current state of ASDM adoption in the Czech Republic. In this stage, our aim was to share certain initial observations with researchers and practitioners, not to provide an all-encompassing analysis. We summarize the key finding as follows: *Scrum clearly dominates among the ASDMs implemented in the Czech Republic, but perhaps it is a different form of Scrum than its originators have had in mind* [29, 31].

We offer a possible explanation. As Scrum is rapidly gaining ground in the world of project management, it is increasingly being added to the repertoire of "traditional" project managers. Previously, these professionals might have used heavy-weight methods such as PMBOK or PRINCE2, possibly together with a "command & control" mentality [15]. The ever-growing popularity of Scrum might have caused that differently from the intentions of its originators, the project managers have tended to implement Scrum in a utilitarian sense – as a "great tool" that appears to be simple and easy (in fact, it appears to be significantly easier than the above methods). However, Scrum is "Simple to understand", but "Difficult to master" [29]. This is to underscore the importance of the "soft" element in Scrum, i.e. psychology of the development team. In that sense, Scrum's simplicity may be merely an illusion.

Regarding the relationship between ASDMs seen as generic "brand labels" and concrete agile practices that are used in reality, the situation is complex. Previous research argues that in the real world practices are frequently used in quite creative ways and hardly ever "by the book" [6]. However, a too-relaxed form of ASDM implementation may easily result in disconnecting the practices from the "parental" ASDM, which they were conceptually bound with. In fact, such a pattern seems to presently be a general trend in software development – some authors even convincingly argue that practices should be officially "liberated [i.e. disconnected] from the methods that use them—their method prisons" [32]. If we are to accept this argument, we will not be surprised by the level of creativity practitioners exhibit when adopting ASDMs for their unique contexts. Nevertheless, a contrarian argument may be as follows. Decoupling the practices from the core values and assumptions embodied by the ASDMs could lead to "ritualistic imitation of certain behavior" [30], entirely missing the ASDM essence [31].

Prior concluding, we admit that this paper suffers from several limitations. First, the analytical apparatus employed here is quite simple. Despite this fact, we believe that sharing the results with the community in a timely manner is important, because the results shed some light upon the somewhat controversial state of ASDM adoption in the Czech Republic. Second, in our survey we employed convenience sampling. While this approach is common in the domain of ASDM surveys [3, 6, 11], the sample size is the main limiting factor also in our case [26]. Connected with this, we made use of social networks for the purpose of survey distribution. This certainly introduced a form of bias, limiting the possibility of participation to those who use that media. Third, from the quantitative data, it is hard to understand the exact reasons behind the "Used to a certain extent" answers. In our subsequent research, we therefore want to focus on the analysis of respondents' perceptions by employing a qualitative lens.

Acknowledgement. This work has been supported by an internal grant funding scheme (F4/23/2019) administered by the University of Economics, Prague.

References

1. Cusumano, M., Maccormack, A., Kemerer, C.F., Crandall, B.: Software development worldwide: the state of the practice. IEEE Softw. **20**, 28–34 (2003)
2. Fitzgerald, B.: An empirical investigation into the adoption of systems development methodologies. Inf. Manag. **34**, 317–328 (1998)
3. Kuhrmann, M., et al.: Hybrid Software development approaches in practice: a European perspective. IEEE Softw. **36**, 20–31 (2019)
4. Kraljić, A., Kraljić, T.: Agile software engineering practices and ERP implementation with focus on SAP activate methodology. In: Zdravkovic, J., Grabis, J., Nurcan, S., Stirna, J. (eds.) BIR 2018. LNBIP, vol. 330, pp. 190–201. Springer, Cham (2018). https://doi.org/10.1007/978-3-319-99951-7_13
5. Birkinshaw, J.: What to expect from agile. MIT Sloan Manag. Rev. **59**, 39–42 (2018)
6. Klünder, J., et al.: Catching up with method and process practice: an industry-informed baseline for researchers. In: 41st International Conference on Software Engineering: Software Engineering in Practice, pp. 255–264 (2019)
7. Kalenda, M., Hyna, P., Rossi, B.: Scaling agile in large organizations: practices, challenges, and success factors. J. Softw. Evol. Process. **30**, e1954 (2018)
8. Ochodek, M., Kopczyńska, S.: Perceived importance of agile requirements engineering practices – a survey. J. Syst. Softw. **143**, 29–43 (2018)
9. Williams, L.: What agile teams think of agile principles. Commun. ACM **55**, 71 (2012)
10. Vijayasarathy, L.R., Dan Turk, C.: Agile software development: a survey of early adopters. J. Inf. Technol. Manag. **XIX**, 1–8 (2008)
11. Rodríguez, P., Markkula, J., Oivo, M., Turula, K.: Survey on agile and lean usage in Finnish software industry. In: ESEM, pp. 139–148 (2012)
12. CollabNet VersionOne: 13th Annual State of Agile report (2018). https://www.stateofagile.com/#ufh-i-521251909-13th-annual-state-of-agile-report/473508
13. Stellman, A., Greene, J.: Applied Software Project Management. O'Reilly Media, Beijing (2005)
14. Schwaber, K.: Agile Project Management with Scrum. Microsoft Press, Microsoft Press (2004)

15. Taylor, K.J.: Adopting Agile software development: the project manager experience. Inf. Technol. People. **29**, 670–687 (2016)
16. Diebold, P., Ostberg, J.-P., Wagner, S., Zendler, U.: What do practitioners vary in using Scrum? In: Lassenius, C., Dingsøyr, T., Paasivaara, M. (eds.) XP 2015. LNBIP, vol. 212, pp. 40–51. Springer, Cham (2015). https://doi.org/10.1007/978-3-319-18612-2_4
17. Kurapati, N., Manyam, V.S.C., Petersen, K.: Agile software development practice adoption survey. In: Wohlin, C. (ed.) XP 2012. LNBIP, vol. 111, pp. 16–30. Springer, Heidelberg (2012). https://doi.org/10.1007/978-3-642-30350-0_2
18. Cesa, L.O.A., Mantovani Fontana, R., Reinehr, S., Malucelli, A.: Are we agile or not? A survey on Brazilian software processes. In: Tonin, G.S., Estácio, B., Goldman, A., Guerra, E. (eds.) WBMA 2018. CCIS, vol. 981, pp. 19–33. Springer, Cham (2019). https://doi.org/10. 1007/978-3-030-14310-7_2
19. Campanelli, A.S., Camilo, R.D., Parreiras, F.S.: The impact of tailoring criteria on agile practices adoption: a survey with novice agile practitioners in Brazil. J. Syst. Softw. **137**, 366–379 (2018)
20. Buchalcevova, A.: Research of the use of agile methodologies in the Czech Republic. In: Wojtkowski, W., Wojtkowski, G., Lang, M., Conboy, K., Barry, C. (eds.) Information Systems Development, pp. 51–64. Springer, Boston (2009). https://doi.org/10.1007/978-0-387-68772-8_5
21. Šochová, Z.: Agile Adoption Survey 2009 (2009). http://soch.cz/AgileSurvey.pdf
22. Průzkum agilního řízení v ČR (2013). https://archiv.etnetera.cz/52591-stahnout_agilni_report_2013/
23. Tománek, M.: Současný stav používání agilních metodik ve světě a v ČR. Acta Inform. Pragensia. **4**, 4–17 (2015)
24. Beck, K., Andres, C.: Extreme Programming Explained: Embrace Change. Addison Wesley, Boston (2005)
25. Fitzgerald, B., Stol, K.-J.: Continuous software engineering: a roadmap and agenda. J. Syst. Softw. **123**, 176–189 (2017)
26. Etikan, I., Abubakar Musa, S., Sunusi Alkassim, R.: Comparison of convenience sampling and purposive sampling. Am. J. Theoret. Appl. Stat. **5**, 1–4 (2016)
27. Schlauderer, S., Overhage, S., Fehrenbach, B.: Widely Used but also highly valued? Acceptance factors and their perceptions in Water-Scrum-Fall projects. In: Thirty Sixth International Conference on Information Systems, pp. 1–19 (2015)
28. Gmeiner, J., Ramler, R., Haslinger, J.: Automated testing in the continuous delivery pipeline: a case study of an online company. In: Eighth International Conference on Software Testing, Verification and Validation Workshops (2015)
29. Schwaber, K., Sutherland, J.: Scrum Guide (2017). https://scrumguides.org/
30. Mäki-Runsas, T.E., Wistrand, K., Karlsson, F.: Cargo cults in information systems development: a definition and an analytical framework. In: Andersson, B., Johansson, B., Barry, C., Lang, M., Linger, H., Schneider, C. (eds.) Advances in Information Systems Development. LNISO, vol. 34, pp. 35–53. Springer, Cham (2019). https://doi.org/10.1007/978-3-030-22993-1_3
31. Hohl, P., et al.: Back to the future: origins and directions of the "Agile Manifesto" – views of the originators. J. Softw. Eng. Res. Dev. **6**, 1–27 (2018)
32. Jacobson, I., Lawson, H., Ng, P.-W., McMahon, P.E., Goedicke, M.: The Essentials of Modern Software Engineering. ACM, New York (2019)

Data Vault Mappings to Dimensional Model Using Schema Matching

Mikko Puonti[1,2](✉) ⓘ and Timo Raitalaakso[1,2] ⓘ

[1] Solita Ltd., Åkerlundinkatu 11, 33100 Tampere, Finland
{puonti,timo.raitalaakso}@iki.fi
https://www.solita.fi/en/
[2] Tampere University, Kalevantie 4, 33100 Tampere, Finland

Abstract. In data warehousing, business driven development defines data requirements to fulfill reporting needs. A data warehouse stores current and historical data in one single place. Data warehouse architecture consists of several layers and each has its own purpose. A staging layer is a data storage area to assists data loadings, a data vault modelled layer is the persistent storage that integrates data and stores the history, whereas publish layer presents data using a vocabulary that is familiar to the information users. By following the process which is driven by business requirements and starts with publish layer structure, this creates a situation where manual work requires a specialist, who knows the data vault model. Our goal is to reduce the number of entities that can be selected in a transformation so that the individual developer does not need to know the whole solution, but can focus on a subset of entities (partial schema). In this paper, we present two different schema matchers, one based on attribute names, and another based on data flow mapping information. Schema matching based on data flow mappings is a novel addition to current schema matching literature. Through the example of Northwind, we show how these two different matchers affect the formation of a partial schema for transformation source entities. Based on our experiment with Northwind we conclude that combining schema matching algorithms produces correct entities in the partial schema.

Keywords: Schema matching · Data flow · Data warehouse · Data vault · Dimensional model

1 Introduction

In a data warehouse, whereas several data sources are integrated as one data set, mapping information is crucial. Most commonly used in data warehouse implementation is Extract-Transform and Load (ETL) process [6].

Business driven development defines data requirements to fulfill reporting needs. These reporting needs are typically modelled with a dimensional modeling [7] technique. To enable parallel work with data transformation (ETL) creation and reporting tools we have created a dimensional model as a prerequisite for actual implementation [11]. Reporting tools need a dimensional model populated with a sample data set. Populating a sample data set to a dimensional model creates data flow mapping

© IFIP International Federation for Information Processing 2019
Published by Springer Nature Switzerland AG 2019
P. Doucek et al. (Eds.): CONFENIS 2019, LNBIP 375, pp. 55–64, 2019.
https://doi.org/10.1007/978-3-030-37632-1_5

information at attribute level, whereas one or many attributes are mapped to one target attribute. As a new interface is introduced to a data warehouse, it is created first to staging layer. A sample data set is mapped from staging layer to the publish layer (Fig. 1B). Mapping may be implemented as a database view or a ETL-transformation that populates tables. In this paper, we are referring to these views and tables as entities.

A data warehouse stores current and historical data in one single place. A data vault model [8] is used for storing history. When the data vault model exists, the transformations implementation between staging layer and data vault is automated by using the process presented in our earlier research [12].

By following the process which is driven by business requirements and start with designing a dimensional model with data, continuing with transformation implementation from a staging layer to a data vault model. The transformation graph forms a data flow. This creates a situation where we have in a place publish layer structure, data vault model and transformation mapping between a staging layer and a publish layer together with a data vault (Fig. 1C). Transformation mapping between a data vault and a publish layer is missing. When producing a durable implementation, a target is to create transformation to the publish layer based on the data vault model. Currently, this is manual work and it requires a specialist who knows the data vault model. A large data warehouse may consist of several hundred entities. Our research is focused on how to help this transformation mapping creation. How may we use the data flow mapping information, which is generated in earlier phases? Is there any particular schema mapping technique useful to solve this manual work and at least partially automate tasks in the current situation? Our goal is easing up the developers work. This is accomplished with finding candidates to be used in schema mappings. We are also finding ways to prune parts of a big data model to be used.

2   Related Work

Ontology matching is a wider research area than our schema matching. We are using ontology matching a name based technique where strings are identical [4]. Our ontologies are database schemas, even when the actual implementation not include a database schemas there are structures where tables (relation) contain attributes.

We are using existing data flow mapping information to generate new replacing transformation mappings together with more commonly researched schema matching methods. The data flow forms an directed acyclic graph. It may be considered form a computer program. It describes the dependencies between all entities in a system. Frank Tip is writing about using program slicing in program integration [14, Chap. 5.2]. We are using such slicing to generate subgraphs assisting transformation generation.

Villányi describes schema matching techniques in service-oriented enterprise application integration in his dissertation [15]. In a hybrid matcher Villányi combine a vocabulary matcher and a structural matcher, where structural matcher uses a neighborhood level structural similarity.

Atzeni et al. introduce meta-mappings as a formalism that describes transformations between generic data structures [2]. This enables mapping reuse, when similar

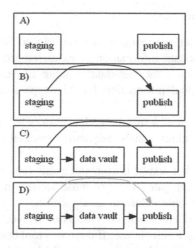

Fig. 1. Transformation stack evolution

information is located in several schemas, whereas our reuse is use data flow mapping for creating new transformation between schemas where transformation is not yet defined.

Golfarelli et al. [5] introduce a starry vault approach to generate a dimensional model automatically from a data vault model. In their paper there are formal definitions of data vault and multi dimensional schemas introduced. Their paper is aiming to find a multi dimensional model from data vault structures. Our approach is to match and generate data flow between two predefined models.

Human effort is needed in schema matching scenarios as existing matching algorithm results are not perfect. Nguyen et al. concentrate on minimizing human effort in reconciling match networks [10]. They stress that after matching there is still a need for a post-matching phase, which is manual correction. Their reconciliation process is an iterative process, whereas our solution is to offer a partition schema for transformation as a selection. Many authors agree that mapping can not totally automate, there is a need for manual corrections [1, 2, 5, 10, 15].

3 Schema Matching and Experiments

In a data warehouse data is in relational form [3], even when NoSQL techniques are used in implementation. A relational database consists of tables and attributes.

A set of tables is grouped together with a schema. Schema is used as an implementation of data warehouse layers, each layer in Fig. 1 is a separate schema. Now we can refine our research question "how to help transformation mapping generation" to form a match schema between a data vault and a publish layer schema.

3.1 Matching Workflow

In a matching workflow, we are using phases introduced Rahm [13]. First phase is preprocessing, where metadata information is extracted from a relational database (Fig. 2a). Relational schema offer metadata: a table name, an attribute name, the attribute data type, additional information for data type and a description field for attribute.

Matching is an execution of a matching algorithm, whereas it can contain several matching steps. These matching can be sequential, parallel or mixing both of those principals.

A combination of matcher results is combining different matcher algorithm values and possibly calculation aggregated value of those values. In a sequential matching a matcher can use earlier matcher values in an algorithm.

A selection of correspondences is in our case a human work phase, which we aim to help with offering matching results in use. If there is a tool built based on our article, it could suggest good matches and human work would be only accept suggestions and creating more complex mappings.

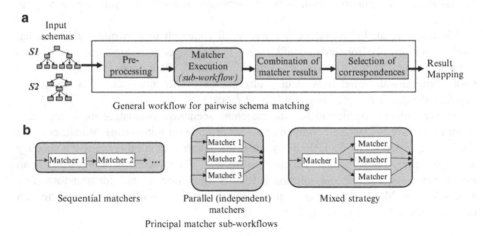

Fig. 2. General match workflow (copied from [13])

3.2 Schema Matching Based on Attribute Names

A matcher compares every attribute name of a data vault with every attribute in a publish layer target attribute. This cross join operation can be easily quite large and this is reason why we suggest to do this few publish layer entities at a time. The preprocess phase in Fig. 3 target subset is chosen. In matcher first pruning is to feed only a partial entity set from the publish layer entities, this may be interpreted as a partition of a second schema [13].

A result of the attribute name matcher is a set of data vault entities, which has common attribute naming compared between data vault and target entities.

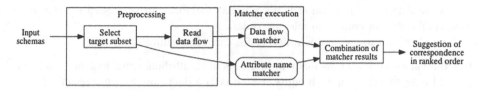

Fig. 3. Match workflow

3.3   Schema Matching Based on Data Flow Mapping

Publish layer entities have data flow mapping for a sample data set. This mapping can be implemented from the data vault or the staging area, nevertheless there is data flow mapping information as presented in Fig. 1B.

Data flow mappings are expressed at attribute level between source and target schemas. Depending on technology used it may be a challenging process to extract that attribute level mapping information, or even worse manually create this mapping information. We suggest expressing data flow information between source and target schema entities, this information is useful and it is easier to extract from ETL-tool or database view metadata information.

The target publish layer entities are chosen as an end point of the subgraph slice. A result of data flow mapping is data vault (source schema) entities, which have corresponding data flow to a publish layer (target schema) entities.

Inside data vault there might exist layers. A raw data vault that is populated straight from staging area. Business data vault [9] is a layer that enriches the data vault model and uses other data vault entities as a source. This piles up the transformation stack and makes the data flow graph deeper. We are using this depth as an indicator of enriched information. Giving a better ranking for business vault entities to be used in the suggested mappings.

3.4   Schema Matching Combination of Attribute Names and Data Flow Mapping

Last phase of our algorithm is a combination of earlier matchers results. Noteworth, these matchers have result sets at different level of granularity. This is presented in Fig. 3 combination of matcher results.

As we are aiming to match schemas between the data vault and the publish layer, this algorithm is for helping creating transformations between these schemas. For human decision, we are presenting potential entities for transformation creation. The earlier matchers enable us to use the following strategy:

- Present all potential entities in order where first is the most prominent candidate
- Present only potential entities, which are common in both matcher result set.

As the data flow information is not always available, our suggested strategy is to present all potential entities in relevant order.

The algorithm to create this ordering for candidate entities.

1. Count at entity level how many attributes is in an attribute name matcher result set.
2. Add a depth value for each entity, which is in a data flow matcher result set.
3. Summarise these result sets.
4. Order the result set according to the value of each entity.

3.5 Northwind Example

As a demonstration of our approach, we use Northwind[1] source data model. We modeled a publish layer schema of order fact and dimensions. The ORDER_F references to CUSTOMER_D, EMPLOYEE_D, ORDER_D and SHIPPER_D. After data vault modeling and transformation population at the phase (Fig. 1C) we get suggestions to new (Fig. 1D) phase transformations as described in (Tables 1 and 2).

CUSTOMER D gets side different false positives from both suggestions but CUSTOMER_H and CUSTOMER_S are found in both sets to be considered as source for mappings. The number of common columns in naming suggestion is higher for these and gets prioritized based on the naming match. Adding the second suggestion set from data flows the results become more convincing. SHIPPER_D gets assurance that CUSTOMER_H and CUSTOMER_S should not be considered as source for mapping. ORDER_F gets suggestions from either ORDER_L or ORDER_BV_L. Data vault model is layered. ORDER_L represent a raw data vault layer and ORDER_BV_L is an entity of business data vault layer. ORDER_BV_L uses another data vault entities as a source for it data. This dependency graph depth is visible in (Table 2) ORDER_BV_L - ORDER_F suggestion row. It is used together with higher score from naming suggestion to choose correct mappings to be implemented.

3.6 Observations from Northwind Example

Both our matchers return side hits - false positives. Attribute naming return overlapping from irrelevant similarity matches. The data flow matcher raises other potential mapping candidates. As the data flow subgraph from used staging entities contains transformations to other data vault entities that are not needed in the desired resulting mapping for a specific target publish layer entity.

With combing results from both approaches we get more precise suggestion for the new data vault publish layer transformations. With our experiments, the false positive groups are some what differing. So exclusion of false positive mapping candidates becomes more convincing. This minimizes the needed human effort while creating the end results.

---

[1] https://github.com/dshifflet/NorthwindOracle_DDL.

Table 1. Transformation suggestions based on naming

MAINENTITY	SOURCEENTITY	TARGETENTITY	C
CUSTOMER_H	CUSTOMER_H	CUSTOMER_D	2
CUSTOMER_H	CUSTOMER_S	CUSTOMER_D	2
SHIPPER_H	SHIPPER_H	CUSTOMER_D	1
SHIPPER_H	SHIPPER_S	CUSTOMER_D	1
EMPLOYEE_H	EMPLOYEE_H	EMPLOYEE_D	2
EMPLOYEE_H	EMPLOYEE_S	EMPLOYEE_D	2
ORDER_H	ORDER_H	EMPLOYEE_D	1
ORDER_H	ORDER_S	EMPLOYEE_D	1
ORDER_H	ORDER_H	ORDER_D	2
ORDER_H	ORDER_S	ORDER_D	2
CUSTOMER_ID_CUSTOMER_L	CUSTOMER_H	ORDER_F	1
CUSTOMER_ID_CUSTOMER_L	CUSTOMER_ID_CUSTOMER_L	ORDER_F	1
CUSTOMER_ID_CUSTOMER_L	CUSTOMER_ID_H	ORDER_F	1
ORDER_BV_L	CUSTOMER_H	ORDER_F	4
ORDER_BV_L	EMPLOYEE_H	ORDER_F	4
ORDER_BV_L	ORDER_BV_L	ORDER_F	4
ORDER_BV_L	ORDER_H	ORDER_F	4
ORDER_BV_L	SHIPPER_H	ORDER_F	4
ORDER_L	CUSTOMER_ID_H	ORDER_F	3
ORDER_L	EMPLOYEE_H	ORDER_F	3
ORDER_L	ORDER_H	ORDER_F	3
ORDER_L	ORDER_L	ORDER_F	3
ORDER_L	SHIPPER_H	ORDER_F	3
CUSTOMER_H	CUSTOMER_H	SHIPPER_D	1
CUSTOMER_H	CUSTOMER_S	SHIPPER_D	1
SHIPPER_H	SHIPPER_H	SHIPPER_D	2
SHIPPER_H	SHIPPER_S	SHIPPER_D	2

4   Discussion and Future Work

In our experimentation, we created a target schema as a database views from the staging layer. The data flow based matcher used this information at an entity level. There are possibilities to extract this data flow mapping information at an attribute level, one option is to use a tool like Queryscope[2]. This would open possibility to create more fine tuned result of the combined matcher described in this paper.

In this paper, we introduce two schema matcher. By adding more schema matchers, it is possible to improve the suggestions. A structural matcher might be beneficial. Link and fact granularities might be used. Link granularity, calculated based on the number of hubs it references, and fact cardinality, how many dimensions it references, could be compared.

---

[2] https://app.sqldep.com/demo/.

Table 2. Transformation suggestions based on data flows

SOURCEENTITY	TARGETENTITY	SCORE
CUSTOMER_H	CUSTOMER_D	1
CUSTOMER_ID_CUSTOMER_L	CUSTOMER_D	1
CUSTOMER_ID_H	CUSTOMER_D	1
CUSTOMER_S	CUSTOMER_D	1
ORDER_BV_L	CUSTOMER_D	2
EMPLOYEE_H	EMPLOYEE_D	1
EMPLOYEE_S	EMPLOYEE_D	1
CUSTOMER_ID_H	ORDER_D	1
EMPLOYEE_H	ORDER_D	1
ORDER_BV_L	ORDER_D	2
ORDER_H	ORDER_D	1
ORDER_L	ORDER_D	1
ORDER_S	ORDER_D	1
SHIPPER_H	ORDER_D	1
CUSTOMER_ID_H	ORDER_F	1
EMPLOYEE_H	ORDER_F	1
ORDER_BV_L	ORDER_F	2
ORDER_H	ORDER_F	1
ORDER_L	ORDER_F	1
ORDER_S	ORDER_F	1
SHIPPER_H	ORDER_F	1
SHIPPER_H	SHIPPER_D	1
SHIPPER_S	SHIPPER_D	1

Future work would be to suggest transformations between source schema (data vault) and target schema (publish layer) entities. At least the result set from the attribute name matcher is re-usable for creating transformation where is one-to-one mapping between source and target attribute. Our target is to reducing manual work by offering a subset of source schema entities for creating transformations, not actually create that data flow.

This paper is talking about a process of creating new or extending an existing data warehouse. A similar approach may be used when replacing an existing direct star schema publish layer data flows by adding data vault modeled enterprise data warehouse layer between a staging and a publish layer. Replacing old ETL tool implementation. Benefits of data vault methodology such as history in satellites and better agile development enablement. The process described in (Fig. 1) fits as is also on such replacement process. Phase (A) Use existing staging and star schema model. (B) Reverse engineer data flow transformation dependencies from old ETL implementation. (C) and (D) phases as described in this paper.

It is inevitable that the data vault model does not have a perfect match for source mapping at some point in data warehouse evolution. These pruned partial matcher results could be used to be a base for new business vault entities. The knowledge of a developer and an access path suggestor[3] could be used to generate links and bridges that satisfy publish layer source information needs.

5   Conclusion

Our research is focused on helping transformation creation between a data vault and a publish layer. For each publish layer entities we create a set of source entity candidates from a data vault schema entities.

As we are following the process which is driven by business requirements, there is a publish layer entity populated with a sample data. This sample data population construct a data flow to the target schema entity.

We examine whether schema matching is based on attribute names enough to suggest correct entities from a data vault schema. Schema matching based on attribute names finds correct entities from a source schema, but still there is room for improvement.

By adding a schema matcher based on data flow mapping we get a result set to enrich an attribute name based matching. Combining the results from these two matchers we may present potential transformation source entity candidates in order where the most prominent one is at first.

This combined algorithm is suitable for building a tool to help transformation mapping creation between a data vault and a publish layer. The result set from algorithm offer correct source entities for transformation mapping sources.

After choosing source entities for transformation mapping, we could additionally suggest mappings from schema matching based on attribute names as a base for that transformation where a specialist could continue with additional mappings and with the complex mappings.

References

1. Alexe, B., Ten Cate, B., Kolaitis, P.G., Tan, W.C.: Designing and refining schema mappings via data examples. In: Proceedings of the 2011 ACM SIGMOD International Conference on Management of data, pp. 133–144. ACM (2011)
2. Atzeni, P., Bellomarini, L., Papotti, P., Torlone, R.: Meta-mappings for schema mapping reuse. Proc. VLDB Endow. 12(5), 557–569 (2019)
3. Codd, E.F.: A relational model of data for large shared data banks. Commun. ACM 13(6), 377–387 (1970)
4. Euzenat, J., Shvaiko, P.: Ontology Matching. Springer, Heidelberg (2013). https://doi.org/10.1007/978-3-642-38721-0
5. Golfarelli, M., Graziani, S., Rizzi, S.: Starry vault: automating multidimensional modeling from data vaults. In: Pokorný, J., Ivanović, M., Thalheim, B., Šaloun, P. (eds.) ADBIS 2016. LNCS, vol. 9809, pp. 137–151. Springer, Cham (2016). https://doi.org/10.1007/978-3-319-44039-2_10

---

[3] http://rafudb.blogspot.com/2019/01/access-path-suggestor.html.

6. Kimball, R., Caserta, J.: The Data Warehouse ETL Toolkit: Practical Techniques for Extracting, Cleaning, Conforming and Delivering Data. Wiley, Hoboken (2004)
7. Kimball, R., Ross, M.: The Data Warehouse Toolkit: the Complete Guide to Dimensional Modeling. Wiley, Hoboken (2011)
8. Linstedt, D.: Data Vault Series 1–Data Vault Overview. The Data Administration Newsletter, Baltimore (2002)
9. Linstedt, D., Graziano, K., Hultgren, H.: The new business supermodel, the business of data vault modeling. Lulu.com (2008)
10. Quoc Viet Nguyen, H., et al.: Minimizing human effort in reconciling match networks. In: Ng, W., Storey, V.C., Trujillo, J.C. (eds.) ER 2013. LNCS, vol. 8217, pp. 212–226. Springer, Heidelberg (2013). https://doi.org/10.1007/978-3-642-41924-9_19
11. Puonti, M., Lehtonen, T., Luoto, A., Aaltonen, T., Aho, T.: Towards agile enterprise data warehousing. In: ICSEA 2016, p. 241 (2016)
12. Puonti, M., Raitalaakso, T., Aho, T., Mikkonen, T.: Automating transformations in data vault data warehouse loads. In: EJC, pp. 215–230 (2016)
13. Rahm, E.: Towards large-scale schema and ontology matching. In: Bellahsene, Z., Bonifati, A., Rahm, E. (eds.) Schema Matching and Mapping, pp. 3–27. Springer, Heidelberg (2011). https://doi.org/10.1007/978-3-642-16518-4_1
14. Tip, F.: A survey of program slicing techniques. J. Program. Lang. **3**, 121–189 (1995)
15. Villányi, B.J.: Schema matching techniques in service-oriented enterprise application integration. Informatikai Tudományok Doktori Iskola (2016)

Shadow IT Management Concept for Public Sector

Lada Šedivcová (Nesvedová)^(✉)⬤ and Martin Potančok⬤

University of Economics, 130 67 Prague, Czech Republic
lada.sedivcova@gmail.com

Abstract. Shadow IT represents a software, hardware, or any other solution used by employees within organizations that has not received any prior formal approval from the IT department to be used. Currently, the issue of Shadow IT is increasingly under discussion and is beginning to be explored in the private sector. However, this issue is not addressed comprehensively in the public sector. The main aim of this paper is therefore to propose a Shadow IT management concept for the public sector. The proposal of Shadow IT management concept identified problematic areas related to Shadow IT discovered during a case study in connection with the main aim of the paper. There are 7 areas designated as A1 to A7. The recommended approaches and solutions are set for these problem areas. Shadow IT Management Concept was created based on the case study (including interviews with main stakeholders).

Keywords: Enterprise IT management · Management concept · Shadow IT

1 Introduction

Shadow IT is a software, hardware, or any other solution used by employees within organizations that has not received any prior formal approval from the IT department to be used [1]. The issue of Shadow IT is currently under discussion and is beginning to be explored in the private sector [2]. However, this issue is not addressed comprehensively in the public sector.

According to Gartner [3], up to one third of investments in IT development are managed and funded outside the IT department and its budget. This is very often caused by cloud solutions or mobile applications. These are services that are immediately available and can therefore be relatively easily deployed without IT expertise. On the one hand, Shadow IT can be an innovative element that pushes companies into new technology solutions [4], but on the other hand it can also be a source of trouble if solutions are provided outside the IT department without being informed by IT department managers and not following strategies and official procedures [5].

Nowadays, employees can bring their own devices into the corporate environment. This trend is known as Bring Your Own Device (BYOD). Some of the applications that employees can bring might be a disruption to the entire infrastructure and vulnerability of the agenda system and intrusion into the internal network may occur [6]. Therefore, it is essential that BYOD policy is implemented and it does not cause Shadow IT.

Furstenau also emphasizes the importance of the issue: *"Shadow IT is becoming increasingly important as digital work practices make it easier than ever for business*

© IFIP International Federation for Information Processing 2019
Published by Springer Nature Switzerland AG 2019
P. Doucek et al. (Eds.): CONFENIS 2019, LNBIP 375, pp. 65–73, 2019.
https://doi.org/10.1007/978-3-030-37632-1_6

units crafting their own IT solutions" [5]. For IT departments, it is necessary to determine when users decide to implement the Shadow IT process and start to manage this process [7]. IT as such, including infrastructure (hardware, software, network resources and other services that are interconnected), should be developed, managed and controlled by the IT department [8]. Fürstenau [9] states in his study that the most common problems are architectural. More than half of the systems may suffer from inconsistent data, non-scalable technical platforms, unstable servers, or hardware components. The architecture of IS/ICT is, according to Bruckner [10], very important, as it creates a relatively stable IS/ICT solution framework. It constitutes a means of communication, ensures the stability of IS/ICT development, takes into account the requirements for IS/ICT properties and allows to minimize the costs of incorrectly assigned projects. One of the most widely used frameworks in practice are ITIL, TOGAF and Zachman. For example, ITIL is a set of business information management practices through services. It is a library of more than 40 volumes published by the British government agency CCTA in 2013 [11], but currently belongs to AXELOS [12].

Despite its complexity, ITIL does not provide sufficient coverage for Shadow IT. The topic has been addressed by several authors, e.g. Pettey [13], Silic et al. [1], Zimmermann [14], but only with the application to the private sector. In the private sector, companies are able to deal with the issue in different ways, but the public sector seems to be an interesting issue. This is mainly due to the impossibility of immediate intervention. Public administration processes do not allow flexible responses to required changes [15]. In the case of public organizations, this topic has not been comprehensively addressed and is therefore an interesting area for research.

For these reasons, the main aim of the paper is to propose a Shadow IT management concept for the public sector.

2 Methodology

Shadow IT Management Concept was created based on a case study, partial results for one type of public organization [16], the Multidimensional Management and Development of Information Systems (MMDIS) [10] and Management of Business Informatics (MBI) [17] models. Different organizations from the public sector were selected for the case study. For the purposes of the case study, higher local government units - regional authorities were addressed. The Vysocina Regional Authority showed the greatest interest in the outputs of the case study and also provided documents that are not publicly available. Close cooperation took place especially with the head of the department of informatics.

As part of the case study, interviews with stakeholders (employees, managers, IT employees and IT managers) were conducted. Respondent groups were distinguished by job position - managerial level in the IT field, positions on managerial level in another field and positions that are not on any of the previous ones (these are positions of common end users, e.g. clerk, accountant, lawyer, etc. The total number of respondents was 35, of which 9 were men and 26 were women. The average length of one interview was 60 min. The beginning of each interview was unstructured to get as much information and as many opinions and information on organizations from the public sector as possible, followed by a semi-structured part with questions about Shadow IT. Other sources of information included strategies of organizations and their structures. The research is fully consistent with the definition of a case study as a qualitative research method within the exploratory and theory-building phase presented by [18] and [19]. The structure of this paper corresponds to the above.

3   Shadow IT Criteria and Reasons for Existence

3.1   Shadow IT Criteria

Since employees (users) can ignore the central IT system, the performance of the specific organizational units of the public sector may be influenced.

According to Rentropa and Zimmermann [14], the so-called evaluation model is used for systematic quality assessment and Shadow IT evaluation criteria. It is therefore appropriate to clarify this model in the case of Shadow IT to find ways to map and respond to the occurrence of Shadow IT. The evaluation model will be used to formulate questions for the interview, which is one of the selected collection methods in our case study.

To define Shadow IT criteria, it is necessary to identify specific Shadow IT cases and associated organizational processes in the first step. These instances are then analysed and evaluated. This evaluation makes it possible to establish basic control over the Shadow IT and to draw up effective strategies to control the Shadow IT. Because this model is developed for the Shadow IT mapping in the private sector, it has been adapted for the public sector to cover specifics and influencing this sector [20]. Evaluation criteria based on [14] are presented in Table 1 and are further described below.

Table 1. Shadow IT criteria, based on [14]

Criterion	Sub-criterion	Sub-criterion
Relevancy	Strategic relevance	
	Criticality	Business processes
		IT security
		Compliance
		IT services management
Quality	System quality	Software
		Technical processes
	Quality of services	
	Quality of information	
	Quality of processes	
Size	Utilization of resources	
	Number of users	
	Shadow IT components	
Innovative potential		
Parallel		

C1 Relevancy

This criterion described Shadow IT along with its relevance to the organization's processes. It carries value and risks. This criterion is therefore subdivided into sub-criteria. (1) Strategic importance is necessary to assess how strong the impact on the region's strategy and strategic decisions regarding IT infrastructure is. (2) Criticality: the use of Shadow IT can influence several things, such as IT security risk, compliance, and inefficiencies in business and business processes. Significance in erratic behaviour brings a degree of risk in many areas. This sub-criterion relates specifically to business processes, IT security, IT service management at different levels of criticality.

C2 Quality

This is an important criterion for assessing the quality of Shadow IT. It refers to the technical quality of the system itself, the quality of IT services and the information generated. These main dimensions of quality represent the success of information system research. On the other hand, it is also necessary to look at the quality of processes where there is a potential occurrence of Shadow IT.

In the case of Shadow IT, it is the quality of hardware and software and the quality of process creation and design. Quality can be defined by models such as Capability Maturity Model Integration (CMMI) [21] or other standards.

Quality of service is a criterion that occurs in the context of Shadow IT, especially for IT department services. The quality of services can be evaluated e.g. on the basis of ITIL [22]. Thanks to best practices in IT service management, existing processes can be better managed, monitored, measured, evaluated and continually improved.

C3 Size

The size criterion can be used to estimate the extent of the Shadow IT in an organization. The size of Shadow IT refers to the use of Shadow IT resources and expertise, distribution and penetration with components and service services. Partial criteria are: (1) Use of resources and professionalism. (2) Number of users. (3) Shadow IT components. (4) Service processes.

C4 Innovative Potential

It is necessary to assess the innovative potential of the Shadow IT. On the one hand, Shadow IT offers the opportunity to introduce new technologies or improve processes in the research environment. On the other hand, Shadow IT may not be technologically suitable.

C5 Parallel

The parallel is an important criterion that assesses how Shadow IT runs in parallel to an existing, official IT system. This means how the identified Shadow IT replaces the official IT solution in the departments where it is used. It may also be the case that Shadow IT complements the IT system.

3.2   Reasons for Existence

The authors define various reasons for the existence of Shadow IT and therefore this chapter analyses reasons from multiple source regardless of the industry.

According to Bayan [23], the reasons are as follows: (1) Shadow IT is enforced due to a pressure to significantly reduce IT spending and an increasing demand for IT solutions for infrastructure problems. These pressures lead to a growing IT volume of unfinished projects. It is necessary to respond to the needs of other departments, many of which depend on IT projects to achieve the goals of the organization. (2) Shadow IT is a solution for specific needs. In some cases, these needs must be met quickly. Also, the return on initial investment pushes the department to realize shadow projects. This is partially because initial investments do not address the project lifecycle, support or infrastructure costs. (3) Shadow IT is stimulated by the fact that Shadow IT solutions seem faster. Some departments are pushing the IT department because they believe that another employee would do the job faster and without some of the IT department's demands.

Author Hulsebosch [24] sees the reasons for the emergence of Shadow IT as follows: (1) Business and IT weaknesses due to a lack of communication between them. Lack of communication leads to a mismatch between users and IT providers in the environment, leading to a decision as to whether the cost of resolving this issue is lower than the cost of circumventing it. (2) The absence of an official solution due to various binding documents or laws, some IT solutions are not possible, which may lead to recourse to the Shadow.

A combination of different facts leads to the emergence of specific Shadow IT. Individual causes of Shadow IT are closely related to the management of the whole organization or IT department. Due to inefficient processes associated with the required solution, mismatch between IT and business departments, or new policies in the organization, the potential incidence of Shadow IT increases. An example of a typical Shadow IT product is cloud-based SaaS (Software as a Service) [6].

In his study, Hulsebosch [24] lists categories that identify the reasons for Shadow IT. Particularly speaking about (1) No official IT solution. (2) The official solution is not extensive enough. (3) Official IT solution is not easily accessible. (4) The official solution is perceived as more expensive. (5) Employees are too strict. (6) Employees underestimate the risks. (7) It is very easy to use Shadow IT and opportunities are created for employees to use it.

4   Shadow IT Management Concept

The proposal of Shadow IT management concept contains problematic areas related to Shadow IT, which were discovered during the case study in connection with the main aim of the paper. There are 7 areas designated as A1 to A7. The recommended approaches and solutions are set for these problem areas.

The model is inspired by MMDIS [10] and MBI [17] models and methodologies. Both concepts define the process from global goals to the design of individual in-format projects. Based on the content analysis of the documents, it is a simplified model similar to those of the regions mentioned in their strategic plans. The model is complemented by Shadow IT problem areas, which are coloured in red. These areas are marked A1 to A7, which are further detailed (Fig. 1).

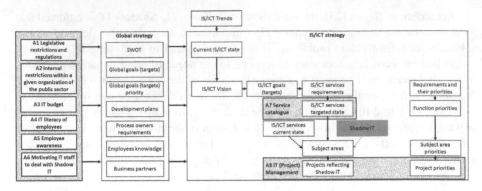

Fig. 1. Shadow IT management concept

A1 Legislative Restrictions and Regulations

The IT department has to take into account legislative restrictions and regulations when developing its own internal procedures. All internal employees must then follow these internal procedures. Since it contains various orders and prohibitions, it is necessary to take into account the needs of its employees in its creation, thus eliminating the risk of Shadow IT occurrence. The recommendation is to actively make comment in the legislative process.

A2 Internal Restrictions Within a Given Organization of the Public Sector

Protection of the internal network and official architecture is a priority for the public sector. Especially due to cloud storage, data leakage or loss may be imminent and therefore these tools (SaaS) are prohibited in public administration. If the IT department is able to respond to employees' requests in time, potential use of Shadow IT can be avoided. The IT department should meet the demands of employees or entire departments. It should be the initiator of the change and achieve it by working with employees outside its department.

A3 IT Budget

With a sufficient IT budget, Shadow IT detection tools, security assurance and tools that eliminate the occurrence of Shadow IT can be acquired or developed. These may be, for example, licenses of programs that are often used by employees but not authorized by the IT department.

A4 IT Literacy of Employees

IT employees might be trained by organizing or attending trainings and seminars on different topics. Furthermore, it is also necessary to motivate employees to attend this training. Training areas can vary according to the identified threats, such as security training from the SW and HW point of view (related BYOD issues) and strong instruction on internal regulations. Internal regulations should be available to all employees and it should never happen that the CIO does not inform their employees about these regulations.

A5 Employee Awareness
It is important that CIO or IT department should always inform employees about how the IT requirements management is addressed and where to find all the supporting documents, internal regulations, etc. Within this staff policy, training and development policies can be set, both in managerial positions and in other subordinate positions. Various sources are used to determine the level of employee awareness. Examples include questionnaires, observations, task analyzes, etc. [25].

A6 Motivating IT Staff to Deal with Shadow IT
The motivation of existing workers can be addressed based on various techniques that fall within the psychological theme. An example of the neglected component of motivation of human behavior may be based on the well-known Maslow's pyramid of needs [26]. Typical incentives for work motivation according to Růžička [27] include: work evaluation, group evaluation (appreciation of performance of a given employee by appreciation, respect, etc.), working conditions, financial reward, possibility of independent work.

A7 Service Catalogue
There should be a catalogue of ICT services. There are clear rules for managing operations and developing services [28]. The most important rules are: (1) Each service must have its own administrator, technical administrator and operator. (2) Clear rules must be in place, based on a binding and approved service architecture. (3) It is necessary to monitor investment and operating costs of individual services. It is also necessary to monitor the scope and quality of these services. In connection with the Shadow IT, it is also appropriate to measure employee satisfaction with the services - whether they adequately cover their needs.

A8 IT (Project) Management
If an analysis of needs and setting new goals in the field of IT (in response to the elimination of the occurrence of Shadow IT) is to be created, it is essential to define whether the project management of the given region is functionally or process-oriented. The demands on IT management arise mainly from the economic, business and operational needs of the region, along with the new possibilities of ICT. Pressure on the performance of IT has lead to the emergence of various methodologies and models. The previously mentioned ITIL library is one of the procedures for informatics management that can be used.

5 Conclusion

The main aim of the paper was to propose a Shadow IT management concept for the public sector. The proposal of Shadow IT management concept contains problematic areas related to Shadow IT, which were discovered during the case study in connection with the main aim of the paper.

There are 7 areas designated as A1 to A7 (legislative restrictions and regulations, IT budget, IT literacy of employees, employee awareness, motivating IT staff to deal with

Shadow IT, service catalogue, IT management). The recommended approaches and solutions are set for these problem areas.

The proposed Shadow IT Management concept should be used by public sector organizations to work effectively with Shadow IT and above all to eliminate risks.

Acknowledgements. This paper was written thanks to the long-term institutional support of research activities by the Faculty of Informatics and Statistics, University of Economics, Prague.

References

1. Silic, M.: Shadow it–Steroids for Innovation. Available SSRN 2633004 (2015)
2. Raden, N.: Shedding light on shadow IT: Is Excel running your business. DSSResources com 26 (2005)
3. Grásgruber, L.: Role IT oddělení a jeho manažera se mění—IT Visions. In: ITVisions.cz (2015). http://www.itvisions.cz/2015/10/role-it-oddeleni-a-jeho-manazera-se-meni/. Accessed 20 Sep 2019
4. Silic, M., Back, A.: Shadow IT–a view from behind the curtain. Comput. Secur. **45**, 274–283 (2014)
5. Fürstenau, D., Rothe, H.: Shadow IT systems: discerning the good and the evil (2014)
6. Zatřepálek, T.: Analýza problematiky stínového IT. České vysoké učení technické v Praze. Vypočetní a informační centrum (2016)
7. Chua, C., Storey, V., Chen, L.: Central IT or shadow IT? Factors shaping users' decision to go rogue with IT (2014)
8. Voříšek, J., Basl, J., Buchalcevová, A., et al.: Principy a modely řízení podnikové informatiky. Vysoká škola ekonomická v Praze, Nakladatelství Oeconomica, Praha (2008)
9. Fürstenau, D., Sandner, M., Anapliotis, D.: Why do shadow systems fail? An expert study on determinants of discontinuation (2016)
10. Bruckner, T., Voříšek, J., Buchalcevová, A.: Tvorba informačních systémů; Principy, metodiky, architektury. Grada Publishing, a.s., Praha (2012)
11. Gála, L., Pour, J., Toman, P.: Podniková informatika: počítačové aplikace v podnikové a mezipodnikové praxi. Grada, Praha (2006)
12. Axelos: About AXELOS (2019). https://www.axelos.com/about-axelos. Accessed 20 Sep 2019
13. Pettey, C.: Don't let shadow IT put your business at risk - smarter with gartner (2016). https://www.gartner.com/smarterwithgartner/dont-let-shadow-it-put-your-business-at-risk/. Accessed 3 Nov 2019
14. Rentrop, C., Zimmermann, S.: Shadow IT evaluation model. In: 2012 Federated Conference on Computer Science and Information Systems (FedCSIS), pp 1023–1027. IEEE (2012)
15. Zákon: Zákon č. 129/2000 Sb. o krajích (krajské zřízení) (2000)
16. Šedivcová (Nesvedová), L.: Návrh metodického postupu pro práci s Shadow IT ve veřejné správě na úrovni krajů České republiky. Vysoká škola ekonomická v Praze (2017)
17. MBI: MBI - management of business informatics. Manag. Bus. Inf. (2015). http://mbi.vse.cz/. Accessed 29 Nov 2015
18. Myers, M.D.: Qualitative Research in Business & Management, 2nd edn. Sage, London (2013)
19. Yin, R.K.: Case Study Research: Design and Methods, 4th edn. Sage publications, Thousand Oaks (2009)

20. Stemberger, M.I., Jaklic, J.: Towards E-government by business process change—a methodology for public sector. Int. J. Inf. Manag. **27**, 221–232 (2007)
21. Clerc, V., Niessink, F.: IT Service CMM: A Pocket Guide. Van Haren Publishing, Hertogenbosch (2004)
22. ITIL: SPRI. The Stationery Office (TSO), London (2007)
23. Bayan, R.: Shed light on shadow IT groups. techrepublic.com 9 (2004)
24. Hulsebosch, M.A.C.: Cloud Strife: an analysis of cloud-based shadow IT and a framework for managing its risks and opportunities (2016)
25. Kocianová, R.: Personální činnosti a metody personální práce. Grada Publishing a.s., Praha (2010)
26. Simons, J.A., Irwin, D.B., Drinnien, B.A.: Maslow's hierarchy of needs (1987). Accessed 9 Oct 2009
27. Růžička, J., Nový, I., Provazník, V.: Řízení profesní kariéry zaměstnanců. Vysoká škola ekonomická (1993)
28. Vláda, Č.R.: Usnesení vlády České republiky č. 889. Usn vlády České republiky (2015)

A Systematic Analysis and Synthesis of Case Study Based Agile Scaling Research in the Context of Digital Transformations

Everist Limaj[(✉)] and Edward W. N. Bernroider

Institute for Information Management and Control,
Vienna University of Economics and Business (WU), Vienna, Austria
{everist.limaj,edward.bernroider}@wu.ac.at

Abstract. Over the past decade, agile scaling concepts in organizations have gained considerable momentum and renewed attention especially from business practice. While agility has its roots in software development, the concept of agile at scale aims at more generally applying agile practices in organizations across different industries. Academic research is serving this development in different disciplines, most notably the management and information systems fields. This short paper takes stock of the last 12 years of scholarly research by developing a systematic content analysis of 26 case studies dealing with agile scaling concepts in the context of digital transformation. In the attempt to narrow the gap between research and practice, we focus on case studies as a strategic research methodology providing rich insights of complex real-life processes such as agile scaling. The findings synthesize the current state of knowledge in this regard and offer new research avenues contributing to the present agile scaling discourse.

Keywords: Systematic literature review · Agile scaling · Digital transformation

1 Introduction

Since the publication of the Agile manifesto [1], many so-called agile transformations of organizations have been implemented worldwide [2]. Most commonly, these change initiatives are driven by the need of organizations to keep up with the trends of the digitalization era (i.e. in-depth understanding of customer requirements, rapid creation of novel digital services, ongoing process renewal, and updates of business models) [3]. Usually utilized in software development teams, agile at scale is being adopted in other industries at different management and operational levels shaping new organizational forms [4]. Agile at scale can be understood as a process of diffusing the initial adoption of agile principles and methods to more organizational structures [5]. The increasing application of agile concepts at the organizational level has also resulted in a growing amount of agile scaling case studies provided by scholarly research. Yet, to date, (as we highlight in the next section) research lacks a compelling (i.e. rigorous) assessment of this emergent literature.

© IFIP International Federation for Information Processing 2019
Published by Springer Nature Switzerland AG 2019.
P. Doucek et al. (Eds.): CONFENIS 2019, LNBIP 375, pp. 74–84, 2019.
https://doi.org/10.1007/978-3-030-37632-1_7

This article seeks to fulfil this gap by conducting a thorough examination of the accumulated agile scaling body of research in relation to case studies, which provide *"an in-depth exploration from multiple perspectives of the complexity and uniqueness of a particular project, policy, institution, program or system in real life"* [6, p. 21]. We purposefully chose to restrict our selection to case studies only, as we intend to develop practice-based scientific knowledge to narrow the gap between theory and practice in the agile domain [7]. Accordingly, based on guidance from Webster and Watson [8], we selected 26 case studies from the agile scaling literature and analyzed them by means of a concept-centric review. The resulting concept matrix contributes to the agile scaling discourse in providing a synthesis of extant research and motivating new research avenues. The remainder of this article proceeds with an examination of previous literature reviews conducted in the agile scaling area. Next, we describe the methods used for data collection and analysis before presenting the result of our systematic literature review. The article concludes by discussing insights for promising directions of future research.

2 Past Literature Reviews on Agile Transformation

For our examination of prior research conducting literature reviews in relation to agile scaling, we identified 9 peer-reviewed publications listed in Table 1, which shows their publication years, review scopes and types of review. Notably, only three industry specific reviews are included (one related to healthcare, two to software industry), while six studies are comprehensive in scope reviewing agile literature across industries. Besides, only two articles actually use methodologically rigorous literature review guidelines (i.e. systematic reviews), while the others give scarce information on selection criteria and methods of analysis. The most commonly investigated topic is concerned with agile challenges [papers No. 2, 3, 6, 7, 9 in Table 1]. Other common topics include agile strategies [papers No. 1 and 4], agile capabilities [papers No. 1, 4, 5], agile success factors [papers No. 3 and 6], agile benefits [papers No. 7, 9], and agile research streams [paper No. 8].

Most commonly identified agile challenges seem not new to organizational change research (e.g. resistance to change, difficulties to plan, changing the culture and lack of investments [2, 16]). More recent issues include controversies with the agile framework, struggle to manage agile methodologies, and difficulties to measure agile value, coordinate multiple teams and integrate non-agile functions. Yet, with few exceptions [2, 10], previous reviews scarcely formulate emergent research topics associated to agile challenges in practice.

With regard to the topics of agile strategies and capabilities, Tolf and Nyström [9] highlight proactive, reactive and embracive strategies as well as five core capabilities (inter-organizational links, market sensitivity, self-organizing employees, elastic organic structures, and timely delivery) needed for healthcare organizations to cope with external uncertainty. Besides, Appelbaum et al., in two publications argue that organizational agile transitions require change at all levels (e.g. strategy, processes, and people) while hinting that there is little information on how to develop agile capabilities.

Table 1. Summary of previous reviews on agile scaling

Paper no.	Year	Author(s) [Reference]	Review scope		Type of review	
			Comprehensive	Industry specific	Systematic	Other
1	2015	Tolf, Nyström [9]		×		×
2	2015	Gregory, Barroca [10]	×			×
3	2016	Dikert, Paasivaara [2]		×	×	
4	2017	Appelbaum, Calla [11]	×			×
5	2017	Appelbaum, Calla [12]	×			×
6	2017	Paterek [13]	×			×
7	2017	Abdalhamid and Mishra [14]		×	×	
8	2018	Sońta-Drączkowska [15]	×			×
9	2018	Putta, Paasivaara [16]	×			×
Total number of articles			**6**	**3**	**2**	**7**

Considerable research has been devoted to point out agile success factors (e.g. management support, customized agile approach, piloting, training, agile coach, communication and transparency, mindset and alignment, team autonomy, culture of continuous learning, and community of practice [2, 13]) and agile benefits (e.g. increase in quality, transparency, collaboration, productivity and alignment [16, 17]. However, one concern is that most of these success factors and benefits are identified from experience reports that have a tendency to emphasize positive views [2].

With regard to research streams, the review of Sońta-Drączkowska [15] proposes five themes, agile in software development, agile in project management, agile organization, hybrid approaches and agile in innovations. The authors recognize that agile concepts are dispersed in a wide range of domains, hence more studies are needed especially to link agile projects with the organizational level [15].

To summarize, while previous literature reviews have provided helpful insights (especially identifying agile challenges and success factors), there still seems to be gap in prior review work providing an overview on how scholars have covered scaling agile in case studies in relation to how scaling agile is defined, understood and applied.

3 Data Collection

Our data collection follows a rigorous process guided by previous research on conducting systematic literature reviews [8, 18, 19]. We focused article selection on case studies that provide information on agile scaling in a digital transformation context, and, thus address the cross section between management and IS research. To guarantee objectivity in the selection procedure, we developed a research protocol describing the search strategy including the databases used for the search, and inclusion and exclusion criteria (Table 2).

Table 2. Research protocol (Source: adapted from [20])

Dimension	Description
Research databases	The databases used for the search process were based on recommendations by Levy and Ellis (21), and include ProQuest, Science Direct, IEEE, ACM, JSTOR, Wiley, Lea Journals, EBSCOhost and AIS library
Publication type	Only peer-reviewed full papers
Language	Only papers published in English
Methodology	Only case studies
Date range	As the research on this topic is relatively recent, the range of our examination was limited to the time frame of 2007 to 2019. We consider this 12-year period representative of the adaptation of agile at scale
Search fields	Title, abstract and keywords section
Search terms	Boolean search combining terms: ("scaling agile" OR "agile at scale") AND ("digital transformation" OR "digitalization" OR "organizational transformation" OR "organizational change")
Inclusion criteria	Only articles that consider agile as a management practice, or those positioned in an agile transformation context, or those that deal with organizational change by scaling agile
Exclusion criteria	Articles were removed considering agile only as a method for software development or as an operational issue, and not at the organizational level (e.g. focusing only at a project level or team level)
Data analysis and synthesis	We used techniques of grounded theory to code the data, identify patterns and map relationships. The qualitative software NVIVO supported this process

Our initial search in databases using filters described in the research protocol resulted in the extraction of 1,073 articles. We controlled for other potential relevant publications that where not found directly from the database search by conducting a backward and forward reference search adding 117 articles potentially in scope. Next, we read the title and abstract of all identified items to remove duplications and studies that are outside the research scope. Further, we read the full text of the remaining articles (157 in total) to evaluate if they met the full criteria described in the research protocol, which resulted in 111 selected items. Of those, 26 articles using a case study methodology were used for our content analysis. Figure 1 illustrates the selection process of the case study articles used for the systematic literature review and outlines the timeframe of their publication. The later shows that from 2016 there has been more effort from research to document agile case studies.

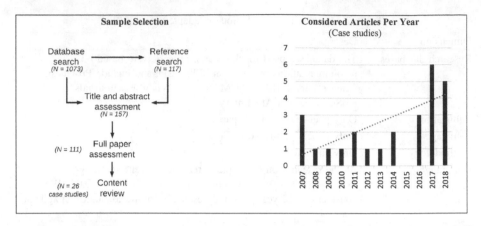

Fig. 1. Illustration of the systematic review process and timeframe of the selected case studies

4 Analysis

The analysis is based on guidance from Webster and Watson [8] and consists in synthetizing the selected literature based on a concept-centric morphological box that we developed following the procedure recommended by Mayring [22]. Correspondingly, we differentiate between three clusters linked with nine main categories as illustrated in Table 3 and describe in the following.

Table 3. Morphological box for analyzing case studies of agile transformations

Classification of case studies					Comprehension of agile transformation		Application of agile transformation	
Publication type	Literature domain	Object of the study	Study design	Study focus	Definition of Agile	Main topic (Agile…)	Industry branch	Organizational size

The first cluster, 'classification of case studies' aims to portray general aspects of the selected articles and includes the following deductive categories: publication type, literature domain, objective of the study, study design and study focus. With regard to the category 'publication type', we differentiate between 'journal' and 'conference' publication. As noted in the research protocol (see Table 2), other publication types have been excluded from the selection. The category 'literature domain' indicates the scientific field of each article. The category 'object of the study' points out the analytical frame of the case and the various positions that can be taken on the object of the study, differentiating between 'theory-testing', 'theory-seeking', and 'storytelling' [23]. The category 'study design' identifies the temporal structure of how change is studied [24]. Typically, research studies take either a 'snapshot perspective' examining "*a target event in a present moment in time,*" or a 'process perspective' examining "*the evolution of an event over time*" [25]. The last category of the first cluster points out that researchers studying an agile transformation process typically focus on one (or a combination) of strategic aspects of change (e.g. culture, leadership, dynamic capabilities), organizational aspects of change (e.g. models of organizing individuals and teams), and/or operational aspects of change (e.g. software development and requirements management) [26].

The second cluster, 'comprehension of agile transformation', focuses on understanding how agile is viewed and investigated from researchers and is composed of the following deductive categories: definition of agile and main topic of the study. The category 'definition of agile' aims to grasp how the concept of agile is specified (or not). Extant research typically considers agile either as a method (or an approach) (i.e. stipulating a method-notion) or acknowledge agile as a capability (i.e. stipulating a capability-notion). The category 'main topic of the study' is to highlight information about dominant agile themes that have been investigated in prior studies. The third cluster, 'application of agile transformation' depicts current application of agile transformation initiatives including two categories: industry type, and organizational size. 'Industry type' organizes case studies based on the sector groupings. 'Organizational size' distinguishes the case organizations considered in the examined study as either small and medium sized enterprises (SMEs) or large corporations.

5 Result

The concept matrix of agile transformation resulting from the analysis of the selected literature is presented in Table 4. The classification of case studies based on their 'publication type' reveals a somewhat proportional division between *journal* (54%) and *conference* publication (46%). Distinctively, the 'literature domain' category shows that agile studies are largely rooted in the *Information System* field (81%) with a few contributions in the research areas of *Strategic Management* (8%), *Production Management* (4%), and *Computer Science* (4%). Within the 'object of the study' category, authors mainly seek for *theory-seeking* (46%) and *storytelling* (46%). Much less, only 8% seek for *theory-testing* [27, 28]. With regard to the 'study design', most authors follow a *process perspective* (77%) to structure their investigation, while a *snapshot perspective* (23%) has been used less [29–34]. Lastly, the 'study focus' category reveals that 19% of the articles consider (fully or partly) all three aspects of the agile transformation (i.e. *strategic, organizational, and operational*) [32, 35–38]. Further, 12% have a combined focus on *organizational and operational* aspects [39–41], while slightly more articles (19%) have considered *strategic and organizational aspects* together [5, 16, 26, 42, 43]. Lastly, 8% of the articles focus on *strategic aspects* only [31, 44], whilst 15% focus on *organizational aspects* only [33, 34, 45, 46].

The analysis highlighting the comprehension of agile transformation in terms of the category 'definition of agile' reveals an assertive tendency (42%) to conceptualize (or refer to) agile as a *method* (or likewise, as an approach). Specific definitions related to this group of articles explain agile as an approach adopted to "*regularly produce high quality software in a cost effective and timely manner via a value driven life-cycle*" [41, p. 4], and agile transformation as the "*switch from a different development approach or work organization concept to agile methods*" [5, p. 3]. On the other hand, 15% of the

Table 4. Result of the concept matrix of agile transformation case studies

Category	Concept	Articles →	Cloke (2007)	Fry and Greene (2007)	Hodgkin and Hohmann (2007)	Doz and Kosonen (2008)	Ganguly and Nilchiani (2009)	Korhonen (2010)	O'Connor (2011)	Hallikainen (2011)	Pikkarainen and Salo (2012)	Korhonen (2013)	Capodieci and Mainetti (2014)	Paasivaara and Lassenius (2014)	Chen and Ravichandar (2016)	Gregory and Barroca (2016)	Turetken and Stojanov (2017)	Heikkilä and Paasivaara (2017)	Hobbs and Petit (2017)	Jovanović and Mas (2017)	Jovanović and Mesquida (2017)	Laanti and Dolla (2017)	Razzak and Richardson (2017)	Fuchs and Hess (2018)	Kalenda and Hyna (2018)	Karvonen and Sharp (2018)	Mikalsen and Moe (2018)	Paasivaara and Behm (2018)
Classification of Case Studies	Publication type	Journal		X	X				X	X		X	X	X	X	X	X	X	X		X				X			X
		Conference	X	X	X				X	X	X									X		X	X	X	X	X	X	X
	Literature domain	Information Systems	X	X	X			X			X	X	X		X		X	X	X	X	X	X	X	X	X	X	X	X
		(Strategic) Management					X								X													
		Production Management					X																					
		Computer Science													X													
	Object of the study	Theory-testing						X							X													
		Theory-seeking			X	X						X		X			X	X		X	X	X		X	X	X	X	
		Storytelling	X	X	X				X	X	X	X		X			X	X			X			X		X		X
	Study design	Snapshot Perspective		X									X		X		X		X		X		X					
		Process Perspective	X		X	X	X	X	X	X	X	X		X		X		X		X	X		X	X	X	X	X	X
	Study focus	Strategic				X					X					X	X	(X)		X	X			X	X	X	X	(X)
		Organizational	(X)		(X)				(X)	(X)	X			X		X	X	X	X	X	X	X	X	X	X	X	X	X
		Operational	(X)		(X)						X					X	X	X	X	X							(X)
Comprehension of Agile Transformation	Definition of Agile	Method-notion	(X)	(X)	(X)				(X)	(X)	(X)			(X)			(X)	(X)	X			X					(X)	(X)
		Capability-notion					(X)	X																			(X)	(X)
	Main topic (Agile…)	Challenges								(X)		X			X	X			(X)						X	X		X
		Success factors	X	X	X					X	X	X			X	X	X		X			X			X	X	X	X
		Conceptualization					X																	X	X			
		Metrics							X	(X)						(X)	X						(X)					
		Scaling Model															X	(X)		X		X		(X)				
		Change Performance							X			X							X	(X)		X						
		Roles/Teams																(X)		X								(X)
Application of Agile Transformation	Industry branch	Software		X													X								X			
		Telecommunications			X		X		X	X		X			X	X		X				X						X
		Financial services																	X						X		X	
		Education							X																	X		
		Retail																							X			
		Mass Media	X	X																								
	Organizational size	SMEs																	X							X		
		Large	X	X	X	X	X	X	X	X		X		X	X	X	X	X	X	X	X		X	X	X	X		X

Note = x: fully applies and (x): partly or indirectly applies

articles conceptualize agile as a *capability*. Studies of this kind refer to agility broadly as the ability to move quickly and in a simple way [47], or somehow more detailed as the capacity to apply agile methods to digital transformations in order to create, react to, embrace, and learn from change while enhancing customer value [38]. Looking at the 'main topic' category, seven archetypes are evident. The dominant topic studied has been *agile success factors* (46%) followed by *agile challenges* (31%). In many cases, these two topics have been investigated together [26, 31, 35, 41, 43, 48, 49]. Further, the topics of *agile metrics*, *agile scaling models*, and *agile change performance* have been equally studied (19%). The least investigated topics have been agile conceptualization and agile roles/teams (12% each).

With regard to analyzing the application of agile transformation in terms of the category 'industry branch' six groupings were made. The prevailing setting were the case studies have been conducted is in the *telecommunications* (31%) branch [27, 28, 31, 32, 44, 45, 49, 50]. The second group of cases are dispersed equally in the *software industry and financial services* (12% each). Some attention has been given to studying agile transformation in *education*, and *mass media* (8% each), while only one case could be identified in *retail* [5]. In terms of the category 'organizational size', there is a clear dominance of articles assessing the transformation in *large organizations* (92%), whilst the remaining 8% of them explore agile change in *SMEs* [30, 46].

6 Discussion

We discuss our findings in light of recent agile practitioners' concerns as pointed out by Gregory and Barroca [36]. Our aim was to identify topics that deserve more attention from research. Accordingly, we spot the three priority areas 'Governance of Agile Scaling', 'Dealing with Legacy Systems', and 'Capabilities for the Agile Way', and elaborate them before pointing out some methodological limitations.

Firstly, extant work has not yet established compelling governance and oversight mechanisms needed to handle agile scaling. This issue is nowadays evermore imperative as agile transformation seems to follow atypical change patterns [5] and requires a shift from the traditional leadership styles [10, 36]. The literature addressing strategic aspects of the transformation, which map to our category 'study focus' highlight the importance of defining the necessary goals of the transformation, which require oversight and a customized process model [35, 37] as well as developing new roles and requirements for renewed management practices [31, 32, 42]. The governance role is imperative in envisioning, formulating and communicating change facets but recent evidence shows a lot of hurdles in this respect [26]. Hence, researchers should devote particular attention to develop opportune governance mechanisms that can benefit leaders to guide and control agile transformation initiatives.

Secondly, a critical challenging area with sparse information relates to dealing with legacy systems during the agile transition. Failure to establish a clear approach to handle legacy systems often results in organizations trying to work in an agile way in a non-agile environment (i.e. with traditional organizational structures) [36]. Surprisingly, when analyzing the 'Agile main topics' investigated in previous studies, the legacy system issues seem to be largely overlooked. We call for future work to explore adequate strategies that enable a smooth transition and continuous integration of legacy systems into the agile world.

Thirdly, there is little investigation on the capabilities needed to succeed in the agile way of working. Extant research propounds the view that renewed skills and a quick learning environment are compulsory to absorb agile practices and new organizational forms [36]. Inevitably, new organizational capabilities at various levels (e.g. ordinary or dynamic) are required at different stages of the agile change. Yet, our findings indicate very little practice-grounded research studies that increase our understanding about this set of new capabilities that benefit agile scaling and subsequently add value to the organization. What is more, apart from a few exceptions [26, 51] identified in the intersection between the 'capability-notion' and the related 'conceptualization' studies in the concept matrix, there seems to be also a lack of theoretical contributions grasping the capability construct in the agile transformation context. Therefore, more research is needed utilizing various lenses (i.e. practical or/and theoretical) to grasp distinct, emergent capabilities vital for the agile journey and to suggest appropriate ways to develop them.

Although our search process included 9 scientific databases, the analysis is limited to 26 selected articles that were found using a case-study methodology. We did not conduct an exhaustive author search, which could have potentially resulted in more selected publications. In attempt to examine highly qualified research findings, we restricted our selection to peer-reviewed papers only. However, nearly half of the selected articles were published in conference proceedings (considered less mature than journal publications). For future investigations within this research stream, more IS journal papers using different methodologies can be considered.

References

1. Beck, K., et al.: Manifesto for agile software development (2001). http://www. agilemanifesto. Accessed 31 Oct 2019
2. Dikert, K., Paasivaara, M., Lassenius, C.: Challenges and success factors for large-scale agile transformations: a systematic literature review. J. Syst. Softw. **119**, 87–108 (2016)
3. Bharadwaj, A., et al.: Digital Business Strategy: Toward a Next Generation of Insights. MIS Q. **37**(2), 471–482 (2013)
4. Denning, S.: How to make the whole organization "Agile". Strat. Leadersh. **44**(4), 10–17 (2016)
5. Fuchs, C., Hess, T.: Becoming agile in the digital transformation: the process of a large-scale agile transformation. In: Thirty Ninth International Conference on Information Systems, San Francisco (2018)
6. Simons, H.: Case Study Research in Practice. SAGE, London (2009)
7. Yin, R.K.: Case Study Research. Sage, Thousand Oaks (2003)
8. Webster, J., Watson, R.T.: Analyzing the past to prepare for the future: writing a literature review. MIS Q. **26**(2), xiii–xxiii (2002)
9. Tolf, S., et al.: Agile, a guiding principle for health care improvement? Int. J. Health Care Qual. Assur. **28**(5), 468–493 (2015)
10. Gregory, P., Barroca, L., Taylor, K., Salah, D., Sharp, H.: Agile challenges in practice: a thematic analysis. In: Lassenius, C., Dingsøyr, T., Paasivaara, M. (eds.) XP 2015. LNBIP, vol. 212, pp. 64–80. Springer, Cham (2015). https://doi.org/10.1007/978-3-319-18612-2_6
11. Appelbaum, S.H., et al.: The challenges of organizational agility (part 1). Ind. Commer. Train. **49**(1), 6–14 (2017)
12. Appelbaum, S.H., et al.: The challenges of organizational agility: part 2. Ind. Commer. Train. **49**(2), 69–74 (2017)
13. Paterek, P.: Agile transformation in project organization: knowledge management aspects and challenges. In: 18th European Conference on Knowledge Management ECKM2017. International University of Catalonia, Barcelona, Spain (2017)
14. Abdalhamid, S., Mishra, A.: Adopting of agile methods in software development organizations: systematic mapping. TEM J. **6**(4), 817–825 (2017)
15. Sońta-Drączkowska, E.: From agile project management to agile organization? – a literature review. Przedsiębiorczość i Zarządzanie **6**(1), 231–242 (2018)
16. Putta, A., Paasivaara, M., Lassenius, C.: Benefits and challenges of adopting the scaled agile framework (safe): preliminary results from a multivocal literature review. In: Kuhrmann, M., et al. (eds.) PROFES 2018. LNCS, vol. 11271, pp. 334–351. Springer, Cham (2018). https://doi.org/10.1007/978-3-030-03673-7_24

17. Putta, A.: Scaling agile software development to large and globally distributed large-scale organizations. In: Proceedings of the 13th International Conference on Global Software Engineering, ICGSE 2018, Gothenburg, Sweden (2018)
18. Tranfield, D., Denyer, D., Smart, P.: Towards a methodology for developing evidence-informed management knowledge by means of systematic review. Br. J. Manag. 14(3), 207–222 (2003)
19. Okoli, C., Schabram, K.: A guide to conducting a systematic literature review of information systems research. Sprouts: Work. Pap. Inf. Syst. 10(26), 1–49 (2010)
20. Alexander, A., Walker, H., Naim, M.: Decision theory in sustainable supply chain management: a literature review. Supply Chain Manag. 19(5/6), 504–522 (2014)
21. Levy, Y., Ellis, T.: A systems approach to conduct an effective literature review in support information systems research. Informing Sci. J. 9, 181–212 (2006)
22. Mayring, P.: Qualitative content analysis: theoretical foundation, basic procedures and software solution, Klagenfurt, AT, 143 p. (2014). https://nbn-resolving.org/urn:nbn:de:0168-ssoar-395173
23. Thomas, G.: A typology for the case study in social science following a review of definition, discourse, and structure. Qual. Inq. 17(6), 511–521 (2011)
24. Goldstein, H.: Longitudinal studies and the measurement of change. J. R. Stat. Soc. 18(2), 93–117 (1968)
25. Sandelowski, M.: Time and qualitative research. Res. Nurs. Health 22, 79–87 (1999)
26. Karvonen, T., Sharp, H., Barroca, L.: Enterprise agility: why is transformation so hard? In: Garbajosa, J., Wang, X., Aguiar, A. (eds.) XP 2018. LNBIP, vol. 314, pp. 131–145. Springer, Cham (2018). https://doi.org/10.1007/978-3-319-91602-6_9
27. Korhonen, K.: Exploring defect data, quality and engagement during agile transformation at a large multisite organization. In: Sillitti, A., Martin, A., Wang, X., Whitworth, E. (eds.) XP 2010. LNBIP, vol. 48, pp. 88–102. Springer, Heidelberg (2010). https://doi.org/10.1007/978-3-642-13054-0_7
28. Korhonen, K.: Evaluating the impact of an agile transformation: a longitudinal case study in a distributed context. Softw. Qual. J. 21(4), 599–624 (2013)
29. Fry, C., Greene, S.: Large scale agile transformation in an on-demand world. IEEE, Washington, DC (2007)
30. Capodieci, A., Mainetti, L., Manco, L.: A case study to enable and monitor real IT companies migrating from waterfall to agile. In: Murgante, B., et al. (eds.) ICCSA 2014. LNCS, vol. 8583, pp. 119–134. Springer, Cham (2014). https://doi.org/10.1007/978-3-319-09156-3_9
31. Chen, R.R., Ravichandar, R., Proctor, D.: Managing the transition to the new agile business and product development model: Lessons from Cisco Systems. Bus. Horiz. 59(6), 635–644 (2016)
32. Heikkila, V.T., et al.: Managing the requirements flow from strategy to release in large-scale agile development: a case study at Ericsson. Empir. Softw. Eng. 22(6), 2892–2936 (2017)
33. Laanti, M., Delta, N.: Agile transformation model for large software development organizations. In: Proceedings of the XP2017 Scientific Workshops 2017, XP 2017, Cologne, Germany. ACM, New York (2017)
34. Turetken, O., Stojanov, I., Trienekens, J.J.M.: Assessing the adoption level of scaled agile development: a maturity model for Scaled Agile Framework. Spec. Issue: Recent Adv. Agile Softw. Prod. Dev. 29(6), 1–18 (2017)
35. Pikkarainen, M., et al.: Strengths and barriers behind the successful agile deployment—insights from the three software intensive companies in Finland. Empir. Softw. Eng. 17(6), 675–702 (2012)

36. Gregory, P., et al.: The challenges that challenge: engaging with agile practitioners' concerns. Inf. Softw. Technol. **77**, 92–104 (2016)
37. Jovanović, M., Mesquida, A.-L., Mas, A., Lalić, B.: Towards the development of a sequential framework for agile adoption. In: Mas, A., Mesquida, A., O'Connor, R.V., Rout, T., Dorling, A. (eds.) SPICE 2017. CCIS, vol. 770, pp. 30–42. Springer, Cham (2017). https://doi.org/10.1007/978-3-319-67383-7_3
38. Mikalsen, M., et al.: Agile digital transformation: a case study of interdependencies. In: Thirty Ninth International Conference on Information Systems, San Francisco (2018)
39. Cloke, G.: GET YOUR AGILE FREAK ON! Agile adoption at Yahoo! Music. In: Agile 2007. Computer Society, Washington, DC (2007)
40. Hodgkins, P., Hohmann, L.: Agile program management: lessons learned from the VeriSign managed security services team. In: Agile 2007. IEEE, Washington, DC (2007)
41. Hobbs, B., Petit, Y.: Agile methods on large projects in large organizations. Proj. Manag. J. **48**(3), 3–19 (2017)
42. Jovanović, M., et al.: Transition of organizational roles in Agile transformation process: a grounded theory approach. J. Syst. Softw. **133**, 174–194 (2017)
43. Kalenda, M., Hyna, P., Rossi, B.: Scaling agile in large organizations: practices, challenges, and success factors. Softw. Evol. Process **30**(10), 1–24 (2018)
44. Doz, Y., Kosonen, M.: The dynamics of strategic agility: Nokia's rollercoaster experience. Calif. Manag. Rev. **50**(3), 95–118 (2008)
45. Paasivaara, M., Lassenius, C.: Communities of practice in a large distributed agile software development organization - Case Ericsson. Inf. Softw. Technol. **56**(12), 1556–1577 (2014)
46. Razzak, M.A., Noll, J., Richardson, I., Canna, C.N., Beecham, S.: Transition from plan driven to SAFe®: periodic team self-assessment. In: Felderer, M., Méndez Fernández, D., Turhan, B., Kalinowski, M., Sarro, F., Winkler, D. (eds.) PROFES 2017. LNCS, vol. 10611, pp. 573–585. Springer, Cham (2017). https://doi.org/10.1007/978-3-319-69926-4_47
47. Ganguly, A., Nilchiani, R., School, J.F.: Evaluating agility in corporate enterprises. Int. J. Prod. Econ. **118**(2), 410–423 (2009)
48. O'Connor, C.P.: Anatomy and physiology of an agile transition. In: Agile Conference. IEEE, Salt Lake City, UT (2011)
49. Paasivaara, M., et al.: Large-scale agile transformation at Ericsson: a case study. Empir. Softw. Eng. **23**(5), 2550–2596 (2018)
50. Hallikainen, M.: Experiences on Agile seating, facilities and solutions. In: IEEE Sixth International Conference on Global Software Engineering (2011)
51. Doz, Y.L., Kosonen, M.: Embedding strategic agility: a leadership agenda for accelerating business model renewal. Long Range Plan. **43**(2–3), 370–382 (2010)

Business Process Matching Analytics

Katalin Ternai(iD), Szabina Fodor(iD), and Ildikó Szabó(⊠)(iD)

Corvinus University of Budapest, Fővám tér 13-15., Budapest 1093, Hungary
{katalin.ternai,szabina.fodor,
ildiko.szabo2}@uni-corvinus.hu

Abstract. Organizations study competitors to gain insights into what extent their processes are compliant to processes of other ones. Business process models are usually described in documents and their elements can be extracted by semantic technologies such as process-based text mining method. Business analytics provides a powerful tool to analyze competitors' identified processes through dashboards. Educational institutions gain competitive advantage by establishing international partnerships. They must improve their processes to become more attractive to students. This paper presents a general method using semantic technologies to enhance the examination of competitors' processes and their application in internationalization strategies.

Keywords: Process matching · Semantic business process management · Business analytics · Text mining · Internationalization

1 Introduction

Organizations must be aware of how their competitors behave on the market. Usually, it is difficult to investigate this behavior directly and explicitly. News, speeches, studies about companies can be applied to detect behavioral symptoms on the market (such as acquisition strategies, digitalization endeavors and so on). Organizational and operational rules contain information about business processes fit to organizational strategies. Nowadays, the digital transformation wave poses effects on every knowledge-intensive organization and makes them committed to improve their processes and modify their operational rules. New ideas, best practices can be captured from these kind of published documents. Business analytics toolset is a powerful instrument to analyze competitors' operations through organizational documents. Nevertheless, it would also provide us opportunities to look into what processes have already been transformed by others and in what extent.

This study addresses the important questions of process analysis and investigates whether and to what extent processes of an organization are matched with processes of their competitors. Different approaches are available to reach this goal. Business process management tools have built-in functions to compare business process models with each other. Competitor analysis can be carried on literature reviews, secondary data analysis out, but these activities require mainly human efforts to solve the problem. However, our approach is based on processing organizational documents with semantic technologies such as process ontologies, because we assume that business process

© IFIP International Federation for Information Processing 2019
Published by Springer Nature Switzerland AG 2019
P. Doucek et al. (Eds.): CONFENIS 2019, LNBIP 375, pp. 85–94, 2019.
https://doi.org/10.1007/978-3-030-37632-1_8

models can be extracted from their descriptions with using semantic text mining algorithms [1, 2]. Our method (see in Fig. 1) starts with business process modelling phase in Adonis.

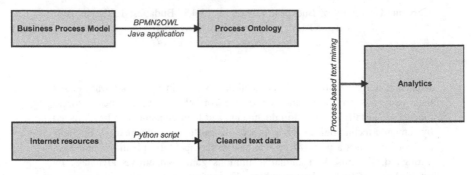

Fig. 1. Our method

In our approach the concept of process ontologies plays a key role on the scene of competitor analysis. Process ontologies have no precise definition in the literature. Some approaches refer to process ontology as a conceptual description framework of processes [3]. Process ontologies are abstract models from this point of view. Task ontologies determine a smaller subset of the process space, the sequence of activities in a given process. Meanwhile the domain ontologies focus on catching the essence of each object of the world and their connections. Process ontology identifies all the artefacts that describe a process, regardless of whether they are structured or not. It allows to build all process elements clearly and unambiguously, linked with the domain ontologies containing specific enterprise concepts.

Hence, they serve as an appropriate basis to capture implicit and explicit semantics of process models hidden in documents. Transformation of business process models into process ontologies makes it possible to process documents in semantic manner. XSLT transformation was used in our previous work, but it ensured us just a semi-automatic method, hence a new Java program was created to make this transformation more automated.

After the model transformation a process-based text mining stage in Python is responsible for identifying process elements in the documents. Text mining is usually considered as a specialized area of data mining but sometimes it just enhances data preparation steps in data mining projects. Its main purpose is to identify patterns within texts. Different approaches are differentiated based on the objective of text mining process and the nature of used methodology. General text mining process contains steps of preparing corpus, pre-processing texts, generating and selecting feature which are followed by data mining steps and interpretation of results [4]. Pre-processing methods usually include collecting multiple documents, tokenizing text contents into individual terms/words, eliminating stop words (e.g. pronouns), identifying root/stem of words and using statistical methods for calculating TF-IDF (term frequency-inverse document frequency) to determine the importance words in collections [5]. Text clusters can be created based on the strengths of relationships between extracted expressions. Ontology learning generates elements of domain ontologies from various kinds of resources with applying natural language processing and machine learning techniques [6]. It relies on statistical, rule-based or mixed methods [7]. According to Kő and Gillani [8] process models provides the contexts, but domain ontologies are applied to extract knowledge by Our process-based text mining method uses preprocessing techniques, n-grams as most likely connected word pairs and the structure of process models to create a dashboard for visualizing the results of process matching. All phases will be described in more detail during presentation of our business case.

This paper presents this general method using semantic technologies to enhance the analysis of competitors' process in the respect of a given business process. Having presented our method, the second section introduces related theoretical works in the field of semantic business process modelling. The third section presents how our method works in practice. The case of the research grant application process was selected to illustrate the applicability of this method as a proof-of-concepts. Limitations and future research steps are highlighted in the fourth section.

2 Related SBPM Researches

The usage of Semantic Web technologies like reasoners, ontologies, and mediators add a completely new viewpoint to business process management. This approach is known as semantic business process management (SBPM) [9]. Process mining is one of its related subdomains.

Process mining deals with data of actual process execution stored in event logs, transactional data etc. "to discover process models, check the conformance of process models to reality and extend or improve process models" [3].

Three common classes of process mining techniques can be summarized as follows:

- **Process Analysis.** The goal of process analysis and process monitoring is to monitor process runs and to analyze their executions with using business intelligence tools. It supports business analysts in identifying deviations in processes and corrective measures to redesign suboptimal processes.
- **Semantic Process Mining.** Process mining includes techniques to extract process models from logs. It focuses on the automatic discovery of information from event logs without a predefined model. The importance of process mining in BPM is widely acknowledged as an important and unavoidable analysis tool to aid the (re-) design and the (re-)configuration of process models. Current process mining techniques are already quite powerful and mature. However, the analysis they provide are purely syntactic.
- **Cross-Organizational Conformance Checking.** Conformance Checking refers to algorithms for verifying whether logs follow the predefined behavior expressed in process model or not. These algorithms require the process model and its instances as well. The main advantage of ontologically defined process instances and models is that they improve the interoperability between information systems.

Organizations aspire to learn from others on how they adapt their processes towards improvement [10]. Process benchmarking, however, is mainly a manual process, requiring the involvement of experts to collect and interpret process-related data [11]. A main problem is that processes are often modeled on different levels of granularity.

Several approaches were elaborated to combine Business Process Management with Semantic Web technologies [12, 13].

In the context of BPR, organizations compare business process models to identify operational correspondences and differences. The approach for measuring the degree of similarity considers linguistic and behavioral aspects of process models to calculate a degree of similarity [14].

There are other works on measuring similarity between semantic business process models. A business process may be modeled in different ways by different modelers utilizing the same modeling language. An appropriate method for solving ambiguity issues in process models caused by the usage of synonyms, homonyms or different abstraction levels for process element names is the use of ontology-based descriptions of process models [15]. This method describes high-level Petri nets in OWL (Web Ontology Language) [16].

Our approach focuses on extracting information from documents instead of logs. Our process-based text mining uses a generic algorithm - extracting business processes from documents using predefined process structures as heuristics. Similarity measures of process models will be useful metrics in a later phase of this research.

3   Case Study: Research Grant Process

Higher education institutions want to rise to higher place in global rankings to become more famous and attract more international students. Internationalization is getting paid more attention because it provides competitive advantages on national and international scene. The number of participations on international research and conferences reflect the intensity of scientific activities at a university. The Research Committee's mission is to create and strengthen enabling conditions for research activities at the international academic level. The research grant application process at our university provides a good basis to apply our method to it and analyzing its matching with the process of other educational institutions. Application time period for this grant is continuous, the evaluation of any complete applications shall be made in five working days. Automatic acceptance is given up to the budget frame, if the application meets the requirements of the Research Committee.

3.1   Business Process Model

In the Process modeling phase the previously described business process have been implemented on the BOC ADONIS platform[1]. The business process model, the working environment, the document model and the IT system model have been

---

[1] ADONIS is a BPM tool created at the University of Vienna.

specified. The logical shell of the business process model with the core objects (e.g. task) has been created. The input and output data, the IT system information and the responsible role from the organogram have been linked to the activities (Fig. 2).

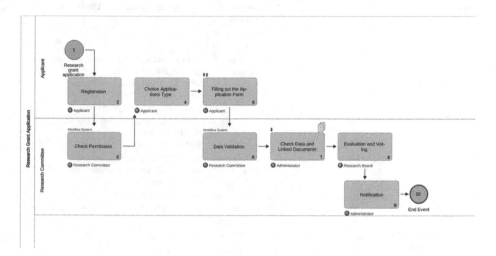

Fig. 2. The BPMN model of our case study

3.2 Transforming BPMN Models (BPMN to OWL)

To represent the business model in the ontology, the representation of ADONIS model language constructs and the representation of ADONIS model elements have to be differentiated. ADONIS model language constructs are created as classes and properties and the BPMN model elements can be represented through the instantiation of these classes and properties in the ontology. The linkage of the ontology and the ADONIS model element instances is accomplished by the usage of properties.

For the transformation process, a prototypical software tool was developed, which transforms a BPMN2.0 into an OWL format. The resulting file contains a partial ontology including classes and individuals of the input file. Every node of the BPMN diagram represents a class and has a parent and can have multiple attributes. All nodes are classes. The top-level class is **owl:Thing** and contains the six child-classes *Documents, IT_system, Roles, Research_Grant_Application, Start_* and *End_Event*. The *Research_Grant_Application* class contains the task elements of the BPMN 2.0 specification. The *Check_Data_and_Linked_Documents* class is one example of BPMN nodes. The developed BPMN ontology contains BPMN elements with their attributes and model associations (see Table 1).

Table 1. Overview of BPMN-OWL correspondence

BPMN	OWL	
	Structure	Current value
OWL classes		
process	super class of tasks	Research_Grant_Application
	subclass of *Start_Event*	
task	subclass of process	Check_Data_and Linked_Documents Check_Permission Choice_Application_Type Data_Validation Evaluation_and_Voting Filling_out_the_Application_Form Notification Registration
adonis:target C_ROLE class	subclass of *Roles*	Administrator Applicant Research_Board Research-Committee
adonis:target C_DOCUMENT class	subclass of Documents	Application_Form Cost_Calculation Travel_Form
adonis:target C_INFRASTRUCTURE_ELEMENT C_SERVICE class	subclass of IT_system	Workflow_system
OWL object properties		
sequenceFlow	followed_by owl:ObjectProperty	
adonis:relation RC_REFERENCED_INPUT_DATA_OPTIONAL_M	input_data owl:ObjectProperty	
adonis:relation RC_REFERENCED_OUTPUT_DATA_OPTIONAL_M	out_data owl:ObjectProperty	
adonis:relation RESPONSIBLE_FOR_EXECUTION	responsible_for_execution owl:ObjectProperty	
adonis:attribute A_ORDER	order owl:ObjectProperty	

3.3 Process-Based Text Mining

The first step of our text mining process was the corpus creation. Descriptions about research grant application processes published by educational institutions were collected by a Pyhton[2] scraper. The script uses beautifulsoup, urlib, re, time Python libraries to download hits provided by the Bing search engine. 'Conference', 'Grant', 'Funding', 'University' keywords were applied to identify related descriptions published on the Internet. Ten other announcements were downloaded manually besides this repository. After reviewing this collection containing 57 descriptions, we detected that our searching method and keywords would be refined to find more relevant hits in the future. At the end, the repository was separated into two datasets with 11 and 8 elements. These datasets contained announcements published by universities in the US and outside US to facilitate regional analysis as well.

---

[2] Python Programming Language: https://www.python.org/.

Text pre-processing steps were executed in the second stage. Process ontology resulted from the BPMN to OWL transformation was handled by our Python script uses owlready2 Python package. Class names of the process steps, documents and roles were collected from this ontology and textblob functions were used in preprocessing the corpus. Bigrams meaning a sequence of two adjacent elements were extracted from each description. The name of process ontology elements was split into words and lemmatized and the collections sets of n-grams were filtered by these terms. For example, in the case of Application Form document, all bigrams containing at least application or form word were gathered. This procedure was iterated in the case of each process steps, documents and roles. Having created these lists, the intersection of remained bigram lists of a given process step and a document was determined to generate and select feature e.g. ['evaluation', 'application'] bigram was identified by the 'Evaluation and voting' process step and by the 'Application form' document. All bigrams from the intersection list, their related process step and document were stored in a CSV file in the case of each announcing institutions. This step was repeated for process steps and roles as well.

3.4 Analytics

Having executed these pre-processing and feature generation procedures in the case of datasets about universities of the US and universities outside the US, Tableau[3] business analytics tool was used to discover interesting information about the research grant application process of each institution. Corvinus Business School operates an online application platform[4] to make this process more flexible. One aim of this process matching was to detect the degree of automatization at each university.

Three charts were created to investigate which documents are required, which the executive roles are and which documents are transmitted in each process steps at our competitors. A dashboard was composed from these diagrams to provide a toolset for stakeholders. All charts can be filtered on a given university. The following figure presents that application form is transmitted during this process in the case of five universities. After filtering data on Indiana University Bloomington (IUB) we can see that they use application website to enhance this process and a board makes the decisions. At Corvinus Business School online application platform is used and the Research Committee deals with the internal grant applications. These findings indicate us that the process of IUB might be similar to ours, it is worth checking later (Fig. 3).

We do scrutinize the following chart (see A part of Fig. 4) to gain deeper insights into what extent the processes of our competitors are automatized. It reveals that Cornell University requires PDF form and DAAD Office prefers online application. These universities are from US and we need to examine the cases of universities outside the US to get a broader overview about this area (see B part of Fig. 4). The results of this process-based text mining do not reveal any signs of automatization in the case of non-US universities.

---

[3] Tableau: https://www.tableau.com/.

[4] Corvinus Business School Online Application platform: http://workflow.business.research.uni-corvinus.hu/.

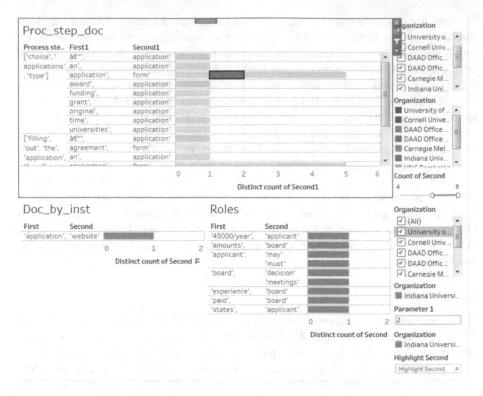

Fig. 3. Dashboard to analyze competitors' processes

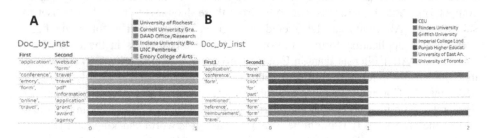

Fig. 4. Transmitted documents per US and outside US university

4   Limitations and Future Research

This paper highlighted a solution to analyze competitors' processes extracted from business documents with using BPMN to OWL Java-based transformation program and process-based text mining. A general algorithm was developed to transform business process models into process ontologies. It was written in Java and it can be parameterized hence it replaces the XSLT transformation in a more sophisticated way.

BPMN elements and their connected OWL model elements were also presented to enhance future development in this field.

A text mining algorithm written in Python showed how competitors' document can be processed based on a reference process model.

This research in the current stage has several limitations. Corpus collected by Bing search engine needs to be refined, cleansed in the future. Same words in the name of different process elements result the duplicates of bigrams - e.g. ['application', 'form'] was identified by the Choice Application Type process step and the Application Form document as well – hence the Count Distinct function was applied to present data on charts. Nevertheless, this paper presented that the concept is acceptable and applicable. However, it is necessary to improve this method to make competitor analysis more effective, accurate and automatized. We are planning to modify our corpus collection method, the names of process elements, validate our BPMN to OWL transformation procedure, extend our text mining algorithm with semantic-based relationship mining [1, 2] or SVM-based algorithms.

References

1. Szabó, I., Ternai, K.: Semantic audit application for analyzing business processes. In: Tjoa, A.M., Xu, L.D., Raffai, M., Novak, N.M. (eds.) CONFENIS 2016. LNBIP, vol. 268, pp. 3–15. Springer, Cham (2016). https://doi.org/10.1007/978-3-319-49944-4_1
2. Ternai, K., Szabó, I.: Semantic application for the internationalization audit of higher education institutions. In: Kő, A., Francesconi, E. (eds.) EGOVIS 2016. LNCS, vol. 9831, pp. 194–205. Springer, Cham (2016). https://doi.org/10.1007/978-3-319-44159-7_14
3. Haller, A., Marmolowski, M., Gaaloul, W., Oren, E.: A process ontology for business intelligence. DERI, Technical report (2008)
4. Hashimi, H., Hafez, A., Mathkour, H.: Selection criteria for text mining approaches. Comput. Hum. Behav. **51**, 729–733 (2015). https://doi.org/10.1016/j.chb.2014.10.062
5. Vijayarani, S., Ilamathi, M.J., Nithya, M.: Preprocessing techniques for text mining-an overview. Int. J. Comput. Sci. Commun. Netw. **5**, 7–16 (2015)
6. Haase, P., Völker, J.: Ontology learning and reasoning—dealing with uncertainty and inconsistency. In: da Costa, P.C.G., et al. (eds.) URSW 2005-2007. LNCS (LNAI), vol. 5327, pp. 366–384. Springer, Heidelberg (2008). https://doi.org/10.1007/978-3-540-89765-1_21
7. Zhou, L.: Ontology learning: state of the art and open issues. Inf. Technol. Manage. **8**, 241–252 (2007). https://doi.org/10.1007/s10799-007-0019-5
8. Ko, A., Gillani, S.: Ontology maintenance through semantic text mining: an application for it governance domain. In: Innovations, Developments, and Applications of Semantic Web and Information Systems, pp. 350–371 (2018). https://doi.org/10.4018/978-1-5225-5042-6.ch013
9. Koschmider, A., Oberweis, A.: Ontology based business process description. In: Proceedings of the CAiSE, pp. 321–333 (2005)
10. Rolstadås, A.: Performance Management: A Business Process Benchmarking Approach. Chapman & Hall, London (1995)
11. Teuteberg, F., Kluth, M., Ahlemann, F., Smolnik, S.: Semantic process benchmarking to improve process performance. Benchmarking Int. J. **20**(4), 484–511 (2013)

12. van Dongen, B., Dijkman, R., Mendling, J.: Measuring similarity between business process models. In: APCCM 2007 Proceedings of the Fourth Asia-Pacific Conference on Conceptual Modelling, Australia, pp. 71–80 (2007)
13. Ehrig, M., Koschmider, A., Oberweis, A.: Measuring similarity between semantic business process models, pp. 1–4 (2007)
14. Maedche, A., Staab, S.: Measuring similarity between ontologies. In: Gómez-Pérez, A., Benjamins, V.R. (eds.) EKAW 2002. LNCS (LNAI), vol. 2473, pp. 251–263. Springer, Heidelberg (2002). https://doi.org/10.1007/3-540-45810-7_24
15. Kalogeraki, E.-M., Apostolou, D., Panayiotopoulos, T., Tsihrintzis, G., Theocharis, S.: A semantic approach for representing and querying business processes. In: Tsihrintzis, G.A., Virvou, M., Jain, L.C. (eds.) Intelligent Computing Systems. SCI, vol. 627, pp. 87–114. Springer, Heidelberg (2016). https://doi.org/10.1007/978-3-662-49179-9_4
16. Bakhshandeh, M., Pesquita, C., Borbinha, J.: An ontological matching approach for enterprise architecture model analysis. In: Abramowicz, W., Alt, R., Franczyk, B. (eds.) BIS 2016. LNBIP, vol. 255, pp. 315–326. Springer, Cham (2016). https://doi.org/10.1007/978-3-319-39426-8_25

Collaborative Networks and Project Management

Online Social Transparency in Enterprise Information Systems: Risks and Risk Factors

Tahani Alsaedi[✉], Keith Phalp, and Raian Ali

Faculty of Science and Technology, Bournemouth University, Poole, UK
{talsaedi, kphalp, rali}@bournemouth.ac.uk

Abstract. Enterprises integrate social networking within their information systems to enhance collegiality, situational awareness, coordination and collaboration amongst their members. Social networking features can be seen in traditional systems such as the online profile, calendar, dashboard, auto-reply and status. More specialised systems enable bespoke features to declare and share and retrieve current and past engagements, team memberships, allocated tasks and priorities. Such social transparency is typically voluntary and not strictly enshrined by organisational governance and norms. Despite its positive connotations, negative consequences such as information overload, social loafing and undesired pressure can be a result of it. We conducted a multistage qualitative study, including focus groups, interviews and observations, to conceptualise online social transparency and explore the risks that stem from its unmanaged implementation. Our research aims to provide the first step towards a systematic method for risk identification and mitigation around online social transparency.

Keywords: Social transparency · Enterprise social software · Enterprise information systems

1 Introduction

In enterprise information systems, it is becoming common for employees to share more information about themselves so that they enhance situational and context awareness and, hence, communication relevance and sensitivity. Enterprise social software (ESS) is an online platform that allows employees to communicate, in real-time, information about their identities, activity streams, assigned tasks, work progress and collaboration with others [1] and it allows companies to improve the business relationships with customers [2]. These platforms used to practice social transparency that we defined in our previous work as *"voluntarily use of online platforms by employees to share their own information about their situation, roles and responsibilities with other members of the organisation"* [3].

At the organisational level, [4] stated that transparency is one of the trends in corporate social responsibilities (CSR) that results in an improvement in enterprise performance, productivity and profit. On the individual level, social transparency is typically to enhance situational awareness, coordination, and collaboration amongst employees. Organisational scientists have long understood that the success of

© IFIP International Federation for Information Processing 2019
Published by Springer Nature Switzerland AG 2019
P. Doucek et al. (Eds.): CONFENIS 2019, LNBIP 375, pp. 97–111, 2019.
https://doi.org/10.1007/978-3-030-37632-1_9

organisations depends on commitments, coordination, and collaboration of their employees [5]. Online social transparency is one of the mechanisms whose effects on employee collaboration and motivation have been proven [6]. Social transparency contributes to building trust and bringing awareness amongst organisation members through intentional information disclosure, group knowledge sharing or individual activity sharing [7]. Thus, social transparency has become a popular requirement for employees before engaging in the activities of others.

Despite the positive connotations, it seems that current digital tools are both primitive and cumbersome. Most of the enterprise social software has substantial shortcomings in regard to their facilitation of online social transparency. The ad-hoc practice of such transparency may lead to adverse effects such as disturbance, information overload and lack of interest [8]. Research on transparency and its effects is rare in the requirements engineering literature. In [9], a conceptual framework is proposed to facilitate the adoption of transparency in responsible organisational business management. It describes what organisations can do to be more transparent and the potential benefits of transparency. An argumentation framework was proposed in [10] to elicit transparency-related requirements. TranspLan language was proposed in [11], and it provides models and templates for specifying transparency requirements within enterprises and algorithms to reason about them in terms of consistency and conflicts. In terms of social transparency, the authors in [12] examined how individuals use information about others' actions in open social software and provide suggestions about the design of social media for large scale enterprise, and imply a variety of ways that transparency can support innovation, knowledge sharing and community building. In [13], it is argued that the online platforms for social transparency are making information visible without careful thoughts to the social inferences the platform design supports. The authors provided a theoretical framework for analysing social transparency and inferences stemming from the change in technology.

Although these works illuminate the potential promise of managing social transparency in the enterprise, particularly in their online platforms, scholars still handle social transparency as an information quality issue. In our work, we address the question of how to manage social transparency as an informed decision and behaviour. We provided earlier our definition of social transparency, and we assume that this transparency is an autonomous decision by organisation members to be open when conveying social information through online platforms.

In this paper, we build on our previous work in [3, 14] and conduct a multi-stage qualitative study (described in Sect. 2) to provide empirical evidence that online social transparency can lead to a negative impact on employees as well as organisations if implemented and conducted in an unmanaged style (Sect. 3). We provide common risks and associate them with certain classifications of online social transparency (Sect. 4). Our results are meant to inform future risks assessment method of online social transparency and, also, the engineering of enterprise social software so that it plays a role in guiding and steering it and make employees decisions about it more informed.

Table 1. Research method stages

Stage	Description	Purpose
1st stage foundations	- Review related literature including organisational transparency, CSCW, Group Dynamics, situational awareness and organisational culture - Two scenario-based focus groups with 14 participants	- To conceptualise online social transparency - To identify essential factors for assessing online social transparency [14]
2nd stage exploration	Semi-structured Interview with 15 Participants	- To build a reference model for the assessment method of online social transparency [3] - To form an initial set of risks and their factors
3rd stage refinement	Observation study, Interviews, Focus group	- To form the final set of risks and risk factors

2 Research Method

A multistage qualitative study was used to investigate the potential shortcomings of applying social transparency within enterprise information systems. We used multiple data collection methods as presented in Table 1. The study aimed to (i) identify the assessment dimensions of online social transparency and (ii) explore the typical risks and risk factors around the unmanaged conduct of it.

All the studies were recorded and transcribed verbatim to support the analysis stage. We used a thematic analysis approach by following the six phases of thematic analysis proposed by [15]. In the analysis stage, we identified the participants' views on their transparency expectations from their co-workers and managers and their concerns about affecting their role, social dependencies and actions. We used the findings of each stage as a template to start with when analysing the next stage and expanded it until we reached the saturation point in all stages. The study was approved by the research ethics committee of the authors' institution.

2.1 Focus Groups Phase

A total of 14 individuals participated in two focus group sessions to explore how they view online social transparency in the workplace, their requirements of it, and how certain modalities and configurations of transparency contribute to risks that affect aspects of their work environment. We recruited participants who worked in organisations where their role involved collaborative work with others online. The participants were given a presentation to familiarise themselves with the context of the research. We developed four scenarios to cover various aspects of transparency such as its content (e.g. intentions, plans and status), its presentation (media and interfaces), its timing and relevance. We used the scenarios in the session to stimulate discussions. Each scenario included questions to be answered individually before discussing it within the group.

2.2 Interview Phase

We used the findings from the focus group stage as a foundation for further investigation. We conducted a semi-structured interview study to (i) confirm and refine the findings that related to the transparency assessment factors resulting from the focus group and (ii) explore families of typical risks related to unmanaged online transparency around those factors. While we used typical scenarios in the focus group study, the interviews were intended to delve into the personal experiences of the participants about online transparency in their workplaces. The interviews phase sought to explore the risk of transparency through the professionals' lived experiences and different work environments. We interviewed 15 participants throughout two stages. We first interviewed participants from diverse work environments, including academia, small companies and call centres. Ten employees agreed to participate in this study (four females and six males) aged between 27 and 43 years. In the second stage, we interviewed professionals in managerial roles. Five managers from various levels of seniority participated in this study that they are a project manager, call centre manager, team leader and two supervisors. We also considered diversity in gender in the second stage, with two females and three males aged between 36 to 52 years.

2.3 Observation Phase

We conducted a two days observation study at two multicultural small-scale companies to further explore the risks and their factors of social transparency in enterprise social software and confirm they exist in real context. The companies use software called Slack (https://slack.com/intl/en-gb/enterprise) for tracking the progress, managing employees' collaboration and improving overall performance. A short interview with employees was conducted after the observation of their behaviour and interaction with the software finished.

After two days of observation, we conducted one focus group in each company. To enrich the results with a diversity of opinions originating from various perspectives, participants with managerial roles and employees were involved. As a result, a total of 10 professionals from the two companies participated in our focus group study, one session with 5 professionals in each company. In addition to the diversity in roles, we considered diversity in gender and age, with three females and seven males ranging from 28 to 49 years old. The focus group included two activities. The first was a scenario-based discussion where the scenarios used are built based on the observations made in the two companies. The second involved an open card sorting activity to organise the risks of online social transparency into groups. The card sorting aimed to confirm and refine the findings with regards to the risks of online social transparency on employees' wellbeing and performance. The card sorting activity included risks generated from participants' answers and risks founded in the second stage. Each focus group lasted for around two hours. The sessions were audio-recorded and transcribed for content analysis.

3 Categories of Online Social Transparency

Social transparency can be classified into three categories based on two factors (i) the awareness of the information provider and (ii) the accessibility level of the information receiver. The awareness of the information provider refers to the conscious choice for the information to be visible. Awareness is a spectrum, and it falls between two edge cases:

- "I revealed" case: It refers to the deliberate sharing of individual information with consent to be visible to others. For example, staffs consciously reveal information about their current status and progress in the task with the purpose that this information will be visible to enterprise members and how it can be usually used.
- "*I did not reveal*" case: It refers to the sharing of individual information without full awareness of the sharing action itself or the audiences of the information shared. For example, a team leader shares information about their team, where members are not aware of that. Another example is about sharing location data and not being aware or able to predict whether this might be occasionally re-shared by others.

Regarding the second factor, we found that online social transparency sharing can be classified into two kinds based on the accessibility level by enterprise members.

- Open accessibility: In which information is accessible by all individuals in the workplace. Staff open online calendar is a typical example where others can see the schedule of their colleagues and what the meetings are about and their location.
- Regulated accessibility: In which information is limited, deliberately or due to connectivity and contextual barriers, to a set of individuals in the workplace. Group conversation and to-do-list is a typical example.

Based on the two dimensions of awareness and accessibility, we found four categories of online social transparency:

- **Open social transparency** refers to sharing information about the self with full awareness and also desire to be visible to others in the organisation. This kind of transparency is typically motivated by increasing awareness in the workplace which will then positively affect the organisational goals. There are several examples of open social transparency in organisations such as staff calendar; staff profiles page, their location and activity status and public posts and conversations.
- **Regulated social transparency** refers to sharing information about the self, which reaches only specific members of the organisation. This kind of transparency regulates the visibility of individual information for various reasons, including the protection from misuse and the reduction of misconceptions amongst members. For example, sharing information about personal difficulties in the work may be of interest only to the teams to which the employee belongs. Busy colleagues may not see them due to applying filters and techniques like muting other's people status. In other words, regulation of accessibility can also be a receiver choice.
- **Unconscious social transparency** refers to the visibility of individual information without awareness from the information owner. This kind of transparency is one of the ethical issues in the workplace as colleagues may share personal information

about an individual without their knowledge. We emphasise here that social transparency has loose contractual settings and access control and relies mainly on personal judgement and organisational and cultural norms. For example, a member of a team may share information about difficulties and their peers' weaknesses or peer's progress in a collaborative task with other teams aiming for external support. Such transparency seems unavoidable even in an ordinary social environment but still undesired as it has a diverse impact on the collaboration between organisational members. A participant highlighted that *"it happened in the joint work when people want to jeopardise the progress or displacing colleagues form their assigned tasks."*

- **No social transparency** refers to the situation where enterprise members are not sharing information about their activities stream, progress, and interest in certain tasks or their relationships with other colleagues. We found this case more in new members who still have not built a trust relationship with peers and management and confidence in their role and contribution to the group. Introversion and extroversion can also be part of the personality.

4   Risks Associated with Online Social Transparency

Our results from the first and second stages of the study indicated that risks are related to the delivery of the information in four aspects: content, timeliness, presentation and intended recipients [3]. The results of our third stage confirmed our previous findings and explored other dimensions of risk factors that need to be considered in the assessment process. Our analysis grouped the risks based on their influence area into (i) performance, (ii) wellbeing and (iii) workplace environment. Two main risk factors seemed to be prominent; the *level* of transparency (Sect. 4.1) and the way it is *practised* (Sect. 4.2).

4.1   Risks Related to Level of Transparency

The level of transparency indicates whether it is adequate, abundant or unsatisfactory. The level is not only determined by the information content but is inherently dependent on the reachability, relevance and interpretability of information. In other words, it is a contextual and subjective measure, determined mainly by the audiences and dependent on their personal, technical and social context. Table 2 presents the main categories of risks revolving around the different levels of transparency.

Risks Related to Excessive Online Social Transparency. Excessive transparency refers to the redundant and repetitive voluntary sharing of information. It refers to pushing information overly in terms of amount and frequency. We reiterate here that the judgement of the level of transparency, in terms of information and their meaningfulness, is not uniform but depends on the recipients personal, task, technical and social context. Examples of these contexts are the recipient's availability, workloads, time, preferences, location, and available communication bandwidth.

Table 2. Examples of risks related to different levels of online social transparency

	Excessive level of Transparency	Normal level of Transparency	Lack of Transparency
Performance	Employee Isolation Lack of collaboration Information overload Slow Decision Making	Loss of interest low engagement Low innovation Social Loafing	Conflict of interest Loss of interest Lack of collaboration
Wellbeing	Inadequate and unprepared Confusion in intentions Stress Pressure	Stress & Pressure Low self-esteem Negative impression Distrust	Lack of belonging Relationship Conflict Annoyance Lack of trust
Workplace Environment	Uncomfortable Place Loss of concentration Loss of professionalism Employees Turnover	Favouritism Disengagement Discouraged employees	Rumours spread Biased opinions Fabricated reactions Information inaccuracy

Performance. Excessive transparency can lead to isolating individuals from others. We noted that participants may avoid collaboration with colleagues who practice transparency more than normal. It was stated that *"having a member with excessive transparency attitude means more unnecessary distraction which may affect the workflow of the team progress"*. Moreover, lack of collaboration may happen as a result of creating information overload due to the excessive transparency of information related to a person's works. Information overload may also slow the decision-making process due to the quantity of information that needs to be processed.

Wellbeing. Excessive transparency may also lead to a risk of making employees feel inadequate or unprepared when they receive too much information, particularly irrelevant information about others' work. A participant stated that *"I may receive information that I do not need to know but because it is sent to me, I feel like it is something I am expected to part of, or to understand"*. It was also showed that too much transparency might create confusion about the ultimate intention of this transparency which, therefore, creates a chance of making mistakes and waste time in the workplace. We noted that employees who are excessively transparent about their good performance run the risk of creating unwanted stress and pressure for employees who may constantly be thinking of how their performance impacts the team productivity.

Workplace Environment. Social transparency in the workplace may make employees excessively open about their personal life more than the work which makes the workplace lose its professionalism. Distraction can stem from excessive transparency and make the workplace an unhealthy and uncomfortable environment for employees who may lose concentration to accomplish their work which in turn increase the rate of employees' turnover.

Risks Related to Normal Online Social Transparency. In this section, we present the risks that may stem from a normal level of transparency. We identify this level as the required level of transparency when the shared information is seen by the audiences as satisfactory and beneficial to certain enterprise goals and activities. We noticed that even if transparency is seen adequate, it might lead to a negative impact on the relationship between enterprise members and the level of trust and interest between them and may need further qualification and support with additional measures to mitigate risks on performance, wellbeing and the workplace environment.

Performance. ESS such as Slack typically have features that allow each member to pin certain messages to appear all the time to all team members as a headline or priority. However, using this feature to be transparent about certain facets such as the long duration or difficulty of a certain task may make colleagues lose their interest to contribute or collaborate in this task. We also found that employees tend to share their personal skills in solving certain problems either to promote their abilities or to make others learn from them. However, this kind of voluntary transparency, despite being relevant and needed, may reduce the innovation and creativity of other employees to find clever solutions and make them more reliant on those who have them. Besides the influence on individual performance, team performance may also be affected by social transparency. For example, our analysis showed that when employees are transparent about their interest in certain tasks; other members may be less motivated to work hard on behalf of the group. This loss of motivation is called social loafing and is associated with free riding. We noted that social transparency might trigger social loafing and free-riding in large groups where more than one member works in the same task or goal and traceability and auditing are harder.

Wellbeing. Employee personal, social and financial wellbeing at the workplace is a requirement for enterprises to address and ensure that their employees remain satisfied, motivated and loyal at work [16]. Wellbeing risks such as stress and pressure may stem from transparency when the information reveals conflict with other member's interest or goals. Transparency about work progress in the public channels in ESS, despite being needed for scheduling and coordination, might reach an employee who is less skilled or has less experience which consequently lowers their self-esteem and may also have a chance to leave a bad impression about others' progress if the information reached a high authority such as project manager. In addition, team collective well-being may also be affected by social transparency amongst the members. We noted that a team could suffer from a distrust problem due to misusing the information that is provided by other team members. For example, employees may share the reasons which slow their progress to eliminate high expectations or to seek voluntary help from other members. Less collaborative colleagues may use this information as a defence strategy and avoid blame on the progress of the whole team in the end. This is because the information in online social transparency are archived and can be retrieved later and processed to generate reports. This is similar to when people use the timeline or post history on social media to retrieve evidence of some social events and behaviours.

Workplace Environment. We found that social transparency may lead to creating favouritism culture in the workplace. Favouritism is defined as special privileges or treatment provided to one person over all of the other employees [17]. Social transparency may develop friendship amongst employees who share similar interests, skills or experiences. This friendship may lead to creating special treatment for some employees over others. The favouritism that emerges from social transparency correlates with a feeling of disengagement from work, feeling discouraged by non-favoured employees. Common risks which were mentioned by our employee participants included nepotism amongst employees and the unjustifiable decisions made based on the special relationships with decision-makers.

Risks Related to Lack of Online Social Transparency. Lack of transparency refers to the unintentional and occasional holding of individual's social information in the enterprise social software. We reiterate here that social transparency is not enforced by the organisational rules and left as a personal choice for staff. We noted that when there is no social transparency, it would be difficult for employees to know what is going on, why certain things are happening, and they may find themselves vulnerable, insecure and afraid of uncertainty. This typically leads to searching for precautionary and defensive strategies and following a more conservative and less creative attitude.

Performance. Lack of social transparency between team members or organisation members means communicating little or no information about colleagues' intentions towards their work, their interests in certain kinds of activities, their availabilities for future collaboration or justifications for unexpected actions. We found that when an employee fails to know about other's intentions such as their priorities and interests in certain tasks, that may create a conflict in performing these tasks and spend significant time in the least priority tasks. Loss of interest and lack of collaboration are other risks that result from lack of social transparency amongst enterprise members. For example, no transparency about interest in performing collaborative tasks may demotivate employees and make them think carefully before engaging in this task.

Wellbeing. We noted that a lack of belonging is one of the common issues that result from a lack of social transparency between peers in the same team. Lack of social transparency has been seen as a reason for relationship conflict because employees are unaware of other members' diverging interests and incompatible preferences which make employees misattribute the intentions of others. As a result, risks such as tension, annoyance, low work satisfaction and commitment, lack of trust and low group cohesion has a high chance to stem amongst employees.

Workplace Environment. Our analysis showed that when social transparency is lacking amongst employees, team leaders and management members, there tends to be a high chance that rumours, biased opinions, inaccurate information and fabricated reactions will become common throughout the organisation processes and particularly employees' communication.

4.2   Risks Related to Transparency Sharing Practice

Research on social transparency describes it in a model where two parties exchange their information, and an observer has an opportunity to engage in these exchanges [13]. In the two companies, we observed the sharing practice amongst employees when conveying social transparency. Risks can be organised around two main types of social transparency practice: asymmetric and symmetric. A summary is presented in Table 3.

Risks Related to Symmetric Online Social Transparency. This type is identified as the reciprocal transparency behaviour where the two parties are, at a certain point of time, transparent about their information and have enough information about each other. By observing symmetric social transparency in ESS, we concluded that the quality facets such as presentation, timing, and relevance of the information are the essential triggers of risks in the workplace.

Performance. Symmetric social transparency in ESS might create information overload to employees who are not interested in this information. In other words, people may not expect or want reciprocal transparency as a return to being transparent. We noted that unmanaged symmetric transparency could increase the distraction from work unless staff are enabled to filter responses to their transparency. Symmetrical social transparency and the perception of others to reciprocate transparency even if not demanded to do so can create a massive information history in the online platform, which may cost the employee time and effort to search for relevant information.

Wellbeing. Conditional reciprocity is an interesting noted behaviour in symmetric social transparency. Employees would be socially transparent when their colleagues are transparent as well. If the other party continually fails to be transparent, it will be reputational, and other employees will stop being transparent with them. That would add pressure on employees to avoid losing transparency of others as well as avoid Fear of Missing Out (FoMO) feelings occurring when they expect a return to their transparency from colleagues. FoMO is described in [18] as "the desire to be continually connected with what others are doing".

Workplace Environment. As mentioned earlier, some employees may not expect or like reciprocal transparency, i.e. transparency from others as a return to their own transparency. A workplace with symmetrical transparency behaviour might be an uncomfortable place for them as it can create a less genuine sharing practice and workarounds. For example, we noted that symmetrical transparency behaviour does not ensure that information itself is also symmetrical in quality, timeliness and format which can increase the chance for reducing harmony and consistency in the workplace. We noted that employees who practice symmetrical transparency might lose the opportunity to learn from their colleagues. For example, when expert employees feel they only need to be transparent about their progress and tasks and hold the information related to the techniques they use knowing that novice colleagues would not be able to reciprocate in that aspect. Symmetrical transparency is also described by some of our participants as a sign of lack of trust in the workplace as employees may not feel secure to be fully and truly transparent but rather pressured to do that.

Table 3. Examples of risks related to Symmetric and Asymmetric Online Social Transparency

	Symmetric Social Transparency ⇄	Asymmetric Social Transparency ⇐
Performance	Information overload Distraction Big information history Time/effort consuming	Insufficient knowledge Delay in progress Low performance and productivity
Wellbeing	Conditional reciprocity Pressure FoMO	Power imbalance Stress Insecure employees Pressure
Workplace Environment	Uncomfortable place Loss learning opportunity Low harmony	Low group cohesion Insecure workplace Unfair workplace

Risks Related to Asymmetric Online Social Transparency. This type occurs when one party is more transparent, in terms of information content and, also timing and proactiveness than other parties. Asymmetric transparency can make a discrepancy in situational awareness. As social transparency is voluntary, there are no regulations to oblige employees to be transparent with each other and how to choose the time and frequency for doing so.

Performance. We noted that there is a chance to reduce collaboration amongst employees who are not transparent or less transparent about their information at the time others are transparent. Risks such as insufficient knowledge base due to inequivalent communication between members of an organisation and low consistency of transparency behaviour play a significant role in delaying the employee's progress, lowering their performance and reducing the overall productivity of the organisation.

Wellbeing. Asymmetric social transparency can create power imbalance as individuals may use others' information as a way to empower themselves or misuse the information for personal benefits such as complaining against an employee to relocate them to a different department. With the characteristics of digital systems, such as data retrieval, real-time and traceability, e.g. sharing a location, these risks are maximised if we compare them to face-to-face transparency. From a collaboration perspective, there is a high chance to reduce collaboration with employees who are not transparent or less transparent about their information compared with their colleagues. Employees may have stress and insecure feelings to collaborate or engage in a work with an employee that is less transparent than them. We found that the asymmetric transparency behaviour adds <u>pressure</u> to employees to cope with the behaviour of more transparent colleagues. A participant declares that this pressure may happen for employees who tend to cope with other behaviour to create a good impression or to avoid any blame for less transparent behaviour.

Workplace Environment. Asymmetric behaviour of social transparency has a chance to <u>reduce group cohesion</u> due to the imbalanced transparency amongst employees. A participant described a workplace with asymmetric transparency as an <u>insecure workplace.</u> It has also been described as <u>an unfair workplace</u> because this behaviour <u>decreases the learning opportunity</u> amongst employees, particularly new or less-skilled employees.

5   Discussion

Work on organisational transparency showed the positive impact of social transparency in motivating peer production and accelerating the decision-making process [19]. As discussed in this paper, social transparency in ESS can enable enterprise members to adjust their inter-relationships with others, expectations, focus, and priorities and be aware of the dynamic contexts of their group and enterprise. The ultimate goal of social transparency is to enable the enterprise to reach its strategic goals and at the same time maintain quality and social requirements such as job satisfaction and perception of openness and fairness [3]. However, in the absence of shepherding and guidance on how individuals practice social transparency via the ESS, especially about the level of transparency (in amount, subject, outreach, and frequency) and the balance of sharing and openness culture amongst all, the intended benefits of it can be easily compromised.

Although the literature in fields like Computer Supported Cooperative Work (CSCW) conceptualised social transparency as information sharing technique, mainly practices within small group settings, we still lack methods to engineer such online platforms to make decisions about social transparency informed, especially across a large scale such as enterprise. For example, an individual would need the system to predict and visualise the impact of sharing certain information and, also, receive impressions and feedback on the sharing, which help them refine future actions. We argued in [3] that EES also needs to provide a more structured way which allows better management of the content of transparency, interaction time and the set of audience, still without contradicting with the free-spirit in social transparency and its voluntary nature and reliance on an openness culture.

Besides the need for automated support to assist individuals in making an informed decision about social transparency, assessing its risks can be integrated into the design phase of social enterprise software, so that common risks are elicited and dealt with in advance as part of the design and its interactive features. For example, capturing the strategic goals and activities of each role in the organisation can become a reference point for decisions around the relevance of information content and hence be a basis for decisions around information overload. We suggest that such an assessment method has to include two phases: the preparation phase and the analysis and actioning phase. We intend to consolidate and validate our proposed phases in future work.

Preparation Phase: This phase is expected to be administered by the system analysts alongside enterprise management, and it shall also include representatives of each role in the enterprise. This phase is to set up the scene and to determine the parties involved in the assessment and loci in the business process where social transparency can be beneficial or detrimental. The decision about transparency risks are subjective and differ from one individual to another and even for the same individual depending on their context. Early in this paper, we defined social transparency as a voluntary act to share information about the individual's own status including goals, activities, priorities, mood, plans, and skills. Therefore, and given the nature of information and the personal differences in risk assessment, we suggest using human-centred techniques which allow capturing such diversity [20]. Examples include the use of user stories, goal modelling, think-aloud and scenarios to both generate test cases and speculated risks. We would need a bespoke version of such techniques to fit the peculiarities and special nature of social transparency, e.g. a domain-specific template for user stories supported with a controlled vocabulary reflecting typical intentions and goals of social transparency. In our previous work [3], we demonstrated that social transparency side-effect becomes evident once it is practised in the day to day life of the enterprise members. Hence, we suggest gathering user stories over some time and merging it with methods like diary studies [21]. User stories collected in real-world context and aided by a simulator can then be used to generate scenarios which will allow the system analysts and management to get real-life examples of the interaction, activities, and behaviour amongst enterprise members and their practice of social transparency in a realistic manner. To document and formalise social transparency and its risks within their organisational context, techniques like goal modelling and BPMN can be used so that formal analysis can be then conducted.

Analysis and Actioning Phase: The user-centred techniques (user stories, diaries, scenarios and think aloud) and the presentation of the knowledge captured through them (goal modelling and BPMN) built in the preparation phase are meant to be the knowledge base for the analysis and actioning phase. Approached involving the actual users of EES and social transparency, such as participatory design approach [22], are preferred given the nature of risks, i.e., being subjective and context-dependent. In [3] we advocated mitigation strategies can lead to further risks. For example, mitigating risks of lack of cooperation due to asymmetric transparency through increasing openness may lead to triggering information overload risk. Therefore, the method would need to look at the chain of risks and their impact and weight, so it allows prioritisation. Moreover, social transparency is not only an individual act, but it also involves all members of the enterprise. Therefore, we suggest that the assessment process has to be performed collectively so that it captures emerging properties and become more sensitive to group dynamics. As such risks can emerge only in a real-world context, despite making all effort to predict them at the design stage, iterative and lifelong risk assessment methods within the enterprise information systems would be needed.

6 Conclusion

In our previous works, we provided the basics of assessing social transparency and its associated risks related to the delivery of information which includes the content, presentation, timeliness and transparency recipients. This paper is complementary to our previous work on assessing online social transparency in the enterprise. We provided categories of online social transparency based on the awareness of transparency provider and the level of accessibility to the information. In terms of the risks of social transparency, we have considered here the influence of the level of transparency and the transparency sharing practice on performance, wellbeing and workplace environment. Our future works will design an engineering method that aid system analysts and enterprise management to assess social transparency implemented in their online platforms.

References

1. Graupner, S., et al.: When social media meet the enterprise. In: IEEE 16th International Enterprise Distributed Object Computing Conference (EDOC), pp. 201–210. IEEE (2012)
2. Pavlíček, A., Doucek, P.: Social media and social CRM. In: Tjoa, A.M., Xu, L.D., Raffai, M., Novak, N.M. (eds.) CONFENIS 2016. LNBIP, vol. 268, pp. 77–87. Springer, Cham (2016). https://doi.org/10.1007/978-3-319-49944-4_6
3. Alsaedi, T., Phalp, K., Ali, R.: Towards an assessment method for social transparency in enterprise information systems. In: The 10th Workshop on Service oriented Enterprise Architecture for Enterprise Engineering (SoEA4EE 2019), co-located with the 23rd IEEE International Enterprise Computing Conference (EDOC). IEEE (2019)
4. Pavlíček, A., Doucek, P.: Corporate social responsibility in social media environment. In: Khalil, I., Neuhold, E., Tjoa, A.M., Da Xu, L., You, I. (eds.) CONFENIS/ICT-EurAsia - 2015. LNCS, vol. 9357, pp. 323–332. Springer, Cham (2015). https://doi.org/10.1007/978-3-319-24315-3_33
5. Gibbons, R., et al.: What do managers do? Suggestive evidence and potential theories about building relationships. In: Handbook of Organizational Economics. Princeton University Press, Princeton (2010, forthcoming)
6. Brandes, L., Darai, D.: The value and motivating mechanism of transparency in organizations. Eur. Econ. Rev. **98**, 189–198 (2017)
7. Schnackenberg, A.K., Tomlinson, E.C.: Organizational transparency: a new perspective on managing trust in organization-stakeholder relationships. J. Manag. **42**(7), 1784–1810 (2016)
8. Laud, R.L., Schepers, D.H.: Beyond transparency: information overload and a model for intelligibility. Bus. Soc. Rev. **114**(3), 365–391 (2009)
9. Parris, D.L., et al.: Exploring transparency: a new framework for responsible business management. Manag. Decis. **54**(1), 222–247 (2016)
10. do Prado Leite, J.C.S., Cappelli, C.: Exploring i* characteristics that support software transparency. In: iStar (2008)
11. Hosseini, M., Shahri, A., Phalp, K., Ali, R.: A modelling language for transparency requirements in business information systems. In: Nurcan, S., Soffer, P., Bajec, M., Eder, J. (eds.) CAiSE 2016. LNCS, vol. 9694, pp. 239–254. Springer, Cham (2016). https://doi.org/10.1007/978-3-319-39696-5_15

12. Dabbish, L., et al.: Social coding in GitHub: transparency and collaboration in an open software repository. In: Proceedings of the Conference on Computer Supported Cooperative Work (CSCW), pp. 1277–1286. ACM (2012)

13. Stuart, H.C., et al.: Social transparency in networked information exchange: a theoretical framework. In: Proceedings of the conference on Computer Supported Cooperative Work (CSCW), pp. 451–460. ACM (2012)

14. Alsaedi, T., Phalp, K., Ali, R.: Social transparency in enterprise information systems: peculiarities and assessment factors. In: The 6th International Conference on Behavioral, Economic, and Socio-Cultural Computing (BESC). IEEE (2019)

15. Braun, V., Clarke, V.: Using thematic analysis in psychology. Qual. Res. Psychol. 3(2), 77–101 (2006)

16. Renee Baptiste, N.: Tightening the link between employee wellbeing at work and performance: a new dimension for HRM. Manag. Decis. 46(2), 284–309 (2008)

17. Arasli, H., Arici, H.E., Çakmakoğlu Arici, N.: Workplace favouritism, psychological contract violation and turnover intention: moderating roles of authentic leadership and job insecurity climate. Ger. J. Hum. Resour. Manag. 33(3), 197–222 (2019)

18. Przybylski, A.K., et al.: Motivational, emotional, and behavioral correlates of fear of missing out. Comput. Hum. Behav. 29(4), 1841–1848 (2013)

19. Marlow, J., Dabbish, L.A.: The effects of visualizing activity history on attitudes and behaviors in a peer production context. In: Proceedings of the 18th ACM Conference on Computer Supported Cooperative Work & Social Computing (CSCW), pp. 757–764. ACM (2015)

20. Giacomin, J.: What is human centred design? Des. J. 17(4), 606–623 (2014)

21. Singer, J., Sim, S.E., Lethbridge, T.C.: Software engineering data collection for field studies. In: Shull, F., Singer, J., Sjøberg, D.I.K. (eds.) Guide to Advanced Empirical Software Engineering, pp. 9–34. Springer, London (2008). https://doi.org/10.1007/978-1-84800-044-5_1

22. Spinuzzi, C.: The methodology of participatory design. Tech. Commun. 52(2), 163–174 (2005)

A Bounding Technique for Probabilistic PERT

Maksim Goman$^{(\boxtimes)}$

Johannes Kepler University, Altenberger Street 69, 4040 Linz, Austria
Maksim.Goman@jku.at
http://www.jku.at/ie

Abstract. Bounding time distributions has been an effective way of improvements of the original PERT method. Analytical enhancement of PERT is often an effective time bounding approach. However, one thing that is missing today is a combination of time distributions which parameters can be effectively obtained empirically and the effective bounding technique for them. We aim at addressing this gap and suggest Cornish-Fisher expansion (CFE) to compute time bounds in formal models like the classical PERT.

We argue that CFE allows us to evaluate analytically approximate time bounds easily without resort to simulations. This bounding approach is useful in case of complex distribution functions of task durations, because analytical derivation of project completion time distribution is tedious. Our example shows CFE usage for uniform time distributions and comparison with time bounds of classical PERT.

Keywords: Stochastic PERT · Bounding technique · Time bounds · Project management · Path duration

1 Introduction

Project Evaluation and Review Technique (PERT) [1] (classical PERT) is known today as a method of project time evaluation. The principal idea is to perform a probabilistic analysis of the project completion time. Unfortunately, there has been a lot of criticism of the classical PERT due to its model assumptions, e.g. [2]. One of the most unfortunate assumption is use of central limit theorem (CLT) to approximate path durations with Gaussian distribution, regardless of distribution function (DF) of individual activity times. CLT appeals to be an easy solution to the complex problem of project time evaluation in a stochastic activity network (SAN). The alternative is aggregation of random time variables along the paths. CLT introduces ambiguity about initial time distributions of tasks in classical PERT, i.e. they had initially beta DF, but going back from the resulting normal distribution of the whole project time we can assume that they could be marginally normal distributions. In this way, there is little use of constructing initial beta distribution of tasks. There are a number of equivalent

© IFIP International Federation for Information Processing 2019
Published by Springer Nature Switzerland AG 2019
P. Doucek et al. (Eds.): CONFENIS 2019, LNBIP 375, pp. 112–122, 2019.
https://doi.org/10.1007/978-3-030-37632-1_10

conditions for data in order that CLT can be applied in the theory [3]. Goman [4] has analyzed the applicability of CLT for classical PERT problems and confirmed the need to verify the CLT conditions for the given data in order to have consistent and reasonable results of classical PERT analysis.

There have been many attempts at using times with Gaussian DF in PERT analysis [5]. Choice of the normal DF was due to simplified modelling and calculations, especially for multivariate case. Computational difficulties called attention to normal distributions many decades ago because manipulation of arbitrary distribution functions (DFs) was hard due to slow computers and lack of readily available software tools for that. Computation time for a project SAN is not an issue today for any realistic size of PERT SAN. Aggregation of known DFs can be done fast using modelling. Moreover, the choice of normal distribution needs more explanations for its negative range and infinite tails of time values.

However, this is not only about assumptions. Basic principles of management are even more important, e.g. what kind of the outcome should the analysis produce to a decision maker (DM) in project management? DM can not expect exact time estimation of possible project time due to unreliable initial time estimations, unknown real distribution types and other uncertainties in the project model. These distributions are only artefacts of the model and follow from some assumptions. In fact, the only thing possible about prospective time analysis is reduction of uncertainty, i.e. more or less accurate estimation of time. The resulting time distribution is obtained from complex aggregation of time distributions of all project activities and can not be verified until certain time in the future. Therefore, any mathematically precise derivations of the resulting distribution are not very vital. Instead, a good guess of the form of the distribution seems more appropriate.

In reality, DM does not need a good approximation of time DF, but a good estimation of time bounds (intervals) for activity start and end times. A good example is critical path method (CPM) that is considered useful today and referred to in textbooks. Although deterministic, it shows the information that a project manager needs and a schedule can be build on it. The same is true for different possible project events like milestones. Because the form of the resulting distribution can be diverse (skewed, non-continuous, discrete), bounds that reflect probability density function (PDF) concentration can be of more value for the DM. A bounding technique that returns quantiles of DF as bounds with certain reliability level can help the DM to manage project in the circumstances of uncertainty. In particular, it can be simple and useful in the pre-project estimations and in the very beginning of a project when lack of empirical data (related to the current project) is an issue. Additionally, a good bounding method should be simpler than derivation of a precise DF or application of a modelling technique.

Analytical bounding techniques have long history [6–11]. There are bounds for PDF and for expected value of the project time distribution. Classical PERT also produces a lower bound of expected value of project completion time. Moreover, classical PERT implies beta distributions to express uncertain time estimations. There is no practically proven method today that can easily operationally obtain time estimations with normal, exponential or beta time distribution. On the opposite, simpler distributions like uniform and triangular are possible to obtain from experts and verify the estimations (e.g. [12]). Analytical bounding is still appealing for its completeness. One of the goals of deterministic CPM method is determination of time bounds of earliest and latest start and end times for each activity in SAN. As DF assumptions are predefined and SAN is given, it should allow computational complexity of $O(n)$ to compute (or recompute) n activity times like those of CPM without modelling for the stochastic PERT problem.

Consideration of uniform or triangular distributions instead of beta distribution is new in this context since they almost have not been considered for PERT problems in the last 30 years. These DFs do not have many useful mathematical properties that simplify aggregation in PERT analysis. However, it is easier to obtain their parameters in practice [12,13]. Johnson [13] has shown that simpler and intuitively obvious triangular distribution can be very close to beta DF and proposed a procedure for its parameter estimation.

In order to set up a basis for classical PERT improvement, we would like to address one piece of the aggregation task in this paper. This is aggregation of a number of serial activity durations for known identical independent distributions (iid.) of activity times. We suggest an analytical bounds for random time aggregation in order to solve this problem *in general* for different possible activity time distributions. This technique can be applied to *consecutive tasks* or to *paths* for their comparison (paths need to be enumerated first). We believe, that it is possible to extend this technique of time analysis to full project graph, but this needs consideration of conditional DF behavior during collapsing of parallel activities or paths. We leave this task for the future.

Our bounding approach presumes application of CFE [14] using known moment generating function (MGF) of activity DFs. This promises an approximation of time quantiles of the real convoluted DF of the last activity in the sequence. In order to verify the quality of our bounds, we consider the case of uniformly distributed activity times. Fortunately, there is a closed form PDF expression for the sum of random variables for this case. Thus, we can resolve any time quantile with PDF. However, we are searching for a better bounding technique *in general*. Therefore, this particular case is convenient for verification of the quality of our bounds because this DF type expresses the largest uncertainty. Thus, we verify the quality of our CFE bounds (quantiles of the sum) as an absolute error in comparison with known analytical solution for the quantiles based on known PDF of the sum of uniform distributions (UD). The CFE technique should work with any DF types, including discrete, mixed or non identical DFs. In case of convolution of other DFs, verification of the bounding error in general can be done with simulation techniques.

Using normal distribution and CLT is still popular and original PERT employs it. In fact, the kernel of the original PERT is nothing else as aggregation of Gaussian random time variables along one critical path (CP). Therefore, we consider it useful to compare CFE bounds and quantiles for a normal DF as in the classical PERT analysis and for another perspective distribution, namely uniform distribution. Nevertheless, we should repeat again that serial sub-paths may not be long enough in order to approximate their duration with CLT.

The paper is organized as follows. In Sect. 2 we define the problem and give necessary theoretical information required for CFE understanding and bounds derivation. In Sect. 3 we provide expressions for determination of necessary DF parameters for CFE application, especially for a sum of iid. uniformly distributed time variables. Bounds are computed and compared to the classical PERT in an example problem in Sect. 4. Conclusion summarizes our findings.

2 Theoretical Background

Problem Definition

Let $\mathbf{A} = (A_1, A_2, \dots, A_n)$ be a vector of random time durations of n project activities $t_1, t_2, \dots, t_n$ (activities on arcs) with defined precedence relations $t_i \prec t_j$, $i \in \overline{1, n-1}$, $j \in \overline{i+1, n}$ from the start node (event) e_0 to the finish node e_n. The activities are performed sequentially. These sequence of activities $\mathbf{A}$ is a subset of all activities of the project and they constitute one possible path or a part of it. We consider the case of UD activity durations $A_i \sim U(a_i, b_i)$ in this paper. The duration of their execution time is the completion time of the last activity t_n before the end event e_n. Naturally, this time is a new random variable $Z = \Sigma_{i=1}^{n} A_i$.

We are interested in concentration of PDF of Z. We introduce the reliability threshold $\alpha \in [0.5, 1]$ for the bounds derivation. The lower bound (LB) and upper bound (UB) of project time are such that the real time can be below (above) the bound with respective probability $P_{LB} = (1 - \alpha)/2 = \alpha'$ and $P_{UB} = 1 - \alpha'$. Thus, the probability that the PDF of the value Z gets into the interval [LB, UB] is α. These bounds are related to one of the most important project management objectives, viz. the LB (UB) is bound of the earliest (latest) start or end times of any activity. The LB and UB of the start time of the specific activity k is a random time variable $\sum_{i=1}^{k-1} A_i$ at the moment just before the activity k begins. The LB and UB of the end time of the specific activity k is a random time variable $\sum_{i=1}^{k} A_i$ at the moment when the activity k has ended.

Moment-Generating Function

For $\forall w \in \mathbb{R}$, MGF of a random variable X is defined as [15]:

$$M_X(w) = E(e^{wX}) = \int_{-\infty}^{\infty} e^{wx} f_X(x) \, dx, \tag{1}$$

Let $Y = bX + a$ be a new random variable for a random variable X and $a, b \in \mathbb{R}$, then the MGF for Y is related to the MGF of X by $M_Y(w) = e^{aw} M_X(bw)$. For our case of an n-dimensional random vector $\mathbf{A}$ with independent components

A_i, n-dimensional row vector $a, \mathbf{b} \in \mathbb{R}$, the random variable $Y = a + \mathbf{b}X$ has the MGF: $M_Y(w) = e^{aw} M_{A_1}(b_1 w) M_{A_2}(b_2 w) \dots M_{A_n}(b_n w)$.

MGF produces k-th moments $\mu'_k = E(X^k)$ of the convolution of n random variables as the value of the k-th derivative at its parameter point $w = 0$.

Cornish-Fisher Expansion

The CFE is a tool for random variables quantile approximation using only its first few cumulants. According to Stuart and Ord [14], the cumulants of the order r of a random variable X are values κ_r, such that $\forall t$

$$exp\left(\sum_{r=1}^{\infty} \frac{\kappa_r t^r}{r!} \right) = \sum_{r=1}^{\infty} \frac{E(X^r) t^r}{r!}. \tag{2}$$

Cumulants of X are connected to moments of X. Cumulant-generating function is $K(t) = \ln(M_X(w))$. Like MGF, a specific cumulant κ_r is obtained from r-order differential of $K(t)$ at point zero: $\kappa_r = K^{(r)}(0)$.

Use of cumulants gives an advantage in the context of our problem. A cumulant of a sum of n independent random variables is the sum of their respective cumulants, e.g. for independent X and Y, $K_{X+Y}(t) = K_X(t) + K_Y(t)$ and this is true for all orders r of cumulants of the sum $\kappa_r(X + Y) = \kappa_r(X) + \kappa_r(Y)$.

Cumulants κ_r of a random variable X can be expressed in terms of its mean value μ and its central moments $\mu_r = E[(X - \mu)^r]$. Alternatively, the same cumulants κ_r can be expressed in terms of only raw (noncentral) moments $\mu'_r = E[X^r]$. Both the cases are summarized in Table 1 [14].

The CFE tries to approximate the quantile q of a target DF taking into consideration higher moments (skewness and kurtosis) of that DF to adjust for its non-normality. Thus, for a normally distributed random variable X with $\mu = 0$ and $\sigma = 0$, Cornish and Fisher [16] derived an expansion that enables approximation of q-quantile $\Phi_X^{-1}(q)$ using the five cumulants of X and quantile function of Gaussian distribution $\Phi_Z^{-1}(q)$, $Z \sim \mathcal{N}(0,1)$. There are several versions of the expansion that use different number of cumulants. The formula that uses five cumulants is as follows (all terms are required) [15]:

$$x^* = \Phi_X^{-1}(q) = \Phi_Z^{-1}(q) + \frac{(\Phi_Z^{-1}(q))^2 - 1}{6} \kappa_3 + \frac{(\Phi_Z^{-1}(q))^3 - 3\Phi_Z^{-1}(q)}{24} \kappa_4$$
$$- \frac{2(\Phi_Z^{-1}(q))^3 - 5\Phi_Z^{-1}(q)}{36} \kappa_3^2 + \frac{(\Phi_Z^{-1}(q))^4 - 6(\Phi_Z^{-1}(q))^2 + 3}{120} \kappa_5 \tag{3}$$
$$- \frac{(\Phi_Z^{-1}(q))^4 - 5(\Phi_Z^{-1}(q))^2 + 2}{24} \kappa_3 \kappa_4 + \frac{12(\Phi_Z^{-1}(q))^4 - 53(\Phi_Z^{-1}(q))^2 + 17}{324} \kappa_3^3.$$

Table 1. Computation of cumulants κ_r from moments of random variable X.

Using central moments	Using raw moments
$\kappa_1 = \mu$	$\kappa_1 = \mu'_1$
$\kappa_2 = \mu_2$	$\kappa_2 = \mu'_2 - \mu'^2_1$
$\kappa_3 = \mu_3$	$\kappa_3 = \mu'_3 - 3\mu'_2\mu'_1 + 2\mu'^3_1$
$\kappa_4 = \mu_4 - 3\mu_2^2$	$\kappa_4 = \mu'_4 - 4\mu'_3\mu'_1 - 3\mu'^2_2 + 12\mu'_2\mu'^2_1 - 6\mu'^4_1$
$\kappa_5 = \mu_5 - 10\mu_3\mu_2$	$\kappa_5 = \mu'_5 - 5\mu'_4\mu'_1 - 10\mu'_3\mu'_2 + 20\mu'_3\mu'^2_1 + 30\mu'^2_2\mu'_1 - 60\mu'_2\mu'^3_1 + 24\mu'^5_1$

3   CFE Application to Bounds of n Activity Distributions

Using concepts of CFE, MGF and basics of probability theory, we derive the simple analytical approximate bounds for random activity time durations. We can use CFE to approximate quantiles of $Z = \sum_{i=1}^{n} A_i$ with means μ_i and standard deviations σ_i. First, we normalize A_i as required by CFE: $A'_i = (A_i - \mu_i)/\sigma_i$. Now $A'_i \sim \mathcal{N}(0,1)$ and central moments of A'_i are obtained from the central moments of A_i with the expression $\mu'_r = \mu_r/\sigma^r$ [15]. Because A_i and consequently A'_i are independent random variables, we compute individual cumulants of A'_i and add the respective cumulants as it was explained in Sect. 2 to get cumulants of $Z' = \sum_{i=1}^{n} A'_i$. Then, we resolve the required quantile q approximation z' of Z' applying the CFE expression (3). The approximated value of the original q-quantile z^* of Z is obtained through de-normalization: $z^* = z'\sigma + \mu$, where $\sigma = \sqrt{\sum_{i=1}^{n} \sigma_i^2}$ and $\mu = \sum_{i=1}^{n} \mu_i$.

In order to generalize the approach to moment derivation for other distributions in the prospective work, we will consider the ways of raw and central moment derivation in more details below. The central moments of A_i are required for CFE application. However, we can express central moments $\mu_r = E[(X - \mu)^r]$ through non-central moments $\mu'_k = E(X^k)$. Denoting powers k of the mean value μ^k, the required formulas for the central moments are shown in Table 2.

In their turn, raw moments can be obtained from known MGF taking $\lim_{t \to 0}$. However, this is hard for UD. Alternatively, raw moments can be determined for a uniform distribution via straightforward integration of $\mu'_n = \int x^n f(x) dx$ with PDF in the terms of Heaviside step function $f(x) = \frac{H(x-a) - H(x-b)}{b-a}$ [17]:

$$\mu'_n = \int_{-\infty}^{\infty} (H(x - a) - H(x - b))/(b - a)x^n dx = \frac{b^{n+1} - a^{n+1}}{(n + 1)(b - a)}, \qquad (4)$$

that enables to get the expressions of raw moments easier (see Table 2).

Table 2. Computation of raw and central moments of random variable X.

Raw moments	Central moments
$\mu'_1 = \frac{1}{2}(a + b)$	$\mu_1 = 0$
$\mu'_2 = \frac{1}{3}(a^2 + ab + b^2)$	$\mu_2 = E[(X - \mu)^2] = \mu'_2 - \mu^2$
$\mu'_3 = \frac{1}{4}(a^3 + a^2b + ab^2 + b^3)$	$\mu_3 = E[(X - \mu)^3] = \mu'_3 + 2\mu^3 - 3\mu\mu'_2$
$\mu'_4 = \frac{1}{5}(a^4 + a^3b + a^2b^2 + ab^3 + b^4)$	$\mu_4 = E[(X - \mu)^4] = \mu'_4 - 4\mu\mu'_3 + 6\mu^2\mu'_2 - 3\mu^4$
$\mu'_5 = \frac{1}{6}(a^5 + a^4b + a^3b^2 + a^2b^3 + ab^4 + b^5)$	$\mu_5 = E[(X - \mu)^5] = \mu'_5 + 10\mu^2\mu'_3 - 10\mu^3\mu'_2 - 5\mu\mu'_4 + 4\mu^5$

The respective central moments can be determined in the same way for UD via integration of $\mu_n = \int (x - \mu)^n f(x)dx$ (see $\mu = \mu'_1$ in Table 2) with PDF in the terms of Heaviside step function $f(x) = \frac{\mathrm{H}(x-a)-\mathrm{H}(x-b)}{b-a}$ [17]. This approach turns out $\mu_n = \frac{(a-b)^n - (b-a)^n}{2^{n+1}(n+1)}$ and gives the required central moments for the UD case:

$$\mu_1 = \mu_3 = \mu_5 = 0; \ \mu_2 = \frac{1}{12}(b-a)^2; \ \mu_4 = \frac{1}{80}(b-a)^4. \tag{5}$$

4   Illustrative Example

We consider a sequential set of independent tasks with identical UD DFs and obtain approximations of the end time bounds with quantiles for probabilities from $q = 0.1$ to $q = 0.9$ with step 0.1 by means of CFE with five cumulants (3). Results of the classical PERT analysis are also computed. We evaluate the maximum error of CFE and PERT quantile approximation with available expression for PDF $f_Z(z)$ of the sum of n UD. According to the original expression formula for $f_Z(z)$, the lower bound of DFs should strictly equal to zero $B_i \sim U(0, c_i)$ [18]:

$$f_n(z) = \frac{1}{(n-1)! \prod_{k=1}^{n} c_k} \left(z^{n-1} + \sum_{k=1}^{n} (-1)^k \sum_{J_k} \left[\left(z - \sum_{l=1}^{k} c_{jl} \right)_+ \right]^{n-1} \right), \tag{6}$$

where $J_k = \{(j_1, \ldots, j_k); 1 \le j_1 < j_2 < \ldots < j_k \le n\}$; $0 \le z \le \sum_{i=1}^{n} c_i$, $n \in \mathbf{N}$, $z \in \mathbf{R}$ and $x_+ = max(0, x) \, \forall x \in \mathbf{R}$.

We obtain $B_i \sim U(0, c_i)$ after introduction of new variables $c_i = b_i - a_i$: $B_i = A_i - a_i$; $i = 1, 2, \ldots, n$. This is a *shift* of DFs by constants a_i. It is possible to process the random parts B_i with known PDFs and then apply correction by adding $\sum_{i=1}^{n} a_i$.

By definition, a value z^* such that cumulative distribution function (CDF) $F(z^*) = f(Z \le z^*) = q$ is called a quantile of order q, $q \in (0, 1)$. Quantiles for probability q can be evaluated by solving the equality with known PDF $f(z)$ or the respective CDF $F(z)$: $q = F(z^*) = \int_l^u f(z)dz$, where in our case $l = 0$ is the lower bound and $u = z^*$ is the sought upper bound for B_i (q is specified).

We consider two sub problems. One is aggregation of two, five and ten identical DFs. The other is addition of random time variable $B \sim U(1, 3)$ $i = 2, 3, 4$ and several unequal time DFs $\sum_{j=1}^{i-1} A_1 \sim U(1, c_j)$, $c_j = 2, 4, 6$. We consider that very long task sequences or paths without branches are very unlikely in real projects. Resulting quantiles as bounds for UD are shown in Table 3. We compute CFE approximation z^*_{CFE} of quantiles z^* for given probabilities $q = 0.1, \ldots, 0.9$. For comparison, results of classical PERT (PERT z^*) are given as well. Absolute errors of Z^* approximation can be seen by comparing the quantiles obtained with known PDF (6) in "Real z^*" rows and the respective values z^*_{CFE} or PERT z^*.

We also verify the quality of approximations by substitution of the approximated quantile z^* into the integral of the known PDF (6) and observing how different the probability $F_Z(z^*_{CFE})$ from the initial q value is. Absolute errors (abs.error q) of quantiles of orders q between $F_Z(z^*_{CFE})$ and q are also given in

Table 3. Quality of CFE q-quantile evaluation for the number of tasks i.

i	Method	z^* for q for the sum of i of identical DFs $A_i \sim U(1,3)$								
		0.1	0.2	0.3	0.4	0.5	0.6	0.7	0.8	0.9
2	Real z^*	2.894	3.265	3.549	3.789	4.0	4.211	4.451	4.735	5.106
	z^*_{CFE}	2.812	3.155	3.455	3.732	4.0	4.268	4.545	4.845	5.188
	$F_Z(z^*_{CFE})$	0.082	0.167	0.265	0.375	0.5	0.625	0.735	0.833	0.918
	abs.error q	−0.018	−0.033	−0.035	−0.025	0.0	0.025	0.035	0.033	0.018
	PERT z^*	3.715	3.813	3.883	3.944	4.0	4.056	4.117	4.187	4.285
	$F_Z(\mathrm{PERT}\ z^*)$	0.368	0.411	0.443	0.472	0.5	0.528	0.557	0.589	0.632
	abs.error q	0.268	0.211	0.143	0.072	0.0	−0.072	−0.143	−0.211	−0.268
5	Real z^*	8.321	8.887	9.3034	9.663	10.0	10.337	10.696	11.113	12.679
	z^*_{CFE}	7.784	8.291	8.862	9.433	10.0	10.567	11.138	11.709	12.216
	$F_Z(z^*_{CFE})$	0.082	0.167	0.265	0.375	0.5	0.625	0.735	0.833	0.918
	abs.error q	−0.018	−0.033	−0.035	−0.025	0.0	0.025	0.035	0.033	0.018
	PERT z^*	9.288	9.532	9.709	9.859	10.0	10.141	10.291	10.468	10.712
	$F_Z(\mathrm{PERT}\ z^*)$	0.296	0.362	0.413	0.458	0.5	0.542	0.587	0.638	0.704
	abs.error q	0.196	0.162	0.113	0.058	0.0	−0.058	−0.113	−0.162	−0.196
10	Real z^*	17.644	18.445	19.029	19.530	20	20.469	20.971	21.555	22.356
	z^*_{CFE}	16.072	16.703	17.738	18.859	20.0	21.142	22.262	23.297	23.928
	$F_Z(z^*_{CFE})$	0.015	0.035	0.109	0.269	0.5	0.731	0.891	0.965	0.985
	abs.error q	−0.085	−0.165	−0.191	−0.131	0.0	0.131	0.191	0.165	0.085
	PERT z^*	18.576	19.065	19.417	19.719	20.0	20.282	20.583	20.935	21.424
	$F_Z(\mathrm{PERT}\ z^*)$	0.221	0.307	0.377	0.440	0.5	0.560	0.623	0.693	0.779
	abs.error q	0.121	0.107	0.077	0.040	0.0	−0.040	−0.077	−0.107	−0.121
i	Method	z^* for q for $\sum_{j=1}^{i-1} A_j \sim U(1,c_j)$ **and** $B \sim U(1,3)$								
		0.1	0.2	0.3	0.4	0.5	0.6	0.7	0.8	0.9
2	Real z^*	2.632	2.894	3.1	3.3	3.5	3.7	3.9	4.106	4.368
	z^*_{CFE}	2.560	2.832	3.069	3.288	3.5	3.712	3.931	4.168	4.440
	$F_Z(z^*_{CFE})$	0.079	0.173	0.285	0.394	0.5	0.606	0.715	0.827	0.921
	abs.error q	−0.022	−0.027	−0.015	−0.006	0.0	0.006	0.015	0.027	0.021
	PERT z^*	3.322	3.383	3.427	3.465	3.5	3.535	3.573	3.617	3.678
	$F_Z(\mathrm{PERT}\ z^*)$	0.411	0.442	0.464	0.482	0.5	0.518	0.536	0.558	0.589
	abs.error q	0.311	0.242	0.164	0.082	0.0	−0.082	−0.164	−0.242	−0.311
3	Real z^*	4.557	5.022	5.380	5.698	6.0	6.302	6.620	6.978	7.443
	z^*_{CFE}	4.334	4.778	5.202	5.606	6.0	6.394	6.798	7.222	7.666
	$F_Z(z^*_{CFE})$	0.065	0.143	0.248	0.370	0.5	0.630	0.752	0.857	0.935
	abs.error q	−0.035	−0.057	−0.052	−0.030	0.0	0.030	0.052	0.057	0.035
	PERT z^*	5.502	5.673	5.796	5.901	6.0	6.099	6.204	6.328	6.498
	$F_Z(\mathrm{PERT}\ z^*)$	0.337	0.392	0.432	0.467	0.5	0.533	0.568	0.608	0.663
	abs.error q	0.237	0.192	0.132	0.067	0.0	−0.067	−0.132	−0.192	−0.237
4	Real z^*	7.107	7.868	8.462	8.993	9.5	10.007	10.538	11.132	11.893
	z^*_{CFE}	6.562	7.287	8.039	8.775	9.5	10.225	10.961	11.713	12.438
	$F_Z(z^*_{CFE})$	0.051	0.120	0.227	0.358	0.5	0.642	0.773	0.880	0.949
	abs.error q	−0.049	−0.080	−0.073	−0.042	0.0	0.042	0.073	0.080	0.049
	PERT z^*	8.112	8.588	8.932	9.226	9.5	9.774	10.068	10.412	10.888
	$F_Z(\mathrm{PERT}\ z^*)$	0.239	0.323	0.388	0.446	0.5	0.554	0.612	0.677	0.761
	abs.error q	0.139	0.123	0.088	0.046	0.0	−0.046	−0.088	−0.123	−0.139

the Table 3. The same verification is performed for classical PERT approximations $F_Z(\text{PERT } z^*)$ and absolute error is given.

It is obvious that classical PERT that uses CLT approximation is *significantly* worse than CFE approximation unless many identical iid. DFs are considered (and this makes the pattern closer to CLT applicability assumptions). PERT's probability estimation for q quantiles is always worse than CFE for not very equal DFs (and mostly for equal ones) for the most important quantiles ($q = 0.1, 0.2$ for LB and $q = 0.8, 0.9$ for UB) and this difference is impressive, i.e. from 1.5 to 10 times and even more. The difference in time value z^* approximation from the real one may not seem so dramatic, however, due to the scale of time units, the absolute difference can be substantial for the DM. Additionally, CFE underestimates the LB and overestimates the UB, i.e. produces real bounds, whereas classical PERT does vice versa, i.e. underestimates the quantile values from above and below that is undesirable.

5   Conclusion

In this study, we attempted at improving only one problem of PERT analysis, namely obtaining time bounds on a sequential set of tasks. For the general case, we can determine upper and lower bounds using bounding techniques. This can be imprecise in case of CLT approximation in classical PERT or if bounding methods do not take into account specific properties of distributions. If time distributions are known, we can determine upper and lower bounds using CFE.

Using CFE, we derived bounds for iid. sum of uniform DFs of activity times and verified the absolute error with exact analytical solution of the quantile problem. The DF type is not used frequently, however it has an advantage of easily obtainable parameter estimation in practical application. We also compared our result with the results of classical PERT analysis. In fact, original PERT employs CLT approximation and thus uses quantiles of Gaussian distribution. Our experiments show that CFE approximation outperforms classical PERT in evaluation of time of sequential tasks with known DFs. This is absolutely important for bounds with high confidence (e.g. $\alpha \geq 0.8$). It seems that CFE application instead of CLT approximation can improve evaluation of CP in the classical PERT.

To the best of our knowledge, our bounding technique for UD based on CFE is pioneering in the area of PERT analysis. CPM like time bounds for the case of several consecutive activities with uniform DFs enable evaluation of duration of sub-critical paths in a SAN. Moreover, CFE is a universal tool that can be applied to the task with other DF types. The computational complexity is $O(n)$ for a known SAN structure without simulation modelling.

This is the first step in the development of an improved bounding technique for a project SAN. Based on the current results for serial activities, an extension of the bounding technique should be developed for a SAN with converging subpaths. We need to examine conceptual meaning of converging activities into an event before the next common activity after them. Mathematically, this is consideration of a maximum operator for two or more random time variables and choosing the best promising method of DF evaluation for this operator. Another prospective task is evaluation of the bounding approach with triangular time distributions that are also perspective in operational parameter estimation and have been used for project time analysis (e.g. [12]).

References

1. Malcolm, D.G., et al.: Application of a technique for research and development program evaluation. Oper. Res. **7** (1959). https://doi.org/10.1287/opre.7.5.646
2. Roy, D., Roy, R.: Distribution of the activity time in network analysis: a critical revisit with a gamma alternative. Commun. Stat. - Simul. Comput. **42**(6), 1288–1297 (2013). https://doi.org/10.1080/03610918.2012.664231
3. Spanos, A.: Probability Theory and Statistical Inference: Econometric Modeling with Observational Data. Cambridge University Press, Cambridge (1999)
4. Goman, M.: Practical verification of CLT assumption for PERT application. In: Proceedings of the 8th International Scientific Conference on Project Management in the Baltic Countries Project Management Development–Practice and Perspectives, pp. 114–127. University of Latvia, Riga (2019). https://www.balticpmconference.eu/sites/default/files/image-uploads/Proceeding_book_29.04.2019.pdf. Accessed 24 Aug 2019
5. Udoumoh, E.F., Ebong, D.W.: A review of activity time distributions in risk analysis. Am. J. Oper. Res. **07**(06), 356–371 (2017). https://doi.org/10.4236/ajor.2017.76027
6. Devroye, L.P.: Inequalities for the completion times of stochastic PERT networks. Math. Oper. Res. **4**(4), 441–447 (1979). https://doi.org/10.1287/moor.4.4.441
7. Dodin, B.: Bounding the project completion time distribution in PERT networks. Oper. Res. **33**(4), 862–881 (1985). https://doi.org/10.1287/opre.33.4.862
8. Elmaghraby, S.E.: The estimation of some network parameters in the pert model of activity networks: review and critique. In: Advances in Project Scheduling, pp. 371–432. Elsevier (1989). https://doi.org/10.1016/B978-0-444-87358-3.50021-3
9. Kamburowski, J.: An upper bound on the expected completion time of PERT networks. Eur. J. Oper. Res. **21**(2), 206–212 (1985). https://doi.org/10.1016/0377-2217(85)90032-3
10. Kleindorfer, G.B.: Bounding distributions for a stochastic acyclic network. Oper. Res. **19**(7), 1586–1601 (1971). https://doi.org/10.1287/opre.19.7.1586
11. Shogan, A.W.: Bounding distributions for a stochastic pert network. Networks **7**(4), 359–381 (1977). https://doi.org/10.1002/net.3230070407
12. Grey, S.: Practical Risk Assessment for Project Management. Wiley, New York (1995)
13. Johnson, D.: The triangular distribution as a proxy for the beta distribution in risk analysis. J. R. Stat. Soc.: Ser. D (Stat.) **46**(3), 387–398 (1997). https://doi.org/10.1111/1467-9884.00091
14. Stuart, A., Ord, J.K.: Kendall's Advanced Theory of Statistics, Volume 1: Distribution Theory. Arnold, London (1994)
15. Holton, G.A.: Value-at-Risk: Theory and Practice, 2nd edn. (2014). https://www.value-at-risk.net
16. Cornish, E.A., Fisher, R.A.: Moments and cumulants in the specification of distributions. Rev. Int. Stat. Inst. **5**, 307–320 (1937)

17. Weisstein, E.W.: Uniform Distribution. From MathWorld-A Wolfram Web Resource. http://mathworld.wolfram.com/UniformDistribution.html. Accessed 24 Aug 2019
18. Sadooghi-Alvandi, S.M., et al.: On the distribution of the sum of independent uniform random variables. Stat. Pap. **50**(1), 171–175 (2007). https://doi.org/10.1007/s00362-007-0049-4

Impact of Personality Traits (BFI-2-XS) on Use of Shared Online Calendars

Petr Doucek[1] (iD), Antonin Pavlicek[1] (iD), and Frantisek Sudzina[1,2](✉) (iD)

[1] University of Economics, Nám. W. Churchilla 4,
13067 Prague, Czech Republic
[2] Aalborg University, A. C. Meyers Vænge 15, 2450 Copenhagen, Denmark
sudzina@business.aau.dk

Abstract. People use calendars for a long time but stand-alone electronic calendars came along only with personal computers, while shared online calendars are here only for less than two decades. The paper investigates impact of personality (following the Big Five Inventory framework) on use of shared online calendars. Data were gathered in the Czech Republic. The sample consisted of university students. Age, gender, and type of student job were used as control variables. With regards to the results, gender, openness to (cognitive) experience, and type of student job influence the adoption. It is male, more open to experience, and working student who use shared online calendars more.

Keywords: Personality traits · Calendar · Adoption

1 Introduction

Shared online calendars belong to group support software [1]. History of shared online calendars is described in a greater detail in [2]. They ought to enable better collaboration through the possibility of collective use of individual calendars between multiple users [3]. Shared online calendars are useful for scheduling shifts, communicating opening/working hours, their changes, staff vacation and sick days [4]. The issue is that scheduling per se "is often iterative and requires a great amount of coordination" [5]. Calendars are also shared in order to coordinate appointments [6].

When shared with others, calendars provide information about the owner of the calendar. Users tend to have more than one shared calendar in order to manage who has access to what information [6]. Users that used a combination of desktop and mobile calendars perceived much higher effectiveness and satisfaction compared to ones who used only one software tool or a paper-based calendar [7].

On some occasions, it is a bottom-up process - when an organization does not offer it, employees adopt a tool that suits them. [8] describe a case of adoption of a shared online calendar by a mid-level manager in one of a supermarket store in Denmark. Though it was not appreciated by their IT department, most likely for security and governance reasons. It could be considered a case of Bring Your Own Device (BYOD). Although it was not the company's policy in this particular supermarket chain, many companies adopt BOYD in the effort to be more agile and up-to-date.

© IFIP International Federation for Information Processing 2019
Published by Springer Nature Switzerland AG 2019
P. Doucek et al. (Eds.): CONFENIS 2019, LNBIP 375, pp. 123–127, 2019.
https://doi.org/10.1007/978-3-030-37632-1_11

It appears that there exists no research linking use of shared online calendars to personality traits. In order to close the gap, this paper investigates impact of personality traits on use of shared online calendars, while controlling for age, gender, and job type.

2   Data and Methodology

Data were collected using an on-line questionnaire in from December 2017 to March 2018. Surveyed were university students from the Czech Republic. The sample consisted of 478 respondents (272 male, 206 female; 20.5 years old on average), of whom 189 respondents indicated that they use shared online calendars. As for their experience from practice, 12 have a full time within the field of study, 16 have a full time outside the field of study, 164 have a part-time job, 176 have a temporary job (brigade), and 106 only study.

Personalities were evaluated according to John and Soto's Big Five Inventory-2 [9] using a validated Czech translation by Hřebíčková et al. [10]. For this conference paper, only BFI-2-XS [11], i.e. a 15-item version of the instrument was used. The instrument uses a 1-5 Likert scale where 1 means strongly disagree and 5 means strongly agree.

The question for the explanatory variable was "Do you use the following services? Shared online calendars (like Google Calendar)" Possible answers were:

- "No" (coded as 0),
- "Yes, sometimes" (coded as 1),
- "Yes, often" (coded as 2).

Also additional questions were included in the questionnaire but they have not been analyzed in this paper.

Ordinal logistic regression will be used to test influence of age, gender, job type and five personality traits on use of shared online calendars. A multivariate approach will be used. Calculations will be done in SPSS.

3   Results

The research question is if any/which of five personality traits influence use of shared online calendars, while controlling for age, gender, and job type. Ordinal logistic regression estimates for the full model are in Table 1. The model per se is significant, p-value $< .001$, Cox and Snell pseudo-R^2 is .126, Nagelkerke pseudo-R^2 is .148, and McFadden pseudo-R^2 is .071.

Table 1. Full model - ordinal regression.

	Estimate	Std. error	Wald	df	Sig.
[calendar = .00]	3.079	1.303	5.586	1	.018
[calendar = 1.00]	4.111	1.309	9.860	1	.002
Extraversion	.153	.123	1.545	1	.214
Agreeableness	−.262	.140	3.484	1	.062
Conscientiousness	−.056	.143	.155	1	.693
Neuroticism	.043	.114	.140	1	.709
Openness to experience	.257	.127	4.125	1	.042
Age	.053	.047	1.254	1	.263
Gender = male	.701	.208	11.333	1	.001
Gender = female	0a	.	.	0	.
Job type = full time within the field of study	1.892	.612	9.568	1	.002
Job type = full time outside the field of study	.604	.556	1.180	1	.277
Job type = part-time job	1.351	.294	21.102	1	.000
Job type = temporary job	.594	.290	4.211	1	.040
Job type = only study	0a	.	.	0	.

Legend: a. This parameter is set to zero because it is redundant.

Students who are (less agreeable,) more open to experience, men, and working are more likely to use shared online calendars. Ordinal logistic regression estimates for the streamlined model are in Table 2. The model per se is significant, p-value < .001, Cox and Snell pseudo-R^2 is .123, Nagelkerke pseudo-R^2 is .144, and McFadden pseudo-R^2 is .069.

Table 2. Streamlined model - ordinal regression.

	Estimate	Std. error	Wald	df	Sig.
[calendar = .00]	1.851	.655	7.997	1	.005
[calendar = 1.00]	2.872	.662	18.788	1	.000
Agreeableness	−.252	.136	3.447	1	.063
Openness to experience	.290	.125	5.429	1	.020
Gender = male	.730	.199	13.410	1	.000
Gender = female	0a	.	.	0	.
Job type = full time within the field of study	2.040	.601	11.537	1	.001
Job type = full time outside the field of study	.768	.541	2.015	1	.156
Job type = part-time job	1.507	.280	28.920	1	.000
Job type = temporary job	.694	.285	5.941	1	.015
Job type = only study	0a	.	.	0	.

Legend: a. This parameter is set to zero because it is redundant.

The estimates stay almost the same if agreeableness is removed from the model. It is not clear whether agreeableness should be included in the model as it is not clear why more agreeable respondents would use shared calendars less. On the other hand, a short scale was used, i.e. it may be less precise, so p-value of .063 should not automatically mean that agreeableness does not influence use of shared online calendars; in case the trait is measured using a longer scale, the p-value may be lower.

It also cannot be completely ruled out students who work time outside the field of study are using shared online calendars more often than students who only study because it is based only on a relatively small sample (16 respondents). If the standard deviation for the full-time job outside the field of study was like the ones for a part-time or a temporary job, the p-value would be below .05.

4 Conclusions

To sum up, respondents who are more open to experience, men, and working alongside studies are more likely to use shared online calendars. Since virtually all respondents were digital natives, it is not surprising that age was not found to be significant. So, in the future research, which will be aimed at the population of all employed people, age should be included (as a control variable) in spite of not being significant in this particular research.

More research will be needed, esp. with regards to agreeableness - whether it or any of its facets influences use of shared online calendars if it is measured using a longer scale. But more research will be needed also with regards to openness to experience as it is unclear whether people open experience use shared online calendars more because it is a new technology and they are more open to try it, or they are involved in more activities, so they actually have a higher need for coordination.

Acknowledgment. Paper was processed with contribution of grant IGS 27/2019 from the Faculty of Informatics and Statistics, University of Economics, Prague.

References

1. Palen, L., Grudin, J.: Discretionary adoption of group support software: lessons from calendar applications. In: Munkvold, B.E. (ed.) Implementing Collaboration Technologies in Industry. CSCW, pp. 159–180. Springer, London (2003). https://doi.org/10.1007/978-1-4471-0073-7_8
2. Lord, C.: Evolution of the electronic calendar: introducing social calendaring. http://citeseerx.ist.psu.edu/viewdoc/download?doi=10.1.1.510.2442&rep=rep1&type=pdf. Accessed 31 August 2019
3. van den Hooff, B.: Electronic coordination and collective action: use and effects of electronic calendaring and scheduling. Inf. Manag. **42**(1), 103–114 (2004)
4. Hughes, S.E.: Scheduling using a web-based calendar: how teamup enhances communication. Public Serv. Q. **14**(4), 362–372 (2018)
5. Lewejohann, L.: Fill my datebook: a software tool to generate and handle lists of events. Behav. Res. Methods **40**(2), 391–393 (2008)

6. Thayer, A., Bietz, M.J., Derthick, K., Lee. C.P.: I love you, let's share calendars: calendar sharing as relationship work. In: Proceedings of the ACM 2012 Conference on Computer Supported Cooperative Work, CSCW 2012, pp. 749–758. ACM, New York (2012)
7. Wu, D.: Identifying usability issues in personal calendar tools. In: Fong, S. (ed.) NDT 2011. CCIS, vol. 136, pp. 136–146. Springer, Heidelberg (2011). https://doi.org/10.1007/978-3-642-22185-9_13
8. Kerr, D., Talaei-Khoei, A., Ghapanchi, A.H.: A paradigm shift for bring your own device (BYOD). In: Twenty-Fourth Americas Conference on Information Systems, AIS, New Orleans (2018)
9. Soto, C.J., John, O.P.: The next Big Five Inventory (BFI-2): developing and assessing a hierarchical model with 15 facets to enhance bandwidth, fidelity, and predictive power. J. Pers. Soc. Psychol. **113**, 117–143 (2017)
10. Hrebicková, M., et al.: Big Five Inventory 2: Hierarchický model s 15 subškálami. Ceskoslovenska Psychologie (2019)
11. Soto, C., John, O.P.: Short and extra-short forms of the big five inventory-2: the BFI-2-S and BFI-2-XS. J. Res. Pers. **68**, 69–81 (2017)

Security and Privacy Issues

Preventing Additive Attacks to Relational Database Watermarking

Maikel Lázaro Pérez Gort[1(⊠)], Martina Olliaro[2,3],
Claudia Feregrino-Uribe[1], and Agostino Cortesi[2]

[1] National Institute of Astrophysics, Optics and Electronics, Puebla, Mexico
{mlazaro2002es, cferegrino}@inaoep.mx
[2] Ca' Foscari University, Venice, Italy
{martina.olliaro, cortesi}@unive.it
[3] Masaryk University, Brno, Czech Republic

Abstract. False ownership claims are carried on through additive and invertibility attacks and, as far as we know, current relational watermarking techniques are not always able to solve the ownership doubts raising from the latter attacks. In this paper, we focus on additive attacks. We extend a conventional image-based relational data watermarking scheme by creating a non-colluded backup of the data owner marks, the so-called secondary marks positions. The technique we propose is able to identify the data owner beyond any doubt.

Keywords: Additive attack · False ownership claim · Relational data · Robust watermarking

1 Introduction

Internet has made publicly available digital data on large scale, allowing users to fraudulently claim data ownership. In the 90 s, digital watermarking techniques were developed to protect ownership rights of multimedia assets (i.e., images, audio, video, and texts), where a mark is permanently and unalterably placed into the latter. To overcome watermarking and counterfeit data intellectual property, several attacks have been conceived, and efforts in developing effective digital copyright protection mechanisms have been carried out in response. Invisible watermarking techniques increase the likelihood of successful prosecution once a theft has occurred [4]. Robust watermarking schemes are able to survive against watermark (WM) removal attempts and data manipulations (both malicious and benign). Finally, non-invertible watermarking techniques tackle those attacks, which makes possible multiple data ownership claims [6].

At the beginning of the 2000s, watermarking techniques were extended to relational data. As well as multimedia data watermarking, relational data watermarking techniques too had to deal with several attacks attempting both to remove the WM and to carry out false ownership claims [9]. Attacks attempting to raise doubts about data ownership are called additive and invertibility attacks. According to [9], an additive attack is carried out when a malicious user adds his own WM to a watermarked relation and try to claim his ownership. On the other hand, an invertibility attack occurs when a

© IFIP International Federation for Information Processing 2019
Published by Springer Nature Switzerland AG 2019
P. Doucek et al. (Eds.): CONFENIS 2019, LNBIP 375, pp. 131–140, 2019.
https://doi.org/10.1007/978-3-030-37632-1_12

malicious user is able to find a fictitious WM which is in fact a random occurrence from a watermarked relation.

This paper is focused on additive attacks. On it, we first discuss the basics and limitations of previous relational data watermarking techniques dealing with false claims of ownership carried out through additive attacks. Then we extend the image-based relational watermarking scheme presented in [7] by creating a non-colluded backup of the data owner's marks, the so-called secondary marks positions. The latter allows us to restore the owner's WM to determine the rightful data owner in case of been applied additive attacks over the protected data. Finally, we provide experimental results validating the proposed technique.

The rest of this paper is organized as follows. Section 2 discusses preliminaries about watermarking techniques for relational data, particularly the schemes created to deal with additive attacks. Section 3 defines the approach proposed to prevent ownership claim invalidation by means of additive attacks. Section 4 shows experimental results validating our proposal. Section 5 concludes this work.

2 Preliminaries

In this section we present part of the notation we will use throughout the paper, we give an overview of the basics of related watermarking techniques, and we discuss previous approaches proposed to deal with additive attacks.

2.1 Notation

According to Agrawal and Kiernan [2], let R be the relation to be marked, with: tuples r_j such that $j \in [0, \eta - 1]$, primary key PK, attributes a_i such that $i \in [0, v - 1]$, and scheme $R(PK, a_0, \ldots, a_{v-1})$. $r_j.a_i$ denotes the ith attribute of the jth tuple. η and v are the number of tuples and the number of attributes in R respectively. ξ is the number of less significant bits (*lsb*) in the binary representation of an attribute value which can be marked. $\frac{1}{\gamma}$ is the Tuple Fraction (TF) which denotes the fraction of marked tuples, such that $\gamma \in [1, \eta]$. If the usability constraints are ignored, when $\gamma = 1$, all the tuples of the relation will be marked. ω is the number of marked tuples from the η tuples in R defined by the equation $\omega \approx \frac{\eta}{\gamma}$.

2.2 Background

The technique we propose in this paper is based on the image-based watermarking (IBW) approach for relational data presented in [7]. The latter mostly takes inspiration from two previous works: the one of Agrawal and Kiernan [2], and the one of Sardroudi and Ibrahim [13].

In 2002, Agrawal and Kiernan [2] defined the first relational data watermarking technique. Also called AHK algorithm, this approach embeds the marks in one of the ξ *lsb* of pseudo-randomly selected numeric attributes. In particular, once the attributes are determined, together with bit positions, and specific bit values, a meaningless bit pattern constituting the WM is embedded in R. The mark embedding locations depend on a secret key SK known only to the owner of the database. Also, the WM detection does not require either the access to the original data nor the WM, guaranteeing the technique's blindness. However, the AHK algorithm has been proven to be weakly resilient against subset attacks and data transformations. Moreover, the success of the detection phase may be penalized due to the meaningless of the watermarking information, and the data usability may be compromised as database constraints are ignored.

In [13], Sardroudi and Ibrahim defined a relational data watermarking scheme based on the AHK algorithm, that uses a binary image to generate the WM. The final reconstruction of the WM is done by performing a majority voting over each mark, which contributes to avoid the degradation of the WM that attacks based on data modification can cause. To make the scheme resilient against *subset reverse order attacks* [9], the pixels of the image used for WM generation, and the places to embed the marks in R, are chosen by using pseudo-random selection. Due to the pseudo-random nature of those processes, the embedding of the WM cannot be entirely achieved (even if all tuples of the relation are marked, which compromise data usability and make the WM perceptible, violating the imperceptibility requirement [5]).

Finally, as mentioned above, Gort et al., in [7], defined an IBW scheme close to the one presented by Sardroudi and Ibrahim, but able to overcome the limitations of the schemes presented in [13] and [2]. Indeed, Gort et al., increased the capacity of the WM (performing a controlled multi-attribute mark embedding, maintaining the quality of the data). Also, this scheme is proven to be robust against tuple deletion and addition attacks.

2.3   Main Approaches to Deal with Additive Attacks

To deal with additive attacks, proposed techniques are mainly focused on two aspects: (i) taking advantage of the overlapping regions of the multiple WMs embedded in the database relation, or (ii) involving a Trusted Third Party (TTP) in the watermarking processes. Both approaches are based on scenarios that are hard to follow and can be easily compromised in practice. Below, the basics and limitations related to the approaches are given.

Overlapping Regions of Embedding. When an additive attack is performed, we can fall into one of the three following scenarios: (i) the attacker's WM entirely overwrites the owner's WM, (ii) some marks of both owner and attacker's WM have been embedded in the same positions (causing the overlapping of embedding regions), or (iii) the owner's WM and the attacker's WM do not collide at all, i.e., they are not embedded in same positions.

In the case in which the WMs do not collide, all ownership claims will be valid, annulling the process reliability. On the other hand, suspicion may raise if the attacker's WM entirely overwrites the owner's [1, 11]. Indeed, it is not usual that not even a single bit of the owner's WM being found in the data. Moreover, marks of different WMs occupying the same position may have the same value. Thus, an entirely WM overwriting changing all mark values is highly unlikely. Finally, when overlapping regions are present, the ownership claim competition is won by the one who inserted the last WM (i.e., the attacker) [1].

Consider the probability for embedding the marks in the same bits (c.f. Eq. (1) [1]), where, as previously mentioned, ω is the number of bits already marked by the data owner, and γ_A, ν_A, and ξ_A are the parameters used by the attacker to perform the additive attack. If the latter embedding parameters vary (as is expected, considering that if the attacker already knows the value of the parameters used by the data owner would not need to perform an additive attack), a low probability for embedding the marks in the same bits is expected. The more the probability gets closer to zero, the more the ownership assignment process gets more dubious, being even worse if some of the marks colluding present the same values.

$$P\{\text{success}|\omega\} = \left(1 - \frac{1}{2\gamma_A\nu_A\xi_A}\right)^{\omega} \tag{1}$$

Precisely, let A be a digital asset being protected by means of watermarking. The region allowed for the WM embedding in A is given by the function $\mathcal{Z}(\cdot)$, which returns an array of positions (the so-called *primary positions*). The notations W_O and W_A are used to refer to the WM embedded by the data owner and by the attacker respectively. The size of $\mathcal{Z}(A)$, W_O, and W_A can be obtained by using the function $n(\cdot)$. Figure 1 represents the scenarios given above, where the number of overlapping marks between W_O and W_A is given by δ.

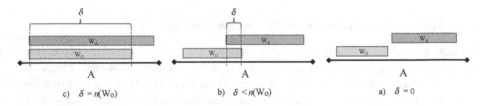

Fig. 1. Possible scenarios considering the overlapping between W_O and W_A.

Figure 1(a) is ruled by the probability of Eq. (1), which is expected to be low, or by the fact that $n(W_A) \approx n(\mathcal{Z}(A))$, which is unexpected if the attacker pretends to preserve the data usability. So, the complete overlapping of W_O by W_A, can be considered as a result of a successful brute force attack rather than by an additive attack. On the other hand, Fig. 1(b) presents the case when some marks of W_O and W_A overlap. This scenario is mostly characterized by $n(\mathcal{Z}(A)) < n(W_O) + n(W_A)$. Also, under the previous condition, the probability of overlapping increases if $n(W_O) \approx n(W_A)$. Figure 1(c) corresponds to the case in which $n(\mathcal{Z}(A)) \gg n(W_O) + n(W_A)$. The latter represents a critical situation since if both marks are embedded in A with no overlapping regions, there is no way to determine which one was embedded first. Such situation cannot be avoided if the attacker uses a low size WM, even though, for the case of relational data it is not expected the attacker using a low size of W_A, since this would compromise its detection over time because of the degradation caused by benign updates. On the other hand, the data owner can successfully evade this situation by increasing the size of W_O as much as the usability of A tolerates.

Trusted Third Party Involvement. Involving a TTP in the watermarking process means allowing a third person to assign the WM to be embedded, considering information from the data owner and adding other persons to the process (e.g., data buyers). Moreover, the TTP can be part of the generation of secret keys, among other important processes. Once the relation is watermarked, the TTP may also store copies of all the data involved [14].

Then, if another person wants to embed a WM on his/her data, comes to the TTP to perform the process. The TTP first checks if there is no other data owner already assigned to that data, and if it is not, proceeds to the WM embedding, secretly storing all data involved in the watermarking process once the task is concluded.

In this context, illegitimate owners may have no intention to present the data to the designated TTP for embedding their WM, or may claim the ownership of the data presenting their own WM to people unaware of the TTP existence. Moreover, involving a TTP is not always possible, can be quite expensive (it demands personal, time, technologies, and equipment) [11], and can lead to confidentiality concerns (e.g., in the case in which the TTP could have access to the data on its readable format). In the end, involving more people in the watermarking processes increases the probability of attacks.

2.4 Related Work

In 2003, Agrawal et al. [1] presented a deeper analysis of [2] in order to handle additive attacks in the AHK algorithm. They introduced Eq. (1) and showed how an attacker can manage to get a low number of overwritten bits with different mark values. Then, they considered both the idea of involving a TTP and of presenting the unwatermarked data, to solve false claims of ownership. Notice that the latter proposal can be easily compromised when the WM scheme can be inverted by creating a fake original data set and a fake WM [3].

In 2004, Li et al. [11] proposed to perform a WM embedding which aims to reach out into the maximum allowable distortion, thus reducing the possibility for the attacker to embed a second WM. This approach resulted to be vulnerable when $\xi_A \leq \xi$. Also, the attacker can always involve different parameters that allow his WM to be embedded without causing more distortion (e.g., by trying to preserve the attribute values distributions such as in [15]). On the other hand, Zhou et al. [17] presented an IBW technique where the WM to embed is generated from a binary image. This allows the generation of low aggressive WMs, and to embed a highly structural signal that can be restored if attacks modifying the data are performed. The resilience of this technique to additive attacks is based on the involvement of a TTP.

In 2009, Gupta and Pieprzyk [8] defined a reversible watermarking technique, which allows obtaining the original data once the WM is extracted. The resilience of this technique to additive attacks is based on the involvement of a TTP. Notice that, in this case, once the WM is extracted the data will remain vulnerable to false ownership claims and other malicious operations. In 2010, Manjula and Settipalli [12] presented a technique that bases its resilience to additive attacks on tracking the overlapping marks. As previously mentioned, the success of this proposal will depend on the parameters used for the embedding of both WMs. Finally, in 2011, Hamadou et al. [10] presented a fragile technique that also bases its resilience to additive attacks on the involvement of a TTP.

3   The Extended Embedding Approach

In order to deal with false ownership claims by means of additive attacks, we exploit the WM overlapping regions (c.f. Fig. 1(b)), and we define a non-colluded backup for the owner's marks by extending their embedding locations, determining the so-called secondary locations. In the case additive attacks are performed, the mark values stored in primary locations are corrected using the correspondent values recovered from secondary locations, making possible the identification of the WM.

3.1   Location Linking Structure

Figure 2 graphically shows the relation among the WM, the primary embedding locations, and the secondary ones. Each mark will be embedded multiple times on different primary locations $p_k^i : k \in [0, X_i - 1]$, being X_i the number of primary embedding for each mark. All primary locations corresponding to the same mark m_i, belonging to W_O, will be stored in the set $P_i : i \in [0, n(W_O) - 1]$. Linked to each primary location there is a set of secondary locations Sp_k^i, where each element is identified as $s_j : j \in [0, \ell_{k,i} - 1]$, being $\ell_{k,i}$ the number of secondary embeddings linked to the primary embedding k of the mark i.

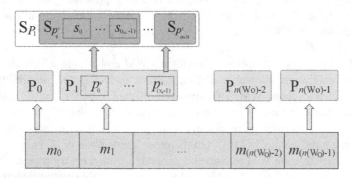

Fig. 2. Link between primary and secondary embedding locations.

Elements of secondary positions sets corresponding to different primary positions of the same mark can present elements in common (i.e., $Sp_a^i \cap Sp_b^i \geq \emptyset : a \neq b$), which enhances the possibility of properly restore the original mark value in the case in which it has been overwritten by an attacker. Eventually, the same secondary position can be assigned to different marks if they present the same value (i.e., if $(m_d = m_e) \rightarrow S_{P_d} \cap S_{P_e} \geq \varnothing : d \neq e$). On the other hand, the same secondary position can never be assigned to marks with different values, which will contradict the mark restoration even if no attacks are performed, compromising the WM synchronization and even its detection (i.e., if $(m_d \neq m_e) \rightarrow S_{P_d} \cap S_{P_e} = \varnothing : d \neq e$).

3.2 Watermarking Processes

The technique we propose is an extension of the conventional relational data watermarking technique in [7], performing an image-based WM generation and the embedding of the marks into the so-called primary locations. We propose, in this work, the module in charge of finding non-colluding locations for the secondary embedding, and the mechanism to embed the mark on those places.

Secondary locations depend on the virtual primary key of the tuple corresponding to the primary location (the virtual primary key *vpk* consist of a value generated to perform the WM synchronization involving the secrecy and privacy of the secret key *SK* and data identifying the tuple being analyzed, e.g., the relation's *PK*). This way, a strong link between the locations is created, avoiding the consequences of just increasing the embedding by changing the parameter values. The link among embedding locations allows higher control of the data usability during the WM embedding and improves the mark restoration effectiveness against additive attacks, compared to traditional approaches.

The starting point for secondary locations are those tuples satisfying the expression *vpk mod*$\gamma = 0$. Let us represent a generic tuple used for a first embedding as r_F. The ψth neighboring tuples to r_F (above and below of it) satisfying *vpk mod*$\gamma \neq 0$ (to avoid collusion with first locations) and $\varphi \neq -1$ will be considered for secondary embedding of the mark embedded in r_F. The symbol φ represents the variation of *vpk* with respect to its neighboring tuples. If the *vpk* constitutes a local minimum, then $\varphi = 0$ and the attributes considered for the mark embedding will be those below the mean of the numerical attributes of the tuple. For the case when *vpk* is a local maximum, then $\varphi = 1$ and the attributes considered for the embedding will be those above the mean of the numerical attributes of the tuple. The parameters controlling the collusion among locations in our approach are ψ and γ.

The WM extraction is performed similarly to the embedding but in the opposite direction (from the watermarked data to the reconstruction of the WM). The same parameter values are used and it is not necessary the original unwatermarked data nor the original source employed for the WM generation. Once a mark is extracted, the extraction of its copies stored on the correspondent secondary locations is performed. Next, a majority voting is performed over the values extracted from the secondary locations and the primary mark. In case the values do not match, it is assumed that an additive attack was performed and the approach proceeds to the WM reconstruction.

4   Experimental Results

4.1   Experimental Setup

We perform the experiments over the numeric relational dataset *Forest Cover Type* [16]. For the validation of the approach the first 30,000 tuples of the dataset were employed, as well as the 10 first attributes, to follow the methodology used in previous works and establishing fairly comparisons when the case demands. For the WM generation, the binary images shown in Table 1 were used.

Table 1. Images used as WM source.

Name	Sample	Size (pixels)
World Wildlife Fund (WWF)'s logo		40 x 45
Chinese character Dào's image		20 x 21

For measuring the differences between the embedded and extracted WMs is it employed the Correction Factor (*CF*) Eq. (2) where each pixel of the image employed to generate the embedded WM (given by Img_{org}) is compared to the ones of the image generated from the extracted WM (given by Img_{ext}). The symbols h and w represent the height and width of the images. The maximum value of *CF* is 100, which indicates the exact match of both images.

$$CF = \frac{\sum_{i=1}^{h} \sum_{j=1}^{w} \left(Img_{org}(i,j) \oplus \overline{Img_{ext}(i,j)} \right)}{h \times w} \times 100 \tag{2}$$

4.2   Robustness Against Additive Attack

Table 2 shows how by applying our approach the data owner's WM can be rebuilt from secondary embedding locations despite both watermarks being embedded over the same primary locations. In the table, *Embedded W_O* is the data owner's WM being embedded in the relation, *Embedded W_A* is the attacker's WM, *Unresilience W_O* constitutes the signal extracted by the watermarking technique with no secondary embedding locations, and *Resilience W_O* the WM recovered by applying our approach. For each case, the correspondent *CF* is also shown. The red pixels represent missed marks due to the partial embedding as a consequence of *pseudo-random selection*. The experiment was performed changing the WMs belonging to both, the attacker and the data owner, to appreciate the role played by the WM's sizes.

Table 2. Images generated from the robustness experiments.

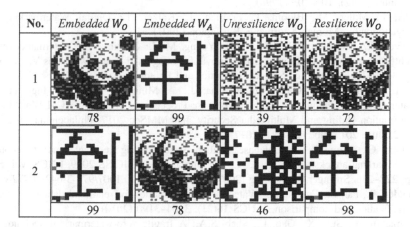

No.	Embedded W_O	Embedded W_A	Unresilience W_O	Resilience W_O
1	78	99	39	72
2	99	78	46	98

Finally, given that the complexity of our approach directly depends on the amount of data being protected, our scheme describes a performance proportional to the tuples of R, represented by $O(\eta)$.

5 Conclusion

In this paper, we proposed a watermarking technique for relational data based on secondary embedding locations to achieve resilience against additive attacks. Based on the analysis of the approaches proposed to deal with false ownership claims, we introduced a method that does not require involving a Trusted Third Party, avoiding the vulnerabilities and downsides of that type of solution. We were able to detect the presence of additive attacks and recover the owner's WM, gathering evidence to uncover the false claim of the attacker. As future work, we aim to analyze the relational watermarking technique we proposed in this paper with respect to *invertibility attacks* and extend it in order to completely prevent possible false claims of ownership.

Acknowledgements. This work was partially supported by the Ph.D. grant No. 714270 and the project grant No. PN 2017-01-7092 from CONACyT, Mexico.

References

1. Agrawal, R., Haas, P.J., Kiernan, J.: Watermarking relational data: framework, algorithms and analysis. VLDB J. Int. J. Very Large Data Bases **12**(2), 157–169 (2003)
2. Agrawal, R., Kiernan, J.: Watermarking relational databases. In: VLDB 2002: Proceedings of the 28th International Conference on Very Large Databases, pp. 155–166. Elsevier (2002)
3. Barni, M., Bartolini, F.: Watermarking Systems Engineering: Enabling Digital Assets Security and Other Applications. CRC Press, Boca Raton (2004)

4. Berghel, H., O'Gorman, L.: Protecting ownership rights through digital watermarking. Computer **29**(7), 101–103 (1996)
5. Cox, I., Miller, M., Bloom, J., Fridrich, J., Kalker, T.: Digital Watermarking and Steganography. Morgan Kaufmann, Burlington (2007)
6. Craver, S.A., Memon, N.D., Yeo, B.L., Yeung, M.M.: Can invisible watermarks resolve rightful ownerships? In: Storage and Retrieval for Image and Video Databases V, vol. 3022, pp. 310–321. International Society for Optics and Photonics (1997)
7. Gort, M.L.P., Uribe, C.F., Nummenmaa, J.: A Minimum distortion: high capacity watermarking technique for relational data. In: Proceedings of the 5th ACM Workshop on Information Hiding and Multimedia Security, IH&MMSec 2017, Philadelphia, PA, USA, 20–22 June 2017, pp. 111–121 (2017)
8. Gupta, G., Pieprzyk, J.: Database relation watermarking resilient against secondary watermarking attacks. In: Prakash, A., Sen Gupta, I. (eds.) ICISS 2009. LNCS, vol. 5905, pp. 222–236. Springer, Heidelberg (2009). https://doi.org/10.1007/978-3-642-10772-6_17
9. Halder, R., Pal, S., Cortesi, A.: Watermarking techniques for relational databases: survey, classification and comparison. J. UCS **16**(21), 3164–3190 (2010)
10. Hamadou, A., Sun, X., Gao, L., Shah, S.A.: A fragile zero-watermarking technique for authentication of relational databases. Int. J. Digit. Content Technol. Appl. **5**(5), 189–200 (2011)
11. Li, Y., Swarup, V., Jajodia, S.: Defending against additive attacks with maximal errors in watermarking relational databases. In: Farkas, C., Samarati, P. (eds.) DBSec 2004. IIFIP, vol. 144, pp. 81–94. Springer, Boston, MA (2004). https://doi.org/10.1007/1-4020-8128-6_6
12. Manjula, R., Settipalli, N.: A new relational watermarking scheme resilient to additive attacks. Int. J. Comput. Appl. **10**(5), 1–7 (2010)
13. Sardroudi, H.M., Ibrahim, S.: A new approach for relational database watermarking using image. In: 5th International Conference on Computer Sciences and Convergence Information Technology, pp. 606–610 (2010)
14. Sencar, H.T., Memon, N.: Watermarking and ownership problem: a revisit. In: Proceedings of the 5th ACM Workshop on Digital Rights Management, pp. 93–101. ACM (2005)
15. Sion, R., Atallah, M., Prabhakar, S.: Rights protection for relational data. IEEE Trans. Knowl. Data Eng. **16**(12), 1509–1525 (2004)
16. Colorado State University: Forest covertype, the UCI KDD archive. Information and Computer Science. University of California, Irvine, June 1999. http://kdd.ics.uci.edu/databases/covertype/covertype.html
17. Zhou, X., Huang, M., Peng, Z.: An additive-attack-proof watermarking mechanism for databases' copyrights protection using image. In: Proceedings of the 2007 ACM symposium on Applied Computing, pp. 254–258. ACM (2007)

Semi-automated Information Security Risk Assessment Framework for Analyzing Enterprises Security Maturity Level

Blerton Abazi[1]([⊠]) [iD] and Andrea Kő[2] [iD]

[1] University for Business and Technology UBT, Prishtina, Kosovo
blerton.abazi@ubt-uni.net
[2] Corvinus University of Budapest, Budapest, Hungary
andrea.ko@uni-corvinus.hu

Abstract. While organizations spend millions of dollars on developing security systems at the highest level, one of the most significant areas of weaknesses, and loss remain their employees. Lack of employee training and security expertise, therefore, can cause huge loss, despite other measure being put in place. Cyberattacks are often able to commit cybercrime due to a lack of qualified cyber-security staff and the limited number of IT staff employed to keep pace with continuing security development and advancement. Testing, training and employing staff therefore is a critical measure for all organizations to reduce the vulnerabilities yet seems to be an area still not fully addressed. Businesses and organizations need to provide training to promote understanding for staff at every level, so they are aware of their roles and responsibilities in protecting against security threats. However, this is a colossal undertaking, and until this learning gap is resolved, financial institutions must continue to fight and efficiently manage cybersecurity threats. The aim of the current research paper is to present and propose a semi-automated risk assessment framework and a security maturity model, which can be helpful for auditors, security officers and managers. It is based on the ISO 27001 and utilize the relevant standards as well. The related risk management solution is a web-based software application. The current study targeted information security in Kosovo, specifically in the banking sector, IT industry and insurance field.

Keywords: Information security and privacy · Risk assessment · Enterprises · ISO 27001

1 Introduction

The violation of information and data breaches is not a new concept and did not first emerge when companies began to convert their protected data digitally. Violations have existed as long as individual, companies or organizations have kept any data, or stored private information. For example, paper-based medical files could be easily shared without authorization and sensitive documents not correctly stored. At these times, many businesses and organizations did not have policies and procedures in place to protect individuals and guide employees in the safe handling of data. According to De

© IFIP International Federation for Information Processing 2019
Published by Springer Nature Switzerland AG 2019
P. Doucek et al. (Eds.): CONFENIS 2019, LNBIP 375, pp. 141–152, 2019.
https://doi.org/10.1007/978-3-030-37632-1_13

Groot [1] publicly disclosed data breaches increased dramatically in the 1980s, 1990s, and in the early 2000s when public awareness of the potential for data breaches began to grow. The bulk of information regarding data breaches focuses on the period from 2005 to the present day. This is mainly due to the advancement of technology and the spread of electronic data across the globe. The result of this is the threat of data attack regarded as a significant concern for organizations, companies and consumers. Due to the advancement of technology, a violation on today's information can impact on hundreds of thousands, if not millions of individual consumers and even more personal data, all from a single attack on a company. By 2020, over one-third of all data will be stored or pass through the cloud. In 2020, data production is estimated to be forty-four times higher than that in 2009 while experts estimate a four thousand and three hundred percent increase in annual data production by 2020 [1]. While individuals are responsible for the majority of data creation (around seventy percent), eighty percent of all data is stored by companies [1]. Security experts always try to keep up with the changes over time, but with fast-changing technology, it is impossible without external aid as a "third party" to help improving future security (Table 1).

Table 1. Data violations over three years [1]

Year	Number of records compromised	Violations that are made public
2016	4,814,941,681	823
2017	2,051,572,640	853
2018	1,038,130,252	699
Total	7,904,644,573	2,375

In 2005, only one hundred and thirty-six data breaches were reported by the Privacy Rights Clearinghouse. However, more than 8,908 data breaches have been made public since 2005, with more than 11,239,817,282 individual data having been violated up until 2018. In the last three years alone, there have been 7,904,644,573 data breaches, showing a comparatively high value compared to previous years. However, it is essential to note the Privacy Rights Clearinghouse only reports the offenses where the number of documents violated is unknown. Therefore, these figures are not a comprehensive summary of all data violations, with the total violated data likely to be much higher. When it comes to information security and data breaches, the financial aspect of the information must also be considered. Thus, according to the latest IBM and Ponemon Institute report [2], the cost associated with data attacks has increased dramatically since 2013. In the United States, the attack price on data is estimated to average $7.35 million, whereas, worldwide, this attack price is $ 3.62 million on average according to Ponemon Institute [2]. These reported costs data are for the financial year 2017, and a significant increase is further seen according to the 2018 report. It is estimated that the cost has also increased to $ 3.9 million in attack data.

Given these consequences, each business or organization must take the necessary measures to protect itself from such cyber-attacks, improve risk assessment practice.

The aim of this paper is to present and propose a semi-automated risk assessment framework, which can be applied by IT auditors to prepare a security risk assessment report and by the enterprises to analyze their maturity level in the field of security risk assessment. The framework is based on the ISO 27001 and utilize the related standards. The related risk management solution is a web-based software application and will be validated by companies from banks, IT and insurance companies.

2 Literature Review

2.1 Information Security Management System and Its Integration to the Organization

Diversity of opinions and factors influencing the process of IT adaption to information security needs is emphasized in many papers [3]. The literature has identified several factors affecting this process, and most of them have listed factors such as senior management, government, IT consultants and organizational behavior [4]. Organizations are often affected by the models and standards that are implemented on information security within the same industry, but not all the models and standards are implemented in the same way. For small organizations that operate with small staff and which distribute information with key staff only, the implementation of information security does not seem to be a necessary option. However, companies where information is distributed to more people simultaneously, it is impossible to manage them without a proper system, thus, presenting the problem of data vulnerability. The third group of organizations is on where the main product is information [5].

Information Security Management System is defined by ISO 27001 as a set of policies and procedures for systematically managing an organization's sensitive data. The goal of an ISMS is to minimize risk and ensure business continuity by pro-actively limiting the impact of a security breach. Organizations have different approaches when deciding to implement an information security system. Some organizations see information security systems as a competitive edge in the market that can provide them with greater credibility in their client relationship, as well as an increase of credibility in their organization and products. Another group of organizations implement information security systems only when they see that their competitors are operating in the same way. The aforementioned views create cultural diversity within organizations of the same industry, and no doubt enables them to improve.

2.2 Maturity Models

To ensure security, it is essential to build security in both design phases and adaptation of a security architecture that provides that security rules and connections are set up accurately. Security requirements must relate to business goals through a process-oriented to access. The process should consider many of the factors that affect an organization's goals. There are at least four areas that affect security in an organization.

First, governance organizations are a factor that affects the security of an organization. Second, organizational culture affects the implementation of security changes in the organization. Thirdly, system architecture may pose challenges for enforcing security requirements. Finally, service management is considered as a challenging implementation process. To identify and explore the strength and weaknesses of an organization's security, several maturity models have been developed [6].

We identified several maturity models for risk assessment in information security that could be adapted and implemented in any organization [7]. Large organizations usually have in place several risk assessments processes at the same time. Those risk assessment processes are decentralized from management and led by departments. For this reason, the need to create a centralized system of risk assessment across different processes and in this case, in the field of information security is necessary. The centralization of the process enables the creation of more accurate reports through which potential threats and vulnerabilities within our system can be identified. To evaluate the security of information, various developments have been seen through mechanisms that are adapted from the recognized engineering field. One of these mechanisms is the measurement of information security through the maturity process [8] and based on this maturity process and to elaborate the concepts of information security maturity, three maturity models have been analyzed, respectively: ISM3 (Information Security Management Maturity Model), SSE-CMM (System Security Engineering Capability Maturity Model), COBIT Maturity Model and NIST Maturity Model. Although the aim and scope of coverage for maturity appraisal differ, maturity models are process-oriented standards, which are based on maturity levels. Processes adhere to a quality standard for each maturity level while documenting and document management is required to ensure that the selected processes comply with the standard. The most popular maturity model is Software Engineering Institute's (SEI) Capability Maturity Model (CMM) for software development and the successor Capability Maturity Model Integration (CMMI) [9]. There are several risk assessment systems which help the companies, but these are usually not dedicated for an audit report preparation and they do not provide recommendations according to the risk assessment results. According to the literature [10], there is a gap between the implementation of the information security standards in business sector needs and objectives of the standards.

To determine a maturity level through a risk assessment process [11] influenced the improvement of preconceptions about information security domination as a discipline where "security should be a process rather than a product". Schneier [11] describes this process as a must to understand all the real threats to the system, and by creating security policies tailored to existing threats, through easier mechanisms for data protection can be developed. Maturity models are considered as a standardized approach on driving activities, processes and commitment to the desired destination and goals [12]. In recent years, many maturity models have been developed, with the same aim to improve processes.

3 Information Security Risk Assessment

As part of the risk management structure, risk assessment process identifies and evaluates the risk to information security by determining the probability of occurrence and the resulting impact [13]. Through the risk assessment process, it is possible to identify threats, classify assets and rate the system vulnerabilities, which support effective implementation of controls [14]. According to literature, we can separate risk assessment models into quantitative and qualitative. Quantitative models are those which are based on measurable data to determine the asset value and associated risk to calculate objective numeric values for each of the components that are collected during the risk assessment process. Qualitative methods are based mostly on the descriptive categories such as low, medium, high, or any other method of scaling. This method assesses the impact of the likelihood of the identified risk [14]. Both methods have their advantages and disadvantages to risk management approach, which also depends on the size of organizations. Organizations usually try to adopt the quantitative methods, because it is more easily measurable, but small-sized organizations with limited resources may decide to use qualitative approach as the best methods for their needs.

The deliverable from a qualitative assessment should be a report of which assets and systems are most important to various parts of the business. The assessment team won't necessarily know the financial impact of these systems were compromised, but they will understand which business units would be affected and how much productivity would be lost in different risk scenarios. Additionally, the assessor would understand the impact to the company's reputation and any PR considerations if a risk were realized and became publicly known. When developing the information security risk assessment methodology for an organization, it's essential to realize that both quantitative and qualitative analyses are needed for a well-rounded view on risk management process. Risk management processes require not only understanding impact but creating a risk management framework that sets the acceptable level of risk to enable functioning business operations.

The advancement and complexity of technological networks create opportunities for more attacks and breaches into security systems, causing large direct and side damage such as financial loss, reputation damage, etc. [15]. Adding this to the need for a proper data protection strategy in an organization, information security management is one of the most important area. While organizations are offering their clients access to multiple information systems, the possibility of security threats are growing, and the need to have secure systems gets special and important emphasis [16]. While many researchers and organizations deal with the issue of information security mainly in the technical aspect, respectively its integration into corporate governance, non-technical issues are rarely considered as one of the issues to be included in business strategies [17].

Most of the security information "shakes" are caused by incidents inside the organization, which means that the internal staff is identified as the first and most security threat to information security [18, 19]. Increasing the need for more secure systems and the need for our data to be handled with the utmost security is that the information security study surpasses the technology gap by increasing awareness of the role of management in data security [20, 21]. Also, given the fact that security information systems development is not enough to stop attacks and damages to information, an effective information security system that includes policies and a robust review of information security policies are key factors for a good protection [22]. As a result, management's role is more focused on the development and execution of information protection policies, training delivery, investment in information infrastructure development and business and IT alignment [23].

3.1 Semi-automated Risk Assessment Solutions

Organizations have a broad set of security requirements. Organizations security and information security management is built from a complex interconnection between business objectives, IT strategy, institutional arrangements and requirements [24]. According to our current research conducted with organizations in Kosovo, completing these requirements is a waste of time and the likelihood of error is large because organizations lack digital, automatic or semi-automatic processes to perform tasks related to information security management. The risk assessment process should be related to what we want to measure, and, in this section, we can interconnect the part of the security controls that we want to evaluate through the risk assessment. Based on the ISO 27001 specification, a total of 133 security controls represent all the areas for information security management. However, not all can be automated through certain tools. A security-control is automated if it can perform the required operations without human intervention in the process. This implies that the best way to automate security controls is through semi-automation. According to Montesino and Fenz [24] and based on the criteria outlined by them, the identification of semi-automated controls can be made through the following criteria:

- Actions and monitoring of audits require only readable and process able resources that cannot be considered as potential training to understand the need to look at and interact with the human factor
- Controls can be automated using one of the relevant security applications.

4 Research Overview

This study aims to propose a risk assessment framework and a related workflow that can be utilized in a semi-automated way in the organization to create an audit report and evaluate security risks. The proposed framework is intended to utilize the model of ISO 27001 and its technical implementations. The objective of the study is to analyze the assessment methods of vulnerability in information security and to propose an effective model after analyzing the existing maturity models.

Our research is based on the evaluation of four maturity model frameworks i.e. ISM3, SSE-CMM, COBIT Maturity Model and NIST Maturity Model. The gaps in the current maturity models identified through the literature review are such as the price of implementation because of the commercial standards such as ISO 27001 and ISM3 [25]. Another issue is the lack of customization and the attempt to implement one-size fits all standard through which small organizations faces difficulties. In these organizations there are processes offered by the standards which are not used and also the period of implementation takes long time due to many administration procedures until the final implementation (NIST, ISO 27001, SSE-CMM) [26]. More issues mentioned in literature review, includes the lack of guidance and complex structures of implementation in a case of COBIT 5, while the number of case studies is limited [27].

Additionally, we collected information about the gaps through surveys at the investigated companies in Kosovo. 70 IT managers filled in it mainly from banks and insurance companies in Kosovo. We distributed the survey to all organizations in the region, and got back responses from all of them. Our risk assessment framework was developed using the information gathered in gap analysis based on the survey results. The framework took ISO 27001 as a main framework and the focus is on technical parts of the framework rather than the documentation process. The currently prevailing IT risk management approaches as a good example witnessed through the literature. It is necessary for risk professionals and auditors to have a maturity model through which they can check if the investigated risk management practice meets with the expectations and produce the required results. Many risk management programs have built on risk maturity model which can be broken down into many other sections focusing on core attributes [28]. Recently, there is an increased interest for the maturity models in the research community and its practical implications [29]. In this regard, the current research will try to find the answer for the following research questions:

How can we develop the semi-automatic risk assessment system? How risk assessment systems can be extended to provide a list of recommendations by identifying the list of areas with a lack of suitable security measures through an automated risk or semi-automated assessment solution?

For the above-mentioned research questions, we developed a software application that apply semi-automated information security risk assessment method and compile a list of recommendations from the assessment findings. The system prototype was created based on the findings from the literature, comparison of maturity models and interviews with individuals of the companies from IT sector, banking sector and insurance companies.

5 Risk Assessment Maturity Framework Prototype

With the help of quantitative and qualitative data analysis and through the identification of gaps in the literature, a software application was developed which apply semi-automated information security risk assessment method after the compilation of recommendations from analytical findings. The system prototype is based on the literary findings, comparison of maturity models, and analytical findings from the quantitative and qualitative data collected from participants from companies of IT, banking and

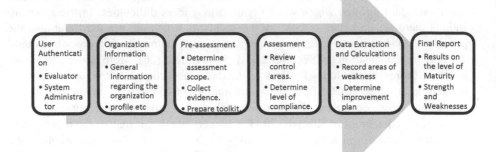

Fig. 1. Risk assessment framework - functional design

insurance sector. Based on studies on risk assessment in information security, we have a wide range of models used in identification, assessment and risk analysis processes: FAIR, OCTAVE, CURF, CRAMM, CORAS, RISK IT, however they have several shortcomings [30] (Fig. 1).

The software is a web-based application developed in PHP programming language and the database is MySQL. The web-based application is optimized for use on every device ranging from personal computers to smartphones with the technology of auto responsive content. This application aims to be user friendly and easy to navigate but the issue of less memory and internet consumption will be solved by implementing the backend-oriented layout using the HTML5 and CSS3 mostly for design and very few images. On completion of the questions from the companies and organization, this system has a report generation with the recommendations function.

The current proposal forwards a framework which is more user-friendly easy to be used and adaptable to develop any risk assessment questionnaire. The application is made up of several blocks that represent the respective functions as well as are interconnected with other parts of the system. This is an incremental and iterative development that is implemented as a new concept and is in line with the idea of the on-the-job development. Characteristics of the framework are defined on two levels. The overall level definition establishes the foundation and framework; it indicates particularities and critical issues that need special attention. The detailed level specification defines requirements with full particulars. These documents are prepared simultaneously for the present one. Specifically, the database design will seek to:

- Minimize data redundancy meaning information is not duplicated in several places making it hard to maintain
- Provide easy access to the data including the ability to handle ad-hoc queries
- Provide security for the data
- Allow constraints that ensure data integrity.

Until now the following sections are functioning:

Companies Profile: This section helps us to obtain data for company profiles (industry, number of employees, annual turnover etc.) subject to the questionnaire.

Surveys: This is the main part of application; through this section questionnaires can be managed. In this section, we can add new questions from the database, categorize questions, or even change the type of the questions.

Assessment: In this section we can see the list of assessments we have conducted so far. Particularly in this section we can make a comparison between different assessments for the same company. For example, if company X has conducted the assessment in 2017 and 2018, then through the compare assessment option we can see the progress that the company has made in certain sections.

Dashboard: Presents visualized data and statistics.

Questions: Through this section we can add new questions, modify the existing ones, or even change the form of the question.

Accounts: Is the administration and configuration part that enables us to administer the system by create new users or adding specific roles to the existing users.

5.1   Vulnerabilities Rating System

To have a qualitative information security risk assessment, we must provide a scoring metric which will be separated for different security controls, this vulnerability rating system is the backend of the proposed solution. The results generated by our proposed framework will be based on a system of estimation of the probabilities that will be calculated in the backend. This system is designed to provide organizations with a better understanding of which identified high-priority vulnerabilities need to be closed. In our research we have analyzed the CVSS (Common Vulnerability Scoring System) which is a risk assessment solution designed to identify the common attributes of several security issues. The reason we choose to analyze CVSS is that it includes standardized vulnerability score that may be meaningful across organization and also it is essential that CVSS is an open framework model and any metric is open and

Table 2. Risk assessment proposed scoring model

Level	Score
Min level	1
Min-mid level	2
Mid-level	3
Mid-max level	4
Max level	5

available to all users while also it helps organizations to prioritize the risk. According to the structure and function of CVSS and as well based on our proposed framework, we have created a score-based model 1 to 5 as follows (Table 2):

Each of the security control groups have a summarization of their result based on the user selections. The resulting score serves to guide the affected organization in the allocation of resources to address the vulnerability. The higher the severity rating, the more significant the potential impact of an exploit and the higher the urgency in addressing the vulnerability. While not as precise as the numeric CVSS scores, the qualitative labels are very useful for communicating with stakeholders who are unable to relate to the numeric scores.

In the dashboard of the system, statistics present the number of companies that have carried out the risk assessment, the number of questions, how many questionnaires have been conducted and how many questions have been answered are displayed. Further statistics are visualized on the dashboard, such as the most frequent answers, the most prevalent security issues from all questionnaires and so on. Companies can place themselves in this risk assessment landscape, and they get feedback about the fields need improvements from controls aspects (Fig. 2).

Fig. 2. System dashboard

6 Conclusion

In this research paper we presented an approach, model and solution for the information security risk assessment especially for the banking sector, insurance companies and IT industry in Kosovo. This framework can be helpful for auditors, security officers and managers in the investigation of their companies' security maturity level. The model is based on the ISO 27001 and utilize the relevant standards as well. The related risk management solution is a web-based software application, which we presented in Sect. 5. The framework supports the identification some of the biggest gaps that organizations have in security implementation. The use of the questionnaire in the system helped to identify exactly the points in which most organizations encounter problems, while the application helps solving these problems through offering the appropriate controls at the lowest cost. While the dependence of people on different platforms is on the rise, the risk this data will be exposed is likely to increase.

Thus, research data reflects an interesting, current state of information protection. A growing number of companies continue to feel threatened by cyberattacks, and the media frequently report attacks on data being made for larger companies such as Facebook and Google. The more in-depth analysis of these two companies has reflected that regardless of the value of the company, each company continues to struggle with security risks. Therefore, in addition to the above-mentioned risks of data destructions, companies need to consider the reality that such attacks can happen. It is imperative that every company with an online presence considers the need to protect their data, whether due to the protection of the business or its users. Finally, management support plays an essential role in the success of IS. It has been shown the need for management to make a risk-based decision and support the goals of IS, for it to be successful in the long-term. The current study targeted information security in Kosovo, specifically in the banking sector, IT industry and insurance field, where businesses and organizations face several risks from a range of threat types. Next phase of the research is dedicated to the prototype testing and fine-tuning of the system.

References

1. De Groot, J.: The History of Data Breaches. https://digitalguardian.com/blog/history-data-breaches
2. Ponemon Institute: 2018 Cost of Data Breach Study, Global Overview (2018)
3. Businge, J., Serebrenik, A., van den Brand, M.: An empirical study of the evolution of eclipse third-party plug-ins. In: Proceedings of the Joint ERCIM Workshop on Software Evolution (EVOL) and International Workshop on Principles of Software Evolution (IWPSE), pp. 63–72. ACM, New York (2010)
4. Joshi, A., Bollen, L., Hassink, H., De Haes, S., Van Grembergen, W.: Explaining IT governance disclosure through the constructs of IT governance maturity and IT strategic role. Inf. Manag., 0–1 (2017). https://doi.org/10.1016/j.im.2017.09.003
5. Burgeois, D.T.: Information Systems for Business and Beyond. Saylor Foundation (2014)
6. Talabis, M., Martin, J.: Information Security Risk Assessment Toolkit Practical Assessments Through Data Collection and Data Analysis. Syngress (2012). ISBN 9781597497350. ISBN 9781597499750
7. Ge, X.Y., Yuan, Y.Q., Lu, L.L.: An information security maturity evaluation mode. Procedia Eng. **24**, 335–339 (2011). https://doi.org/10.1016/j.proeng.2011.11.2652
8. Dzazali, S., Zolait, A.H.: Assessment of information security maturity: an exploration study of Malaysian public service organizations. J. Syst. Inf. Technol. **14**, 23–57 (2012). https://doi.org/10.1108/13287261211221128
9. Poeppelbuss, J., Niehaves, B., Simons, A., Becker, J.: Maturity models in information systems research: literature search and analysis. Commun. Assoc. Inf. Syst. **29**, 506–532 (2011)
10. Von Solms, B., Von Solms, R.: From information security to…business security? Comput. Secur. **24**, 271–273 (2005). https://doi.org/10.1016/j.cose.2005.04.004
11. Schneier, B.: Secrets and Lies: Digital Security in a Networked World. Willey (2004)

12. Ngwum, N.I.: Information Security Maturity Model (ISMM) Information Security Maturity Model. A dissertation submitted to The University of Manchester, pp. 1–136 (2016). https://doi.org/10.13140/RG.2.1.2432.8729
13. Nazareth, D., Choi, J.: Information security management: a system dynamics approach. In: Americas Conference on Information Systems (2012)
14. Macedo, F.N.R.: Models for Assessing Information Security Risk, pp. 1–64 (2009)
15. Hu, Q., Hart, P., Cooke, D.: The role of external and internal influences on information systems security - a neo-institutional perspective. J. Strateg. Inf. Syst. 16, 153–172 (2007). https://doi.org/10.1016/j.jsis.2007.05.004
16. Nazareth, D.L., Choi, J.: A system dynamics model for information security management. Inf. Manag. 52, 123–134 (2015). https://doi.org/10.1016/j.im.2014.10.009
17. Lapke, M., Dhillon, G.: A semantic analysis of security policy formulation and implementation: a case study. In: Association for Information Systems - 12th Americas Conference on Information Systems, AMCIS 2006 (2006)
18. Gaunt, N.: Practical approaches to creating a security culture. Int. J. Med. Inform. 60, 151–157 (2000). https://doi.org/10.1016/s1386-5056(00)00115-5
19. Singh, A.N., Picot, A., Kranz, J., Gupta, M.P., Ojha, A.: Information Security Management (ISM) practices: lessons from select cases from India and Germany. Glob. J. Flex. Syst. Manag. (2013). https://doi.org/10.1007/s40171-013-0047-4
20. Stine, K., Barker, W.C., Gulick, J.: Volume I : Guide for Mapping Types of Information and Information Systems to Security Categories, vol. I (2008)
21. Soomro, Z.A., Shah, M.H., Ahmed, J.: Information security management needs more holistic approach: a literature review. Int. J. Inf. Manag. 36, 215–225 (2016). https://doi.org/10.1016/j.ijinfomgt.2015.11.009
22. Diver, S.: Information Security Policy - A Development Guide for Large and Small Companies. Information Security, SANS Institute (2007)
23. Radack, S., Kuhn, D.: Managing security: the security content automation protocol. IT Prof. 13, 9–11 (2011). https://doi.org/10.1109/MITP.2011.11
24. Montesino, R., Fenz, S.: Automation possibilities in information security management. In: Proceedings of 2011 European Intelligence and Security Informatics Conference, EISIC 2011, pp. 259–262 (2011). https://doi.org/10.1109/EISIC.2011.39
25. Stevanovi, B.: Maturity models in information security. Int. J. Inf. Commun. Technol. Res. 1, 44–47 (2011)
26. Becker, J., Niehaves, B., Poeppelbuss, J., Simons, A.: Association for Information Systems AIS Electronic Library (AISeL) Maturity Models in IS Research. Maturity Models in IS Research (2010)
27. Zhang, S., Le, F.H.: An examination of the practicability of COBIT framework and the proposal of a COBIT-BSC model. J. Econ. Bus. Manag. (2013). https://doi.org/10.7763/joebm.2013.v1.84
28. Sophia, W.: How Can Risk Maturity Model Benefit Your Risk Management. https://www.riskmethods.net/en/blog/How-Can-Risk-Maturity-Model-Benefit-Your-Risk-Management/ 112
29. Khaiata, M., Zualkernan, I.A.: A simple instrument to measure IT-Business alignment maturity. Inf. Syst. Manag. 26, 138–152 (2009). https://doi.org/10.1080/10580530902797524
30. Abazi, B.: A novel approach for a risk assessment maturity framework based on ISO 27001 (2019)

Conceptual Model of the Automated Decision-Making Process in Analysis of Emergency Situations on Railway Transport

Akbala Abuova[1] , Valeriy Lakhno[2] , Nurzhamal Oshanova[3(✉)],
Bagdat Yagaliyeva[4] , and Andrew Anosov[2]

[1] Kazakh University Ways of Communications, Almaty, Kazakhstan
[2] National University of Life and Environmental Sciences of Ukraine,
Kiev, Ukraine
[3] Abai Kazakh National Pedagogical University, Almaty, Kazakhstan
nurzhamal_o_t@mail.ru
[4] Yessenov University, Aktau, Kazakhstan

Abstract. The article substantiates the need of the use of intelligent computer technologies in order to automate the process of analysis of emergency situations on the railway transport. There were considered the analysis variants with automatic generation of recommendations for managers for ES elimination in order to reduce time to develop and to make an informed decision. It is shown that during the analysis of emergencies on the railway transport a particular importance has the development of methods for creating decision support systems (DSS) based on the modeling of transient technogenic emergencies as a complex dynamic process taking into account cause and effect relationships. There is substantiated the necessity of the implementation of a modular software product for the intellectual analysis of emergency situations and the development of operational recommendations for managers on their liquidation. There was made the tasks detalization performed after the receipt of information on the development of the situation. On the basis of detailed tasks, there was created a conceptual model of the decision-making process. Developed a new formalized description of the model for the task of recognizing the situation and making primary decisions. The model differs from the known ones in that it takes into account the information dependencies of the situation parameters that are available to the decision maker. This makes it possible to formalize the decision-making process for recognizing and predicting a situation.

Keywords: Decision support system · Emergency situation analysis · Automatic generation of recommendations · Conceptual model

1 The Introduction

Preparation, adoption and implementation of management decisions on the implementation of organizational and technical measures aimed at ensuring coordinated actions of structural units on emergency situations on railway transport with the aim of eliminating the consequences of an emergency for the shortest possible period of time

© IFIP International Federation for Information Processing 2019
Published by Springer Nature Switzerland AG 2019
P. Doucek et al. (Eds.): CONFENIS 2019, LNBIP 375, pp. 153–162, 2019.
https://doi.org/10.1007/978-3-030-37632-1_14

is the main task of the operational headquarters. The operational headquarters of the enterprises of Kazakhstan Railways (KRT), associations, state enterprises, railway transportation directorates, institutions, organizations and structural units are created for direct management within their competence. Today railway transport control points (RTC), in fact, is the relevant situational centers for emergency response control and represent a hierarchical system, reflects the railway transport control structure. Actions of heterogeneous subdivisions of the functional subsystem of railway transport for the localization of dangerous situations and the elimination of their consequences are determined by significant complexity, which is due to the influence of diverse hazardous factors of such situations on people, equipment and the environment, as well as the complexity of organizing the management of these units in the difficult conditions of their work. The solution of such problems is impossible without the widespread use of computerized systems, including expert (ES) and decision support systems (DSS).

In order to automate the assessment of the situation resulting from the occurrence and development of emergencies, it is necessary to have a large amount of information about the nature of the development of emergencies in time and space, the status of special units and the results of their actions, provision with material and technical means, personal protective equipment, etc., and this amount of information is continuously growing with the development of the situation. In order to minimize the consequences of emergencies in the context of the rapid growth of information flows and lack of time, the need arises to create a clearly created system of automated operational information and analytical support for analyzing the situation, developing and making decisions on emergency response control with the widespread use of modern computer technology, information technology and DSS. Nowadays, control systems such as situational centers SC have entered the practice of managing complex dynamic multi-link systems [1].

At the same time, under the term center there is understood not only a specially equipped room, but also an appropriate information, telecommunication, software and methodological tools providing the process of information aggregation delivery in order to develop an appropriate solution.

All the above mentioned has led to the choice of the topic of our study, which involves the development of models and methods for constructing intellectualized (intellectual) DSSs for emergencies response on railways transport.

2   Literature Review

Methods for solving control problems in emergency situations and mathematical models of the operational units functioning for its liquidation are considered in [1, 2]. Particular attention was paid to the principles of construction and architecture of automated DSS during fire extinguishing [3, 4], to the aspects of creating an integrated expert and information DSS to eliminate chemical accidents, flood situations and forest fires [5], to the problems of decision support on identifying and eliminating emergency situations on the basis of dynamic expert systems (ES) [4], to the intellectualization of the decision support process in emergency situations at enterprises using information on the state of the environment [5–7]. But it should be noted that many publications

[7–9] do not contain descriptive information related to the prediction of the emergencies development on railway transport in order to make recommendations to managers on the elimination of its consequences [9–11]. Meanwhile, not one of the analyzed works considers the use of specialized intellectualized DSS (IDSS) for the elimination of emergencies at railway transport facilities. The absence of such IDSS significantly complicates the process of analyzing the circumstances that have developed on the railway, increases the time period for making timely, informed decisions by the head of emergency response, which leads to an increase in losses from it.

The above mentioned necessitates reducing time to develop and to make an informed decision by the managers of the emergency response on the railway transport of technogenic nature due to the computerization of processes for identifying such situations.

3   Aims and Objectives of the Research

During the analysis of emergencies on the railway a particular importance has the development of methods for creating DSS based on the modeling of transient emergencies as a complex dynamic process taking into account cause-effect relationships. This is not possible without modern information technology.

In order to achieve this aim, it is necessary to develop a software product that consists of interconnected intelligent modules, and is able to perform an emergency analysis of emergency situations and to give recommendations for managers on their liquidation. In this case, it is necessary to create models for identifying emergencies and the process of developing recommendations for their elimination, taking into account the experience of experts and the requirements of managers [5]. The choice of an intelligent system for analyzing emergencies on the railway transport must be justified on the basis of a specific study of the subject area and on the knowledge of experts in solving such problems.

Therefore, the objectives of the study are: the development of a conceptual model of the decision-making process for assessing emergency situations on the railway transport and forecasting the development of the situation; the development of a formalized description of the model for the module of the designed DSS for the task of recognizing the situation and for automated decision-making.

4   Methods and Models

In their daily professional activities, specialists involved in the elimination of the consequences of complex technogenic or other emergencies on the railway transport, including operational duty services (ODS), are dealing with the task of decision-making. Often the essence of these decisions is to generate possible alternatives, to evaluate them and to choose the best one. The choice of alternatives is based on a large number of conflicting requirements and on evaluating solution variants according to many criteria. The inconsistency of the requirements, the ambiguity of the assessment of the situation, the incompleteness and timeliness of the received information greatly complicate the adoption of the final decision and significantly affect its quality.

Numerous researches [3, 5, 6, 8, 10, 11] show that a decision-maker (DM), without additional computerized support, uses simplified or contradictory decision rules. At the same time, decision-makers are guided only by their own experience and intuition, which as a result can lead to erroneous or inadequate solutions of situations.

Decision making support task is to provide decision-makers with the necessary information about the situation. In this case, it is necessary clearly to formalize the description of the input data processing processes. Today, DSS are a qualitatively new level of automation of decision-making processes in various areas of human activity [1, 3, 4, 8]. They allow to organize intellectual support for the activities of the decision-maker and the ODS at making decisions, for example, in eliminating the consequences of emergencies on the railway transport. The introduction of DSS in the ODS activities on the railway transport would provide decision-makers with intellectual support for decision making and help in the following tasks: an automated support for the process of analyzing input data and supplementing it from various databases with information related to emergency response; a display of all information in an accessible and easy to read form; formation of an initial list of solution alternatives for a specific situation; creation of a situation model, assigning it to one of the well-known classes; prediction of the situation development in time, determination on the basis of this the consequences of primary alternatives; optimization of decisions related to the movement and placement of forces and means involved in emergency response on the railway transport. From the analysis of well-known DSS, it is clear that none of them is universal and cannot provide decision-makers with assistance in solving all the problems facing to them. Therefore, in order to provide intellectual support for decision-making by DM during emergency response on railways transport, the urgent task remains to develop a conceptual model of the decision-making process for assessing emergency situations on the railway transport and the prediction of the situation development, as well as formation of the model description for the module of the designed DSS (or IDSS) for the task of recognizing the situation and automated decision-making.

The development of reliable intelligent software is impossible without the use of high-quality and high-speed, dynamically changing databases and knowledge. At the same time, the input data are given by the vector of arguments containing general information about an emergency of technogenic character on the railway transport.

The knowledge base (KB) should contain generalized knowledge on emergency response (expert experience and regulatory rules), as well as knowledge about a real emergency. This knowledge is automatically found or generated from generalized knowledge (knowledge is presented in the form of fuzzy logical statements, production rules). The developed IDSS should have a unit for data and knowledge processing specific to a particular emergency in order to develop recommendations for its liquidation [2, 4]. Management decisions are made using intelligent modules that use the knowledge base. Intelligent emergency analysis module is the main component of the system, and is able to automate the analysis process.

Based on an analysis of the headquarters activities dealing with the elimination of the consequences of emergency situations on the railway transport, as well as the analysis of previous researches [3, 7, 11], there were completed the details of the tasks solved by the decision-maker (DM) after the receipt of information about the situation. Based on detailed tasks, a conceptual model of the decision-making process was created.

In our opinion, as well as on the basis of the above analysis of previous researches in this field, the most optimal way to automate this process is to use production rules [1]. This will make it possible to create a flexible apparatus for calculating and providing recommendations on the recommended measures, forces and means in case of emergency response. This is especially true in situations where the system user will have a very small amount of input data. The results of the actions of the previous product can be used in the implementation of actions or conditions in the next product until the IDSS provides practical recommendations on the number of measures, forces and means for emergency response. In addition, the use of the production model of knowledge as a basic one allows decomposition of the analysis process. That is, to divide the task into simpler, functionally completed tasks. Therefore, the designed IDSS should have a modular structure, which will make it convenient to operate and will allow to scale new functional modules in its architecture.

Depending on the number of conditions and actions during the functioning of the system in order to eliminate conflict situations, the following types of rules are used: simple - one condition and one action; composed - many conditions and actions; branched - one condition and many actions.

An intelligent analysis involves the determination of emergency response parameters, based on the application of production rules with a postcondition and with the development of recommendations for emergency response.

In order to analyze the possibilities of DSS tasks fulfillment facing to the heads of services involved in the emergencies liquidation process on the railway transport, the tasks were formalized for the subsequent synthesis of models.

The situation place is characterized by the following parameters: v_1 – an indicator that determines the population density of the area (locality) in which an emergency occurred on the railway transport. The more crowded the place of emergency is, the more important is v_1; v_2 – an indicator determining the presence of buildings, structures, institutions with an increased level of danger at the emergency site (factories working with hazardous substances, warehouses that store such substances, etc.). The value of v_2 depends on the hazard level of the structures and their quantity; v_3 – geographical location of the emergency place (for example, in the village). Therefore we will obtain: $V = \{v_1, v_2, v_3\}$.

Many events describing emergencies on the railway transport, we denote as $p : p = \{p_1, \ldots, p_a\}, a = \overline{1, o}$, where p_a – a single event that characterizes an emergency, o – the total possible amount of events in the process of emergency development.

The time of an emergency occurrence (denoted as C) consists of two quantities: $C = \{c_1, c_2\}, c_1$ – the absolute time of an emergency occurrence, which is determined by the date and time of the emergency beginning, and c_2 – the relative time of the emergency, the period of time that has passed from the beginning of the emergency to the moment of receipt of a message about it. The absolute time of the situation relates to the amount of persons who may be participants or witnesses of the emergency and is described by two parameters: time of year ($c_{1,1}$) and time of day ($c_{1,2}$). In this way $c_1 = \{c_{1,1}, c_{1,2}\}$.

The amount of persons who may be witnesses of emergencies is characterized by an indicator K that depends on indicators V, C. The value K increases with an increase of the possible amount of people. The status of the situation S depends on its development, if $S \rightarrow$ min, then the situation is regular, and if $S \rightarrow$ max, the situation is emergency. We denote the set of situations types as $T = \{t_1, t_2, t_3, t_4\}$, where t_1 – is the indicator of the situation that determines the need to involve emergency brigades of railway, t_2 – IOC military personnel, t_3 – immediate response groups (IRG) or investigative-operational groups (IOG), t_4 – the use of other actions not related to the involvement of the aforementioned forces and means. If it is necessary to attract a certain type of force, the value of the corresponding indicator increases, otherwise it decreases. The set of possible solutions for emergency response will be denoted as R, $R = \{r_j\}$, $j = \overline{1, q}$, r_j – one of the possible solutions to a particular situation, q – the total possible amount of solutions.

The formalized description of the model for the task of situation recognition and primary decisions making is described as follows:

$$
\begin{aligned}
&r_j \in R_1, \ if \ S \rightarrow \max \\
&r_j \in R_2, \ if \ t_1 \rightarrow \max, \ S, t_2, t_3, t_4 \rightarrow \min \\
&r_j \in R_2 \cup R_3, \ if \ t_1, t_2 \rightarrow \max, \ S, t_3, t_4 \rightarrow \min \\
&r_j \in R_2 \cup R_4, \ if \ t_1, t_3 \rightarrow \max, \ S, t_2, t_4 \rightarrow \min \\
&r_j \in R_2 \cup R_3 \cup R_4, \ if \ t_1, t_2, t_3 \rightarrow \max, \ S, t_4 \rightarrow \min \\
&r_j \in R_5, \ if \ t_4 \rightarrow \max
\end{aligned}
\tag{1}
$$

where R_1 – set of decisions on the recognition of an emergency situation; R_2 – set of decisions on the involvement of emergency brigades, $R_2 = \{r_{2,1}, \ldots, r_{2,f}\}, f = \overline{1, h}$ where $r_{2,f}$ – decision on the involvement of appropriate emergency brigades, h – maximum number of emergency brigades at the place where the decision-maker (DM) works; R_3 – many decisions on the involvement of IOC military personnel to eliminate emergencies on the railway. $R_3 = \{r_{3,1}, \ldots, r_{3,e}\}, e = \overline{1, g}$, where $r_{3,e}$ – the decision to involve the appropriate detachment (group of detachments) of the IOC military personnel to eliminate the emergency situations on the railway, g – the maximum amount of IOC military personnel for emergency response on railways in the area where the decision-maker works; R_4 – the decision to involve IRG or IOG, $R_4 = \{r_{4,1}, r_{4,2}\}$, where $r_{4,1}$ – the decision to involve IRG, $r_{4,2}$ – the decision to involve IOG; R_5 – many decisions on recognizing a situation such that it does not require the involvement of additional forces and means, $R_5 = \{r_5\}$.

As the situation development prediction we will consider the definition of the operational situation development in time, namely, how the place of the emergency and the events characterizing it will change.

The set of consequences of the chosen decision N are: $N = \{n_1, n_2, n_3, n_4, n_5, n_6\}$ where n_1 – is the successful completion of the situation ($n_1 \rightarrow$ max) or vice versa ($n_1 \rightarrow$ min); n_2 – the transition to a state of emergency ($n_2 \rightarrow$ max) or vice versa ($n_2 \rightarrow$ min); n_3 – the sufficiency of the involved forces and means, if the involved forces and means are sufficient, then $n_3 \rightarrow$ max, if it is necessary to attract additional forces then $n_3 \rightarrow$ min, n_4 – losses from emergencies on the railway and human casualties $n_4 = [n_{4,1}, n_{4,2}, n_{4,3}]$; where $n_{4,1}$ – is the amount of physical losses (casualties during the emergency on the railway), $n_{4,2}$ – the amount of material losses, $n_{4,3}$ – the amount of moral damage, with an increase in the amount of corresponding losses $n_{4,1}, n_{4,2}, n_{4,3} \rightarrow$ max, with a decrease $n_{4,1}, n_{4,2}, n_{4,3} \rightarrow$ min; n_5 – possible amount of losses for the emergency response side on railway $n_5 = [n_{5,1}, n_{5,2}]$, where $n_{5,1}$ – is the amount of physical losses among the personnel of the emergency response side, $n_{5,2}$ – the amount of material losses, with an increase in the amount of corresponding losses $n_{5,1}, n_{5,2} \rightarrow$ max, with a decrease $n_{5,1}, n_{5,2} \rightarrow$ min; n_6 – time for which the situation can be resolved. The faster the situation is resolved, the less important is n_6. If the situation cannot be resolved successfully or it goes into a state of emergency $n_6 \rightarrow$ max.

A formalized description of the model of the problem of predicting the development of the situation and determining the consequences of primary decisions is presented below.

$$
\begin{aligned}
n_1 &= \left(\left(\left((p_{n_1 w} \backslash p_{n_1 u}) \backslash p_{sw} \right), (v_{3n_1 w} \backslash v_{3n_1 u}), v_1, v_2, c_{1,1}, c_{1,2}, c_2 \right), r_j \right); \\
n_2 &= \left((p_{sw}, v_2, v_1, c_{1,1}, c_{1,2}), r_j \right); \\
n_3 &= \left(\left((p_{n_3 w} \backslash p_{n_3 u}), (v_{3n_3 w} \backslash v_{3n_3 u}) \right), r_j \right); \\
n_4 &= \left(\left((p_{n_4 w} \backslash p_{n_4 u}), v_1, c_{1,1}, c_{1,2} \right), r_j \right); \\
n_5 &= \left((p_{n_5 w} \backslash p_{n_5 u}), r_j \right); \\
n_6 &= \left((p_{sw}, v_2, v_1, c_{1,1}, c_{1,2}), r_j \right), \text{ if } v_2, v_1, c_{1,1}, c_{1,2} \rightarrow \text{max}, \quad p'_{sw} \neq 0; \\
n_6 &= \left(\left((p_{n_1 w} \backslash p_{n_1 w}), (v_{3n_1 w} \backslash v_{3n_1 w}), c_2 \right), r_j \right), \text{ if } c_2 \rightarrow \text{max}; \ p_{n_1 u} \neq 0, \ v_{3n_1 u} \neq 0;
\end{aligned}
\tag{2}
$$

where "$\backslash$" - set difference; $p_{n_1 w}, p_{n_3 w}, p_{n_4 w}, p_{n_5 w}$ – events that during the decision r_j contribute to the high value of the corresponding consequence; $p_{n_1 u}, p_{n_3 u}, p_{n_4 u}, p_{n_5 u}$ – events that during the decision r_j do not contribute to the high value of the corresponding consequence; $p_{s,w}$ – events that during the decision r_j contribute to the transition to emergency; $v_{3n_1 w}, v_{3n_3 w}$ – places that during the decision r_j contribute to the high value of the corresponding consequence; $v_{3n_1 u}, v_{3n_3 u}$ – places that during the decision r_j do not contribute to the high value of the corresponding consequence.

In order to solve the problems of recognition and assessment of the situation on the railway and primary decision-making on situation development prediction and the determination of the consequences of primary decisions there is proposed the use of the apparatus of artificial neural networks (ANN). The choice of ANN apparatus is motivated by the fact that the considered problems are weakly formalizable [1, 12–14].

The architecture of the neural network consists of three layers of neurons.

Layer 1. The neurons outputs of this layer determine the degree of belonging of the input variables $x_1, x_2, \ldots, x_7$ to the corresponding sets with a trapezoidal membership function.

Layer 2. The neurons outputs are degrees of truth for each of the rules of the formalized model description. All layer neurons implement the OR operation.

Layer 3. The neurons of this layer are ordinary neurons that perform weighted additions.

The input data vector X contains 7 elements. That is, the neural network has 7 inputs: x_1 – the geographical position of the emergency on the railway transport for emergency groups involved in emergency response; x_2 – the geographical position of the emergency on the railway transport for other groups involved in the emergency response; x_3 – population at the emergency place on the railway transport; x_4 – danger of the emergency place on the railway transport; x_5 – absolute time of emergency occurrence on the railway transport; x_6 – relative time of emergency on the railway transport; x_7 – emergency events on the railway transport.

As a training sample there was used a sample of 1800 elements. From the results of training and testing, it follows that a neural network training using the back propagation algorithm of an error '*trainrp*' allows to achieve one of the best accuracy in the least time. Therefore, in order to solve the problem of predicting the development of the situation and determining the consequences of the primary decisions, there was used an incompletely connected, direct-directed neural network, trained precisely by this algorithm. Initially, the training sample was prepared in MS Excel, and then imported into Matlab, for further network training.

Such tasks have a large amount of possible solutions, and their initial data may be inaccurate, erroneous, or inconsistent. Evaluation of the effectiveness of solutions will be considered the choice of the best solution among all possible. The formalized description of the model of the problem of evaluating the effectiveness of decisions is presented as follows:

$$E_{r_j} = M(N_s, k_s), \tag{3}$$

where E_{r_j} – decision effectiveness r_j, M – method by which an effective solution is sought; N_s – consequences of possible solutions for the situation s, s_k – a set of criteria for assessing the characteristics of a situation s, according to which the effectiveness of possible solutions is evaluated.

The indicated problem refers to the problems of multicriteria optimization, therefore, in order to solve it, it is advisable to apply the appropriate methods described in our previous researches. Based on the analysis of the activities of operational services involved in eliminating the consequences of emergencies on the railway transport, there was carried out the detalization of the tasks performed by them after the receipt of information about the situation. Based on detailed tasks, a conceptual model of the decision-making process was created.

5 Discussion of Results and Prospects for Further Research

There was developed a new formalized description of the model for the task of the situation recognition and primary decision-making. The model differs from the known ones in that it takes into account the information dependencies of the situation parameters that are available to decision-makers at making decisions. This makes it possible to formalize the decision-making process for situation recognition and prediction.

A further prospect of work is the development of a method and model for solving problems of emergency recognition and prediction of its development, as well as primary decision-making based on fuzzy inference and fuzzy ANN, which uses information about the parameters characterizing the situation for automatically generation of many possible solutions.

6 Conclusions

There was substantiated the necessity of using intelligent computer technologies to automate the process of analyzing emergencies on railway transport with automatic generation of recommendations for managers (decision-makers) on their elimination in order to reduce the time to develop and to make an informed decision;

It was shown that at analyzing emergencies on the railway transport a particular importance has the development of methods for creating DSS based on the modeling of transient technogenic emergencies as a complex dynamic process taking into account cause and effect relationships;

There was substantiated the necessity of the implementation of a modular software product for intelligent analysis of emergencies and the development of operational recommendations for managers to eliminate them;

There was carried out the detalization of tasks performed by them after the receipt of information about the situation. Based on detailed tasks, a conceptual model of the decision-making process was created;

There was developed a new formalized description of the model for the task of situation recognition and primary decision-making. The model differs from the known ones in that it takes into account the information dependencies of the situation parameters that are available to decision-makers. This makes it possible to formalize the decision-making process for the situation recognition and prediction.

There was proposed a method for solving emergency recognition problems and predicting its development, as well as primary decision-making. The method differs from the known ones in that it is based on formalizing the description of the model of the corresponding problem and on the rules of fuzzy inference and fuzzy artificial neural network, which uses information about the parameters that characterize the situation in order to generate automatically many possible solutions.

References

1. Lakhno, V., Akhmetov, B., Korchenko, A.: Development of a decision support system based on expert evaluation for the situation center of transport cybersecurity. J. Theor. Appl. Inform. Technol. **96**(14), 4530–4540 (2018)
2. Ivashchenko, A.V.: Mul'tiagentnyye tekhnologii dlya razrabotki setetsentricheskikh sistem upravleniya. Izvestiya Yuzhnogo federal'nogo universiteta. Tekhnicheskiye nauki – T. 116, №. 3 (2011)

3. Gelovani, V.A., Bashlykov, A.A., Britkov, V.B., Vyazilov, Y.D.: Intellektual'nyye sistemy podderzhki prinyatiya resheniy v neshtatnykh situatsiyakh s ispol'zovaniyem informatsii o sostoyanii prirodnoy sredy. M.: Editorial: 304, 3 (2001)
4. Kuznetsov, O.P.: Intellektualizatsiya podderzhki upravlyayushchikh resheniy i sozdaniye intellektual'nykh sistem. Problemy upravleniya, №. 3(1) (2009)
5. Yamalov, I.: Modelirovaniye protsessov upravleniya i prinyatiya resheniy v usloviyakh chrezvychaynykh situatsiy. Litres (2014)
6. Shim, J.P., Warkentin, M., Courtney, J.F., Power, D.J., Sharda, R., Carlsson, C.: Past, present, and future of decision support technology. Decis. Support Syst. **33**(2), 111–126 (2002)
7. Medvedev, V.I., Teslenko, I.O., Kalinichenko, E.A.: New emergency cards for the prevention on liquidation of extreme situation with dangerous goods on the railway. In: International Workshop on Early Warning and Crises/Disaster and Emergency Management, pp. 28–29 (2010)
8. Katsman, M., Kryvopishyn, O., Lapin, V.: Mathematical models of decision support system for the head of the firefighting department on railways. Reliabil.: Theory Appl. **6**(3(22)) (2011)
9. Monoši, M., Ballay, M.: Analysis of risks and technical securing of rescue services at traffic accidents on railway crossing. Advances in Fire, Safety and Security Research 2014 i Editors note, p. 121 (2014)
10. János, B.E.N.Y.E.: The role of information of the population in elimination of accidents involving dangerous substances. Hadmérnök **12**(1) (2017)
11. Buts, Y.V., Kraynyuk, E.V., Kozodoy, D.S., Barbashin, V.V.: Evaluation of emergency events at the transportation of dangerous goods in the context of the technogenic load in regions. Sci. Transp. Progr. Bull. Dnipropetrovsk Natl. Univ. Railway Transp. **3**(75), 27–35 (2018)
12. Akhmetov, B., Lakhno, V.: System of decision support in weaklyformalized problems of transport cybersecurity ensuring. J. Theor. Appl. Inform. Technol. **96**(8), 2184–2196 (2018)
13. Akhmetov, B., Lakhno, V., Yerkeldessova, G.: Algorithm of parallel data processing in the automated dispatcherization system of railway transport movement. J. Theor. Appl. Inform. Technol. **97**(9), 2491–2502 (2019)
14. Akhmetov, B.: Methods and models of self-trained automated systems detecting the state of high-speed railway transport nodes. J. Theor. Appl. Inform. Technol. **97**(9), 2466–2479 (2019)

Author Index

Printed in the United States
By Bookmasters